Dedicated to lovers of music

And chasers of dreams...

FORWARD

I'm in a place between dreaming and awake. It's a surreal place where all around me disappears into a long, narrow tunnel. I fall into a comfortable stare, gazing at nothing and everything at the same time. My vision blurs, my hearing is muffled, and a peaceful calm envelopes me.

I'm standing backstage – waiting to go. I hear the roar of thousands of screaming fans calling for the encore. I close my eyes and allow the moment to take me. I've enjoyed these same moments many times; in dark, smoke-filled nightclubs, bright, glitzy casino showrooms, and today - on this beautiful sunny afternoon - at a packed California fair.

I am nowhere and everywhere. The sounds of the midway barely penetrate my mind. The rollercoaster, the Ferris wheel, the music blaring in the carnival loudspeakers, are all background to my momentary oasis. The sun sinks beneath the horizon, and twilight engulfs the fairgrounds. Off in the distance I hear joyful screams and laughter. The aroma of cotton candy, caramel apples, hotdogs, and sugar doughnuts floods my senses as I breathe in.

I rip myself out of my daze. It's time to go. I look for a towel to wipe the sweat and the last of the makeup from my face. The band stands at the stage entrance and waits for my call.

"One last song, boys!" I shout. "Start it up, Richie," I grin towards our guitar player. He smiles, nods, and heads out onstage. The crowd goes wild. In a few seconds, his guitar begins to talk, followed by a swell from the keyboards, a swish of cymbals, and a low droning on the bass guitar. Some of the hard-core fans react with cheers and screams. They know what's coming. These songs are ingrained in people's minds; they are part of the soundtrack of their lives.

If only I had written them.

The hit songs, the charmed life... if only they were mine. The crowd has come to hear Bon Jovi. But we are not Bon Jovi and I am not Jon. This is all just pretend - make believe. Everyone here knows that - but that's not what's important today.

I take a deep breath and run out onto the stage. The screams get louder and we launch into "Living On A Prayer." The crowd sings along. The moment is pure bliss. It's in these moments I remember why I love being an entertainer. Thousands of living, breathing, reasons are standing in front of me and I reach out to connect with every one of them. Some sit cheering from the back, some dance in the aisles, others shout and sing at the front of the stage. What the experience means for each of them I can't be sure. I'm still humbled by it all and I feel blessed to have my part to play. I immerse myself in the exchange and the crowd responds in joyful synchronicity.

When the show is over, the band takes their final bows, and we leave the stage. Another night, another hotel room, another venue. It's a good life. It's also a strange one – pretending to be someone else for a few hours a night. But that's exactly what I do.

A reporter is waiting backstage and I spend a few minutes to chat with him. It's the usual questions: How did the band start? How did I become a tribute singer? Why Bon Jovi? How did I get started in the music business? I have answered these questions many times and yet it still baffles me to think about the series of events that brought me to where I am today.

"It feels like a lifetime ago, but I actually left the music business to become a schoolteacher." I tell him. "I had already spent more than two decades performing and I had decided my rock 'n' roll days were long gone. So, I turned my attention toward teaching.

"I don't know when the exact moment was when I decided to form a Bon Jovi tribute band." I told him. "I was teaching a Grade 7 class and would sometimes bring my guitar to class to play while my students were working on art projects." I recalled how the kids remarked that I looked and sounded like Jon Bon Jovi. It was something I had heard at times in the past, yet I remember coming home from school on one of these particular days, realizing those kids had sparked something inside me.

I had missed rock 'n' roll and wanted to do something in music again one day. I had seen the tribute band market grow in recent years and toyed with the idea that if I were ever to take the stage again I would probably build a tribute band. The tribute phenomenon was growing strong and the opportunities for musicians were both plentiful and rewarding. Tribute bands, the really good ones, were playing the best venues and travelling the world. When it came down to it, that's all I wanted to do. It was the crux of what I had longed for from the music business all my life, despite what I let myself believe in the early days. I was once a starry-eyed wannabe who lusted for rock stardom and the riches it could bring. Eventually I'd stopped trying to write million-selling hit songs and focused on creating an exciting career as a live performer. What I really wanted was to play cool shows and travel to interesting places. Without a hit song or an album to promote, a tribute band was a great way to pursue those desires. But a tribute to Bon Jovi? I had reservations. Would I be able to pull it off? Sure, the kids thought I looked and sounded like Jon Bon Jovi and it had been a comparison others had drawn in the past, but who in their right mind would take on the task of emulating Jon Bon Jovi? Apart from his amazing career in music, Jon Bon Jovi had built houses for the homeless, provided meals for the hungry, and often played a major role in gathering humanitarian aid in times of disaster. Jon's business acumen, passion, and altruistic nature had become a powerful force. His contributions spoke volumes about his character and he had been a public-relations asset for more than one politician's election campaign. As far as I was concerned, Jon was practically a modern-day saint, and most certainly rock royalty. Who could live up to that? Who would even try?

No, if I was going to create a Bon Jovi tribute band, I had to distinguish between Jon the philanthropic, multi-millionaire CEO, and Jon the singer of a blue-collar rock 'n' roll band. There could be no giant shoes to fill, no saintly deeds to live up to. It had to be about the band and their music. I needed to concentrate my efforts on the Bon Jovi concert experience, and target the sound, appearance, and energy of the band live.

As I pursued the idea further, the Bon Jovi story drew me closer. Their lyrics of inspiration and hope connect with their fans in such a huge way. Those who love Bon Jovi really love them, and it was not long before I began to feel an unanticipated sense of responsibility and accountability towards the band and their legions of fans. If I was going to do this, I had to do it right.

I would make a special effort to be conscientious about the philosophy behind my design. I needed to find the essence of the artist. I would create an authentic Bon Jovi experience for the audience, while being respectful of the positive spirit Jon and his band engenders. I believed a tribute should be a celebration of an artist's career. As a tribute artist, I would have to assume the responsibility of being faithful and complimentary in duplicating the original artist's performance while effectively communicating the essence of the artist's spirit and intent. Lofty goals, perhaps, but it was the only way I would even consider the project. So, it was with these ideals and guidelines I began to build Blaze Of Glory – A Tribute to Bon Jovi.

I knew I had the knowledge and experience in the music business to build a good live act; I'd spent decades writing and singing songs, building bands, and playing shows. But I also knew this tribute would take a kind of work and dedication like nothing else I had done before. In the better part of the year I spent building Blaze Of Glory, I brought all of my experience, ambition, and childhood dreams to the task. My research was exhaustive. I absorbed everything Bon Jovi I could get my hands on. I spent hundreds of hours learning from books and interviews. Laura Jackson's Jon Bon Jovi: The Biography became a huge source of factual material for me, and I found it invaluable in tracking Jon's life.

***

As I learned more about Jon Bon Jovi, I began to feel a kind of kinship with the New Jersey kid who grew up to be a world famous rocker and philanthropist. John Francis Bongiovi and I share similar roots. Jon had spent years aspiring to succeed in music, just as I had, but there were other parallels in our lives as well. We grew up in working class families in small towns. We received guitars at an early age, took lessons, and then quit in frustration. We found mentors to learn from, and spent our teen years writing songs and playing underage in the clubs. We both became leaders of our own bands and share the same dogged determination to become successful in music.

However, our paths would become very different by 1983. In the 30 years that followed, Jon went on to enjoy massive worldwide success and notoriety, while I spent those same years in relative obscurity. I am not a has-been, or a never-was – I am an also-ran.

And I am not alone.

Countless artists struggle for success and never become big stars. I gave rock 'n' roll 30 years of my life. Fame and fortune never happened for me. But I had run the same race. I threw my hat in the ring and jumped on the music biz merry-go-round along with so many others who dreamed of stardom. I enjoyed some success along the way, and in fleeting moments, I got to ride the rollercoaster. But, nothing I ever did came close to Jon's massive success.

Jon Bon Jovi not only proved that rock 'n' roll can be wildly lucrative, but also how an artist can give back to the world in a big way. His story has become one of inspiration to me and I am deeply indebted to him for being able to enjoy success in my career now as an ambassador of the Bon Jovi brand. My dreams of big rock shows and exciting world travel have come true as a Bon Jovi tribute singer. I'm certain I would not have the kinds of experiences I enjoy today if it were not for singing Bon Jovi music. Blaze Of Glory has given me a level of career satisfaction and achievement that has translated into happiness and success in ways I have only recently come to understand.

So, how do two kids with the same dream and similar backgrounds, living in lands of opportunity, chase that same dream and experience such different results? We both worked like dogs.

We both paid our dues. What had gone so wrong for me and so right for Jon? I had many questions and few answers. Maybe my songs weren't good enough. Maybe I hadn't believed in myself enough. I wanted to know what had I done wrong and where I had made my mistakes.

I was certain the answers I sought lay in the respective journeys Jon and I had followed. I went back, looked at both of our lives, and tried to make some sense of it all.

Not all memories are easy to recall. Some can be wonderful, carnival rides, while others are brutal to face. It can be both cathartic and disturbing. The past can be a tricky place to venture when you're standing in the present. Sometimes, what we remember will often clash with what we want to believe happened. Still, I wanted answers - whatever they might bring. I set out to write this book to hopefully get it straight in my head – no matter what the risks. I believed that, in the end, the journey would either help me or hurt me... perhaps, a little of both.

CHAPTER ONE

We were children of the '60s, born into a generation of bold dreamers. We were the last remnants of the post-war baby boom and the world was fast-changing as we entered it. The 1960s saw unbridled idealism spawn radical social reform and a challenge to authority. A politically active stance in liberal thinking arose in stark contrast to that of the generation before. Many '60s parents were activists, pacifists, hippies, and dreamers, fighting against social injustice and oppression. They were waging peaceful battles for freedom and equality, and their dreams of change were becoming reality.

To a young boy growing up in that revolutionary era, everything seemed possible. My freethinking parents instilled in me the idea that if you work hard enough, you can achieve just about anything. Life contained immense possibilities and it fired my young imagination to dream big. I have heard Bon Jovi interviews where Jon spoke about how he felt similarly encouraged in his early days when his parents were first starting out, and how they empowered him to pursue his dreams.

John Francis Bongiovi grew up in a modest home in rural New Jersey to a working class, moderate Catholic, Italian-American family of traditional values. His parents were strong, capable people who inspired in Jon a sense of ambition and possibility while providing a happy and stable home life. Jon's father, John Bongiovi Sr., had been a U.S. Marine, a plumber, and by the 1960s, a hairdresser. John Sr. met his wife, Carol, while they were both serving with the Marines. Carol was an exciting and dynamic woman: a soldier, a beauty queen, and for a short time, a Playboy bunny. Jon's parents were excellent models for ambition and aspiration. They encouraged and empowered him to be anything he wanted to be. That goes a long way for a kid.

The '60s spirit of change marched forward against a backdrop of socio-politically charged popular music that swirled with freedom, activism, and a new introspection across the airwaves. Pete Seeger, Buffalo Springfield, and The Mamas and The Papas were among the many new artists that waved the flag of freedom and idealism. I grew up in an exciting psychedelic world, and I knew I was destined to do something radical too. In my dreams, I saved the world from invading aliens and invented miracle cures for horrible diseases. I climbed tall towers to save beautiful princesses and fought terrible foes to save villages from evil forces. The King of All the Land stood in front of his magnificent castle and proclaimed my heroic deeds, while thousands of onlookers waved their banners and cheered in adoration. The world was safe. I had slain the dragon.

Mom believes my hyperactive imagination as a child was, in part, a product of the stark reality of our humble beginnings. We were quite poor in the early days. I never felt it. When I was growing up we had very little of anything, but I don't remember ever doing without. From what I have read, this is true for Jon as well. I have seen pictures of his house when he was a kid. It was a modest home, although not poor by any means. Regardless, he always speaks of happy memories and encouragement.

My mom instilled in me a sense of limitless possibility. Even now, after a lifetime of chasing what I believed was success, I know a person's financial status does not contribute to happiness or ambition. Lots of people with money are miserable. If your earliest childhood experiences are those of parental support and encouragement, you stand the best chance for happiness, regardless of wealth or poverty.

For many poor kids, stardom can still feel like a possible dream – especially when you feel there aren't a lot of other choices available to you. In 1968, Mick Jagger sang, "What can a poor boy do, 'cept to sing for a rock 'n' roll band?" It was the perfect ode for kids from poor and working class families; if you were born without money or influence, you could still join a band and become a star.

I believed it.

My mom lived with my grandmother when I was born. It was a tiny home on a small parcel of land right next to a trailer court that housed some pretty shady characters. I grew up, literally, on the wrong side of the tracks. As a kid you have no idea – it's just where you live. The house had been in our family for years. It was what we had. My great grandmother bought the place in 1944 for $250. My mom still has the original sale papers. Built in 1914, it was made of railroad ties and pitch.

I was brought home on Thanksgiving Day in 1960. My Uncle Art's wife, all of 17 years old at the time, delivered my cousin Little Art three days later. Our house was always busy, and I have wonderful memories of that crowded, tiny shack.

The house had one room. A large area that served as a kitchen/living room/dining room was flanked at each end by two curtained-off bedrooms, each big enough for one small bed. There was no toilet, no bathtub, no shower, and no hot water. We had an outhouse, where we froze our asses off in the winter, and that reeked in the summer. There was a single electrical line running from a post on the road to our roof. With two fuses, we could only plug in one thing at a time. A wood stove provided our heat and was used for cooking.

Every spring the fire department evacuated us when the creek that ran beside our house flooded. The Baldwins, a reclusive old couple who lived next door, would be carried from their home, still sitting in their rocking chairs, by firemen trudging hip deep in the fetid water. Everyone from our tiny neighborhood would gather to watch. It became an annual tradition.

My childhood was a happy time. I remember a warm house and caring people all around me. I remember laughing, singing, and cheerful faces. I recall Christmases, big dinners, large family gatherings, and presents. I remember always feeling safe. In my memory, we had a happy home with plenty of everything a kid could want. There were probably 10 people living there at any given time. Most importantly, there was always music.

It's the early experiences with music that shape our musical sensibilities. How music is perceived in the home and its importance in the lives of the people around us sets a tone for how deeply it can touch our lives. If at an early age we are inundated with strong appreciation and a spiritual connection with music, it can become our raison d'être.

Maybe there's a genetic component. My grandmother used to say, "The music is in your blood..." She said I came from a long line of musicians and would tell me stories about my musical heritage. My great grandmother was born to German parents and grew up playing eastern European folk songs. Granny told me Gran-Gran was always singing and dancing around the house to old German records, and often went out to the local pubs in North Bay, Ontario, armed with her harmonica. She would sing, play, and accompany others with a guitar or piano, playing traditional songs she had learned from her parents. Granny, in turn, grew up with music, eventually playing guitar, piano, and singing for audiences.

Her youngest son, my uncle Art, played guitar from a young age. Uncle Art knew current tunes that he would play and sometimes teach me. The first song I think I could actually chord and sing was an old folk number called "The Ballad of Lydia Pinkham," which in 1968 became a hit for a group called The Scaffold as "Lily The Pink." Uncle Art later taught me "Sloop John B." and "Leaving on a Jet Plane." "Surfer Joe" was one of his personal favorites, and I learned it because he liked it so much. Maybe Granny was right; maybe music was in the genes.

Jon Bon Jovi had a model for music that likely touched his young soul. Jon's mom had once been Miss Erie, Pennsylvania, and one of Hugh Hefner's famous bunnies; I imagine the show biz gene found its way into Jon at a young age. In Laura Jackson's, Jon Bon Jovi: The Biography, the author describes how Carol Bongiovi would line up with Jon before a full-length mirror, and how the two would have fun watching themselves performing songs.

Having parents who encouraged the arts was liberating. My Dad played guitar around the house in the early days. He and my mom were having problems in their marriage. Mom says he picked up the instrument because he could see how much I enjoyed music and thought it might bring him closer to me – and my Mom. Playing music did not come easy to him, as it did with my uncle Art; he had to work hard at it. Dad was more a motorcycle guy than a musician, and often fixed his bikes in the house, much to Mom's dismay. Mom told me she would come home to the sight of motorcycle parts strewn across the kitchen table and whole bikes inside the house in various states of repair. I think this was part of the breakdown of their relationship. When I asked my mom about this, she listed it as one of the reasons things went sour for them. He left before my fifth birthday, and I never saw him again.

But I still had music. It was all around me in the early days. All of my cousins played musical instruments and sang. Bruce and Myles, Michael, David, and Denis all graduated from Uncle Art's music school; they are still involved in music in one way or another. Mom sang with a country and western band, once on the radio, a few times on television, and often in the barrooms of North Bay.

Mom had a job working at the TV station in Callander, about 10 minutes south of North Bay. She managed to get me onscreen when I was a toddler. She sat me up on a stool in the middle of the set, and I would be the test for adjusting lighting and camera angles. There was a children's segment that ran daily and I became the little kid the puppets talked to. People were fussing around me, bright lights shone in my face. Mom said it was obvious I enjoyed the attention.

As a child, I had a wandering spirit. I was always intrigued about what was over the hill. I would look out into the distance at some landmark and curiosity would overwhelm me. I wondered if there were people out there. What kind of people were they? Did they look and talk like me? I had to find out.

I went on my first road trip at age three. I wandered away from the adults and headed down the road. I must've been a quick mover, because before anyone knew it, I was gone. A search party was sent out, the police were called, and a manhunt was underway. I found my way across the entire town before the police caught up to me. I have a vague memory of a police car pulling up behind me, and a policeman calling my name. I knew I was in trouble so I just kept walking.

"Hey, Teddy!" the officer repeated and I heard the cruiser door open. I looked back and he was smiling.

"Where are you going, son?" he asked. I had no answer ready. In fact, I didn't know. I just wanted to go somewhere I had never been.

"Do you know everyone is looking for you?" the officer asked me, his smile fading. I had not considered anyone would be worried. I was simply focused on the task at hand: exploring. I asked him if I was in trouble. The smile came back and he told me my family was worried and he had come to take me home. I got into the car without further issue. On the way home the police officer stopped at the store and bought me an ice cream cone. We pulled up in front of our little house and I saw my grandmother standing outside the front door with her hands on her hips. I was having the time of my life, riding in a police car and enjoying my ice cream treat. Granny was not impressed.

I was told I made several of these little trips, only to be returned by the police, with a smile on my face and an ice cream cone in my hand. I became adept at sneaking out of the house and caused my poor family no end of worry, or so they tell me. I don't remember that part. What I do remember is the adventure.

Chapter Two

Our little house on Homer was eventually sold to the City of North Bay to create a park surrounding the sewage disposal plant. Granny sold it for $3,000. By then, the house was falling apart. The floors had separated from the walls, the roof leaked, and the outhouse smell was permanently ingrained into the rotted wood. I imagine that's why my grandfather described us as shit poor for all those years. The city demolished the house and then left the area to nature.

Although the Bongiovis were not poor, Carol and John Sr. still had to work hard to improve the quality of life for their family. They managed to buy a house in a decent neighborhood in Sayreville, NJ, some 30 minutes outside of New York City, shortly after Jon's two brothers were born. Around the same time, Mom and I made the move to the big city of Toronto. It was a huge move upwards, and I remember her being excited that things were getting better for us. She was a secretary for Cadillac Fairview – a large construction company – and was making a lot more money. It was actually a pretty good job for someone leaving a blue-collar background for a white-collar world. My mom was good at the job and I remember her being happier than I had ever known. We were both excited about the prospects of a nice place to live in the big city. Cadillac Fairview had purchased properties along upscale High Park Avenue in Toronto and planned to demolish them to make way for large apartment buildings. The houses were set for demolition, but we were able to live in one of the best of them for a year before it was torn down.

The house was amazing. I remember it as a mansion. The exterior was somewhat medieval in style and covered with cultured stone, and it was centrally located on a huge wooded lot. It had an expansive living room with large paintings and elaborate wall coverings, left behind by the previous owners. I would sit and study the faded and frayed remnants for hours on end. There were several huge bedrooms throughout the multiple levels, and I can still picture the arched stucco ceilings reaching beyond my view like a creamy white indoor sky. There was a dedicated breakfast room with French doors adjacent to an opulent dining hall. The place was massive, and Mom would host parties for an eclectic group of friends: actors, journalists, beatniks, and musicians she had met over the years.

Canadian legend Gordon Lightfoot and Much Music founder Moses Znaimer were frequent visitors. I remember music and laughter filling the house on any given night of the week; the Beatles, Bob Dylan, Canned Heat, Pete Seeger, Simon and Garfunkel, and the Byrds jingle-jangled throughout the house. Those records became the warbly soundtrack to my childhood.

I would sit on the floor in the corner of the huge living room, poring over album covers and watching records spin on the turntable. Even today, when I close my eyes, I can see the 12" LPs stacked four or five high under the arm of the record player, and the Capitol and Decca 45s with the little plastic centerpiece stuck in the middle. "I Am the Walrus" and "Nowhere Man" swam through my head as the warm sweet smell of something I couldn't identify covered the room like a cozy blanket. That wonderful smell only appeared at parties. I remember asking about it and being told in a hushed voice that it was incense. I decided I loved the smell of incense, and when I grew up it would always be at my parties too.

That was the '60s for me – eclectic parties, cool music, and lots of incense. Out of all of the music I heard in those early days, the Beatles hit the deepest chord. Something about their sound appealed to me. I was captivated by the fact they were from England. It sounded so exotic. A far away land filled with the likes of Mary Poppins, Winchester Cathedral, Bobbies on Bicycles, and London Bridge.

The TV station Mom worked for in Callander gave her an assignment to interview The Beatles when they played in Toronto. I was ecstatic, and it propelled Mom to instant celebrity status in my mind. She had already been hanging with a cool crowd and I had met so many wonderful and strange people in that big house. But this... this was the Beatles! They stayed at the Royal York Hotel in Toronto and she went with a couple others from the TV station to do the interview. She would later recount the experience to me saying they were "charming, polite, very '60s, and very press savvy." In my head John, Paul, George, and Ringo were singing with Mom in a yellow submarine floating in a psychedelic sea of colorful cardboard creatures.

The Fab Four had been a huge part of my musical awakening and to me they were the biggest rock stars ever. I pestered her to tell me the story over and over again; it must have driven her nuts. I listened to Beatles records for hours after she would re-tell the tale. I daydreamed I was Paul, and sang "Love Me Do" to Mary Poppins while we drank tea under the London Bridge.

That house and those early days on High Park Avenue will forever live in my mind. Whether it was a one room shack on a dirt road or a palatial estate, I always felt warm, loved, and comfortable. Mom says she often cringes when she thinks back to the meager resources we began with and how she often had to leave me alone in order to be able to work to support us. She would drop me off at the subway on her way to work and I would ride the TTC alone to school. Then at the end of the day, I would get back on the subway and meet her at the station near her work.

Today, no parent in their right mind would put a six-year-old on a subway train unescorted; but those were different times. Mom says she shouldn't have done it even then. My mom was the best mom in the world and she did what she had to do. All I can remember is the adventure of the Toronto subway. I felt so grown up riding with all of those adults. I saw many of the same people every day, sitting behind their newspapers. Who knows what they thought. There I was, a little kid singing to himself and smiling at anyone who as much as glanced in his direction. The TTC is where I began to love travel, and I still carry with me those early feelings of high adventure when I travel today.

There was a lot of moving around after that big, beautiful house was torn down. Mom packed me up and we moved to Cleveland, Ohio. I don't remember much about Cleveland. We weren't there for long. I remember brick streets and neighborhood kids who were always yelling and fighting. I remember one particular kid who pushed a little girl down in the street, and when I went to help her up, he stabbed me in the ear with a fork. We moved back to Canada the following week. In 1966, Mom fell in love with Floyd Moore from Deep River, Ontario. She married him the following year. Floyd was an engineer for Ontario Hydro and worked in Kitchener-Waterloo, twin cities located 90 minutes from Toronto.

I hated moving and resented my new step-dad for it. It was tough sharing Mom with him after having her to myself for so long. At first, I put him through hell. I resisted his attempts to get close to me. Then in 1968, he bought me my first guitar. To this day, it is still the best Christmas present I ever received. I will always love him for that. Along with the guitar, he paid for lessons held after hours at my school. I was excited the first couple of times, but it was tough trudging back to school for music lessons after an entire day of being there. The rudiments bored me, and I quit after a month. I came home and threw my guitar under my bed.

In Jon Bon Jovi: The Biography, the author describes how Jon got his first guitar from his mother. Carol Bongiovi purchased the guitar new at a local trade fair. Jon took lessons in a tiny room at a local teaching studio in New Jersey. His teacher fell asleep during lessons and often smoked a pipe, quickly filling the small room and the poor kid's nostrils. Jon choked through the smoke, and tried to keep up with the dry theory and monotonous scale exercises. He too lost interest and quit in frustration.

Jon has often told the story about going home and pitching his guitar down the stairs where it remained abandoned for years. My separation from my guitar wasn't quite as long, but it was months before I would pick it up again. If it weren't for Uncle Art, it might have been the end of my guitar playing days altogether. He coaxed me back in, encouraging and inspiring me with facts and stories about performers and artists. He taught me actual chords and real songs from the radio.

It was years before Jon found his own muse and reconnected with his guitar. Throughout his years in the New Jersey public school system Jon hung out with friends, rode his bike, and enjoyed all the great things about being a kid. His guitar was abandoned in the basement, yet his dreams of playing and performing never left his mind.

I was first introduced to performing arts at Crestview Public

School in Kitchener. We had just made the move from Toronto and I was devastated about having to leave the big city. Mom, my new dad, and I were living in a small two-bedroom apartment on Queenston Ave. in a lower middle-class suburb of Kitchener. I was registered in Grade 2 well after the school year started. I was a kid at a new school and everything felt foreign. Everybody knew everybody – except for me. I kept to myself at first. I was quiet and reserved and tended to speak only when spoken to. I was in a new home, starting at a new school, and I was overwhelmed. Singing became my saving grace.

Amid all the anxiety and displacement, I loved to sing. It felt so good to just open my mouth and hear the sounds that came out. When I sang I felt more in control. It was mine. I owned it. I played with words, melody, and it made sense to me. I always loved the reaction when I sang for my family or with friends. Singing helped me integrate into my new school. I took advantage of any opportunity to sing with my class during music. It was a safe way to connect with other kids and not have to try and make friends one by one.

I talked to a few kids that first year at Crestview, but most of my interactions occurred during class activities. The following year, in Grade 3, I was old enough to be selected for junior choir. I instantly loved Mrs. Trudeau's music class at Crestview. She had prepared a choral version of "Edelweiss" from The Sound of Music. We were separated into baritones, altos, tenors, and sopranos. I remember the teacher taking each section to a corner of the class where they were shown their notes and practiced as a section.

I watched students plug their ears while singing, and it confused me. I asked one of the kids why she was doing this and she told me she was trying to concentrate on her part and not be distracted by all the other singers around her. I was dumbfounded. I couldn't imagine not hearing other voices. It was easy for me to tune myself into the other voices singing different melodies. I had already sung so much, and I knew the sound of my own voice so well I put myself on autopilot so I could listen to the other voices. I could sing my own parts while others around me sang many different things. It was fun and I enjoyed how it felt so effortless. I was excited about being good at singing; it gave me a sense of possibility, a sense of being unique… special.

The teacher put the class at the front of the room in our sections one at a time so we could sing our part to the other sections. It was a strange exercise, and we had no idea why we were doing it. She was featuring everyone in class so the choirmaster could hear all the students sing and scout new talent for the school choir.

The choirmaster was a tall, imposing figure in a suit and tie under a long black robe. He stood, expressionless, at the back of the room as Mrs. Trudeau counted the group in. I sang loud and proud along with the rest of the kids. We only made it to the chorus when the choirmaster approached Mrs. Trudeau. She nodded and told us to stop singing. We were confused. What was happening? What had we done wrong? We waited in silence as Mrs. Trudeau and the choirmaster talked. Then, Mrs. Trudeau turned her attention back to us as the choirmaster took his seat at the back of the class. "Ted…" Mrs. Trudeau began, clearing her throat. My heart pounded wildly and I was sure everyone could hear it hammering in my chest. Oh God no! My mind pleaded. Please don't draw attention to me! I could feel my ears begin to prickle.

"Ted," she continued. "Would you like to sing the song as a

solo?" Every eye in the classroom was on me as the blood rushed to my face. I couldn't speak. Oh God, I had sung so loud! I panicked. They were going to make an example of me by embarrassing me.

"I am so sorry…" I stammered, "…please, I can do it quieter… I am so sorry." Some of the kids snickered and I almost broke down right there and cried.

"Quiet!" Mrs. Trudeau barked at the class. I was humiliated. The entire class was silent and I stood alone with all eyes focused on me.

"Ted," she continued, her voice quiet, but firm. "You weren't too loud. Please calm down." I choked back the urge to start bawling.

"I really want to hear you sing this part alone," She reassured me. "Can you do that?" Her voice was softer now and I thought it all very strange. Mrs. Trudeau seemed not a woman given to softness and compassion and this moment of tenderness shocked us all.

I nodded slowly. "Yes, Ma'am."

She motioned for the rest of the kids to take their seats. I looked to the back at the choirmaster and squirmed alone in the front of the classroom.

"Alright then, let's give it a try shall we?" he called out from his seat. His voice was deep and intimidating. Mrs. Trudeau sat down at the piano and played the first note of the passage.

"Just take your time and sing just like you were doing before," she encouraged me.

I looked around at the classroom. I wasn't nervous as much as embarrassed. I didn't like being singled out. I knew I could sing the part, but I was the new kid. I didn't want the other kids to resent me. I tried to put it all aside and concentrate on the song.

I began to sing, softly and slowly at first. I found my stride with the delicate piece. I formed the vowels wide and emphasized the consonants with all the drama I had inside me. I closed my eyes and let Rogers and Hammerstein take me away while everything else blurred into non-existence. I was alone. Nothing else remained except the song and the sound of my voice. I was no longer a shy and introverted kid afraid to put his hand up in class, or talk to anyone in the schoolyard. This moment was mine and no one could touch it. I sang with everything I had through each verse and chorus. I finished the song and the room was silent. I opened my eyes and 25 kids and two adults stared back at me, transfixed. It was incredible. No one said a word. Then Mrs. Trudeau turned to the choirmaster who had removed his glasses and was wiping the lenses.

I didn't speak. I had no idea what was happening. I only knew it had felt wonderful. It was a beautiful song and I had sung it well.

"Well, Mrs. Trudeau," the choirmaster spoke, not taking his eyes off of me. "It seems," he continued slow and deliberate, "that we have a star in the making. Young man, that was absolutely beautiful."

The class exploded into applause and cheers. I thought my knees would buckle and my hands shook. It was all too much. I ran out of the room and sprinted down the hall to the nearest washroom. I burst open a stall door and threw up.

I spit and cried until I heard someone enter the washroom.

"Hello?" The choirmaster's voice boomed against the tiled walls. He let me cry for a minute without saying a word. I knew he was there and I would have to go out and face him. He waited until my bawling slowed to sniffles and asked me if I was okay.

"I'm fine." I sniffed.

"I have a project for you Ted. I think you might be interested." He spoke in a soft and even tone while I wiped away tears and emerged from the stall.

"We're putting on a school play," he continued. "The play is called Old King Cole. I want you to play the lead. I need someone who is not afraid to sing solo in front of an audience."

Afraid to sing?! At that moment, I was afraid to speak! I could only nod my acceptance. He looked me in the eyes, and smiled.

"And no crying allowed." I smiled back and told him I could do it. I would do it. I explained I was embarrassed because of being singled out in front of my classmates. Singing was the only time I actually wasn't scared, nervous, or shy.

In my little brain I began to understand singing was something I could count on to get me through, even if I was feeling bad. It never failed to lift my spirits. It made me feel strong and invincible. More than anything else in the world, I wanted to sing.

Chapter Three

Rehearsals for Old King Cole began the following week. I had several spoken lines and three songs to sing. I learned about stage marks, upstage and downstage, taking directions and projecting my voice. I loved it all. It became my whole world, and in that short time, I grew into a more confident kid.

I had strength and confidence in rehearsal, in the classroom, and at home. I was a singer, and now an actor. I decided I would do this for the rest of my life and it was going to be great. The show opened the last month of school. We performed three shows over three nights in the small school gymnasium.

Opening night was exciting. Parents and kids gathered in the gym as the lights dimmed. I walked from the back of the auditorium through the center of the audience as music filled the hall. I will always remember the look of pride on my mom's face when she saw me walk in, under the spotlight. I strolled up to the huge cardboard castle at the front of the stage and delivered my lines. I owned the room. I was a performer. The world made complete sense now. I delivered my performance all 3 nights without a single hiccup. That play was a milestone for me and those nights performing Old King Cole bolstered my sense of self-worth.

The confidence I gained from performing made me feel better, but I still found it difficult to make friends. There was this feeling that there was so much I did not understand about life and people. It scared the hell out of me. I contemplated a strange conspiracy of sorts.

I thought most of the kids around me knew what they were doing. I wanted to know their secret. They had friends and happily played their games at recess. I, on the other hand, wanted to know the secret of existence, be the world's first rock star/astronaut, and never vomit or cry again.

By the age of nine, my overactive imagination caught fire, fuelled by tales of science fiction and fantasy. I became a Star Trek addict. The voyages of the crew of the USS Enterprise appealed to my sense of adventure. Besides music, all I was interested in were futuristic societies and space travel. My dreams of stardom shared my nights with dreams of being in outer space. In space or on Earth, singing and playing guitar was still everything to me. I practiced every day and dreamed of being a rock star. I played records on the stereo, cranked them up to ear-splitting volume, and practiced my rock star poses in front of the mirror. I waved to throngs of fans in my bedroom auditorium. I blew kisses and winked at the starlets and supermodels at my feet.

On one bedroom wall, I had Elvis sneering in his black leather outfit from the '68 comeback special. Raquel Welch, from the film One Million Years BC, seduced me from the back of my bedroom door. I'd sit and stare at them while I riffed tunes from Elvis movies on my guitar.

I started bringing my guitar to school with me. At lunchtime, I would sit alone in a corner of the school grounds and write songs. I would strum through chords and sing random words and melodies. My first songs were written in that sports field at Crestview, and I still love driving past there whenever I visit Kitchener. People came and listened. Now and then, some girls would sing along. Sometimes boys would chime in with raspberries and crude adaptations of song lyrics. They would later grow up to be music critics.

I was a regular feature on the playground during recess and

lunchtime. At first, I was reticent to play for lots of kids. I preferred it when there were only a few stragglers. Then I began to enjoy the attention. I padded my little set list with one of my original songs. It was an odd combo of traditional folk with spacy undertones. It's hard to pigeonhole a nine-year-old songwriter, but I thought it was cool with a sci-fi edge. I read a lot of Conan novels around this time. Besides, it was the '60s and everyone was deep.

In the land of Forest Green
The Black Knight laughs while the maiden screams
He turns his head toward the Gods
In anger while in flight
Two stars collide – the men inside
Begin to give the knight a ride
They thrust him down onto the ground
And turn his mind to stone
The winter winds whip through his blood
Then plants begin again to bud
One year has passed since he's been dead
It's time to be reborn

By Grade 5, I played my guitar at school on a regular basis. Girls started to pay attention to me. I don't remember if I was interested in girls before that, other than Raquel Welch. Up until then, girls were like anyone else, just more annoying and bossy. Midway through the year, I noticed they were pretty and some of them smelled nice. I began to enjoy when they came around while I played.

Not everyone was as pleased as I was with the attention I was getting. One day, after a schoolyard performance, a kid approached me and told me I was making enemies with the other boys at school.

They didn't like the notice I was getting from the girls, and I "better watch myself." The kid was bigger and older than me. I nodded and put my guitar away. I don't think he wanted to fight me; he was just telling me how it was. It sounded like a sensible complaint and not something I wanted to scrap over. Besides, I only fought my cousins, and mostly only when they hit me first. Those fights were brutal, even by adult standards. I could never fight like that with someone who wasn't family. It would be just wrong.

Anyways, I wasn't trying to be the Pied Piper. I would play, girls would listen, and sometimes they sang along. There were a few girls I could count on to know what to sing and where. They had heard me a dozen times and we carried the weight of the vocal arrangements in the songs. One day, two of the girls I had sung with came over to talk to me. Collette Zehr, my next-door neighbor, and another girl named Rosy Tickle (I swear that was her name, but I'm unsure about the spelling) joined me regularly to sing. I asked them if they wanted to sing with me on a regular basis. In retrospect, I had asked them to join my band.

"Sure," they said in unison. "Where are we going to play?"

I couldn't believe it. Excited, I explained to them how we had a built-in gig at school as Crestview had several Arts Days throughout the year. Some kids had drawings and paintings, some twirled batons, some performed skits or sang, and others would play an instrument. The girls agreed it sounded great and we should start rehearsal the next day after school.

I had a band.

Collette, Rosy and I rehearsed a set of three songs. The girls sang background vocals and played tambourine and maracas. We practiced at the edge of the soccer field or in empty classrooms. We opened with John Denver's "Leaving on a Jet Plane," and followed with the Beach Boys' "Sloop John B." Our finale was my version of "House of the Rising Sun." I had tweaked it since I had learned to play guitar. The girls added some spooky harmonies, and the whole thing became a hippy version that made me feel grown up and groovy.

During rehearsal one day, we decided we needed a name for our band. I think Collette came up with The Sour Smoochers. We agreed it sounded cool and signed in for the next Arts Day. Rosy asked me later if our band name meant we should kiss each other a lot because her mom wouldn't let her do that. I was stumped. It was my first decision as bandleader. I searched hard for anything to say that wouldn't end with her quitting. I cleared my throat and turned eight shades of red.

"It wouldn't have to be like that..." I paused, "We can just kiss when we want to." She smiled, nodded, and walked away. We performed at several Arts Days that year and it was the best school year I'd ever had.

Then, because of a catchment issue, I was transferred to another school. Collette moved to Toronto and Rosy stayed at Crestview. That was the end of my very first band.

I was optimistic and looked towards the adventure in a new school. I was hopeful I might make some new friends at choir or in a play and maybe start a new band. Somewhere along the way, I might even get the slightest clue about what was going on in the world.

Chapter Four

In Jon Bon Jovi: The Biography, Laura Jackson describes how Jon experienced many of the early passions for music and performing – just as I had. Jon's creativity had bloomed during his school years and the love of playing music had consumed him, just as it had me. Jon had found his way back to playing guitar with the help of a more mature influence, just as Uncle Art rekindled my interest in playing again.

When Jon Bon Jovi was 13, he took lessons from Al Parinello, a local musician who lived down the street from him in Sayreville. Parinello played in clubs and knew lots of songs. He played for audiences in bars and nightclubs and was in a real band. He was a professional musician who was out in the scene and gigging. Parinello found a way to light a spark for the young student almost six years after Jon had thrown his guitar down the stairs. Although his dreams of stardom never waned during the years away from his guitar, Parinello reawakened Jon's desire to become more proficient on the instrument.

The relationship between teacher and pupil got off to a rocky start when John showed up unprepared for his lesson. Parinello had shown Jon how to play "House of the Rising Sun" and had asked Jon to play it for him. Jon hadn't learned the song, and Parinello was not impressed.

"Don't waste my time, kid..." he told Jon, and threatened to stop teaching him. It gave Jon a strong lesson in discipline. Every starry-eyed kid that has ever taken up the performing arts knows both the excitement and frustration of practicing. What keeps you going is recognizing the value of practicing every day – even if it sucks sometimes.

Ask any musician and they will tell you stories of falling asleep with their instrument beside them and practicing scales for hours on end. They'll tell you how they missed out on other fun kid stuff because they were honing their chops and memorizing theory. When you love something, you keep at it relentlessly, even if your fingers bleed. If you can find the Zen in practicing your craft, it can be a satisfying and productive place, and the discipline just becomes a part of you.

* * *

In the fall of 1973, a kid named Les Starkey changed my life. Les showed up one morning in our Grade Eight class at Queensmount Senior Public School, a month or so after the school year started. His thick British accent drew my attention. I had dreamed about England ever since my days in the High Park house. I wanted to go over and talk to him right away, but I waited until after school. I figured I'd catch up with him as he walked home.

I raced across the school grounds on my brand new 10-speed, pedaling in top gear. I spotted him up ahead near the roadway and picked up speed. As I neared him, I suddenly realized I wouldn't be able to stop in time. I gripped my rear brake handle as hard as I could, my rear tire skidding on the grass and gravel. Les spun around, horrified to see me sliding sideways toward him. He put his hands out and shouted "Oh no!" I stopped mere inches away from him. I apologized as I gasped for breath. I was so embarrassed. Les was good-natured about it and we introduced ourselves. Les has retold this story many times over the years and it always goes the same… "I was almost bloody-well killed!"

From that day on, we were good friends. Les was a diehard KISS fan and it didn't take long for him to turn me into one too. The costumes and the characters they created appealed to my sense of fantasy. Their raw energy intoxicated me. Les always got the new KISS album the first day it came out. I would go to his house after school and we would sit and listen to both sides, over and over, while passing the album cover back and forth. We would dissect and discuss what we thought the lyrics meant, or what had inspired the guys to write that bit, or which girl had inspired that other bit. For the first time in my life I had someone to talk to about playing music, rock stars, and rock 'n' roll life.

Les had a special LP rack in his room dedicated to KISS albums. We would go through these albums cover by cover talking about the evolution of the group and where we thought they might be heading next. In those days, the only way you knew what a band looked like was by their picture on the album cover, or from a live performance. KISS played a lot in that part of the country, and over the next six years I got to see them on every tour, up to and including the Dynasty tour of '79. In the '70s, music videos were still many years away, but concert tickets were cheap. We saw every KISS show that came within a four-hour radius of Kitchener.

Toronto, London, Buffalo, and Detroit dates were always within our radar. It was then I really started enjoying the rock 'n' roll road. We took the bus and spent the day wandering around until the concert started. It was so cool to see my musical heroes come to life in a concert auditorium. The power and ferocity of the music coupled with thousands of fans screaming and applauding was like energizing thunder. After the show, we spilled onto the streets with the crowds. There was an electric feel as we walked through the big cities at night, far away from home. It fuelled my wanderlust. I wanted to be one of the guys on stage, singing and playing to thousands. I wanted to get a real rock band together and hit the road. I had read the story of how KISS was discovered in a nightclub and that became my goal. I would put a band together. We would play in the clubs, and we would be discovered.

Jon Bon Jovi was also a KISS fan and would one day open for them across Europe. Jon's rock 'n' roll buddy in those days was Dave "The Snake" Sabo. As with Les and I, they shared a love for music and playing guitar. Dave was one of Jon's first musical accomplices. They swore a pact that if one of them got famous he would help the other out. Jon kept that promise years later when he helped Dave, a founding guitar player in the rock band Skid Row, to secure a record deal with Atlantic Records.

Back in my world, Les Starkey introduced me to an organization and a way of life that would go on to shape the rest of my teenage years. The Kitchener Police Department had created a special boxing and martial arts youth program that was operated by members of the police force. The program was designed to offer young offenders and troubled teens an option to avoid being absorbed into the juvenile social services system. It was a program of self-defense and personal discipline. It gave teens a place to enjoy physical activity and learn about themselves through the rigors of mental training and personal combat. Senior police officers eventually formed a Police Cadet corps that would offer the same developmental program within a military-style cadet organization.

Les joined the corps almost immediately upon his arrival in Canada. He was in a similar organization in England and loved it.

He asked me to come along for a recruitment drive and I did; I had already learned a lot from Les and this police school idea seemed a good way for us to hang out. The following week I went with Les to check it out.

The 2873 Kitchener Waterloo Cadet Organization Police School (KW COPS) operated much like a military academy, and had armories located on Victoria Street in Kitchener. The old building housed Quartermaster stores and a small munitions storage. Offices and lecture rooms surrounded a large open section in the center of the building that served as the unit's parade square. The building was a bit dark and dingy, but there was adequate lighting over the parade square. I found myself a chair at the very back wall behind everyone, and watched the cadets gather at the edge of the square. About forty guys were dressed in dark khaki wool uniforms, light khaki collar shirts, and skinny khaki ties. On their red berets they had shiny brass badges. The uniforms reminded me of old war movies, pictures of my grandfather, and Remembrance Day parades. The guys milled about the edge of the square, talking and practicing various movements. Some groups had everyone doing the movements together and it looked so cool. Les' movements were quick and precise. It gave me a sense of great respect for his ability and discipline. It suited him well. Les had a calm reason in the way he thought and communicated, and yet he was still a total rock 'n' roll fan. I figured it was because he was British and that was how they were.

"Form up!" one of the older guys barked, and the whole roomful of guys converged on the center of the huge floor. Two smaller groups took shape until the entire complement shared equal numbers in each section. Each had twenty guys formed in lines of five; four rows deep – a platoon. Some of the ranking soldiers stood at the front of each section. Two guys that looked about 17 stood under Queen Elizabeth II's picture at the front of the room, facing the two platoons. One was Warrant Officer; the other held a higher rank – a Master Warrant Officer and Company Sargent Major.

"Parade!" he snapped. Every voice in the place went silent. Only the rustling of sleeves was heard as each man placed both hands behind his back in smart fashion.

"Attention!" All 40 guys raised their right legs at the knee ten inches high and slammed their feet down tight against their left. The sound of those 40 boots hitting the concrete is something I will never forget. The Sergeant Major turned about in a single, quick movement, slammed his foot down, and faced the Queen. An older guy, who looked to be in his twenties, came marching around the corner. His insignia was that of Chief Warrant Officer – the Regimental Sergeant Major. He wore a Forge Cap and held under his left arm a three-foot wooden shaft with shiny chrome end caps – his pace stick. He swung his free arm from behind his back and forward to the height of his breast pocket like a perfect pendulum as he marched toward the Company Sergeant Major. He turned, stopped in front of the junior officer, and spoke for a brief moment. He then wheeled away and took position behind the company, whereupon the Regimental Sergeant Major began barking instructions outlining the evening's activities. It was in control and precise. I fell in love with the whole thing and signed up that night. The boxing and Judo programs, combined with the military structure and discipline, were a perfect fit. I was so proud when I received my uniform, and quickly became one of the most spit-and-polish cadets in the Corps. Hundreds of hours of marching and drill followed. My life was filled with outdoor combat and survival exercises, rifle and grenade ranges, and summer camps. Confidence and personal discipline began to fuel my perseverance and determination. I decided I was first and foremost - a soldier. I concentrated all my efforts at succeeding and working my way up the ranks. Music took a backseat, and weeks went by where I didn't even tune my guitar.

The military may have distracted me from my dreams of rock stardom, but it gave me a more confident and controlled state of being. For the next five years, it ruled my world.

When I joined KW COPS I got a military buzz cut. It was the middle of the '70s and everyone else had long hair with feathered bangs. There I was – G.I. Joe. I felt out of place everywhere except with my military friends. I have read how Jon Bon Jovi felt out of place during his school years. He felt ostracized by other kids and was a loner too, in many ways. At least he had long hair and looked cool.

Cadets was the first place where I really started to mix with girls in a way I had never done in school. I joined cadets while I was smack in the middle of puberty. Although women had served in the Canadian Armed Forces since before WW II, there were only two or three girls at KW COPS in the early days, and their training was often held separate and away from the guys. Eventually more girls joined, and that's when my real socialization with the fairer sex began.

KW COPS had a big blue bus to pick up cadets around the city. The ride home was something I looked forward to all week long. After we were dismissed for the night we would pile back into the bus. Whatever length of time you had before your stop came up was the amount of time you had to make your moves.

Girls who got dropped off first rarely got charmed – there just wasn't enough time. Sometimes you would spend the whole ride working your feeble magic and end up with no reward. Other times, if you did your groundwork earlier in the night, you could pair off soon after the bus left the armories. As soon as we pulled out of the parking lot, the senior officer driving the bus would turn out the interior lights and crank the eight-track player. I remember making out with Bernice Chauvin in the back of that bus while Black Sabbath's "Paranoid" blared through the speakers. I felt like Ironman.

I was a different kid around my cadet peers. We were all in it together and we learned about life through a military lens. The girls at cadets didn't intimidate me. They weren't the preppy girls and cheerleaders who turned their noses up at geeks like me. All the guys had short hair and the girls were okay with that. Maybe it's true what they say about a man in uniform. Whatever it was, it was working for me in a way it had never worked before.

I was in the military from age 13 to 18. I learned to drink, I learned about weapons, drill, discipline, and friendship. And I got laid.

I was interested in weapons and I loved to target shoot. I quickly mastered the concentration, focus, breathing, and body-positioning skills required to become an excellent shot and started accumulating awards. I had won my crossed rifles, and eventually crossed rifles and crown, and my scores won me a trip to the Dominion of Canada Rifle Association (DCRA). While at the DCRA I met a female cadet named Debbie; she outranked me and was a year and a half older. One night, after range practice was over for the day and everyone was hooting and hollering in the mess tent, she grabbed me and took me out to the middle of a wooded section at the far end of the range. She knew exactly what she was doing, and for that I was grateful. I was 15 years old and I had never had sex -- at least not with another person. I was nervous and tried to be as cool as possible during the whole thing. My excitement got the better of me and it was over pretty quick. But that night under the stars, on top of my poncho, at the skillful hands of an older woman, I became a man.

I never saw or heard from Debbie again and I can't quite picture her face, but I will remember that night forever.

CHAPTER FIVE

My tenure with cadets saw me graduate into the Canadian Armed Forces Reserve with the Highland Fusiliers of Canada. I rarely sang or played anymore. In my mind, the two worlds couldn't co-exist, so I held rock 'n' roll at arm's length. I was almost embarrassed to talk about rock 'n' roll around my military buddies, and I never spoke about the military to anyone outside of cadets. I felt as long as I compartmentalized my life, I was free to roam each world without fear of contamination. My soldier-self had no time for the inane folly of rock 'n' roll, and my fledgling rock star self wouldn't tolerate the rigid nature of military structure and discipline. School was running a distant third, with football and Glee Club the only things that kept me there. My grades fell, and I skipped classes more and more.

My mom and step-dad separated that year. I tried to act surprised when they told me, but I felt that was just the way things were sometimes. People didn't always stay together. I went to bed that night and thought back to how happy Mom had been at the wedding. Floyd had a good job and would be able to give us a life that Mom never could alone. My brother Christian arrived in December of 1968, and then Patrick completed the set in 1970. I enjoyed having siblings and two parents. We were a real family, and we would last forever. But we didn't.

My parents asked me with whom I wanted to live, and I chose Mom. It was as simple as that. My brothers, who were still quite young, went with Floyd. Mom and I moved into an apartment across town while my brothers and Floyd remained in the family home. It was hoped the younger boys would be less traumatized by my parents' split if things remained as normal as possible. I was excited to be on my own with Mom. It would be like the old times – Mom and me against the world.

I had begun dating a girl named Shelley Hause. Shelley was my first love. She was a year older than me, more mature and in tune with the world. Shelley urged me to get back into music. She believed the military was a safety blanket that held me back from doing what I was meant to do. She pressed me to get out and meet people in the music world, to get focused on my dreams again.

I went to militia less and less and then stopped all together. I spent all my time with Shelley and rock 'n' roll again became the center of my universe. Shelley introduced me to a friend of hers named Norma Jeanne Laurette who had a band called Black Star. They played Christian youth organization dances, competed in various contests, and had been on local TV.

Norma Jeanne Laurette was one of the most cosmic people I had ever met and my first real experience with a true "rock chick." NJ had long, straight, hippy hair and wore peasant blouses with wide bell-bottoms. She had these little feather things in her hair, and reminded me of the hippy girl in the Billy Jack movies. She had this groovy, spacey kind of vibe when she talked. She played electric guitar and her brother Robbie played drums. NJ sang an impressive version of Barbara Streisand's "Evergreen" on a real album with the St. Aloysius Folk Choir. I was blown away.

The church let NJ use the speakers from the congregation room and the stage in the downstairs auditorium. She had a small guitar amplifier on her side of the stage and a slightly larger amp beside the drums. There were two other girls, Cathy Maser and Christine Penzak, who sang background vocals and played percussion for the band. Cathy also played flute and did a string rendition of the flute part in the first number they played, Led Zeppelin's "Stairway to Heaven." The band sounded amazing to me, and I was impressed by the way the girls sang together. When Robbie came in on the drums, it absolutely blew my mind. The sound of his drums and cymbals right there in front of me almost knocked me over. I wanted to play too! I could feel NJ's guitar through her little amp, and the drums were blowing right through me. They ended the song with a final crash and I couldn't help but applaud.

"Why don't you grab that bass and play along?" NJ asked me, and motioned to the guitar case beside the drums. Without hesitating, I went over and grabbed the case. I unpacked the instrument and put the strap around my neck. I plugged it into the amp and slowly turned up the knobs. It was the first plugged-in bass I had ever held. I touched the low string and it boomed through the speaker. It was velvet thunder. It was my Gene Simmons-bass-god-rock-adoration on overdrive.

I pulled the string again and I was hooked. That was it. I was going to be a bass player. I looked up from the fret board and blurted, "Can I join your band?"

Everyone stopped what they were doing and turned to NJ. It was awkward, but it was too late to take it back. Everyone was silent. I waited.

Finally, NJ smiled and nodded. "Congratulations Ted. You're the new bass player!" It was just like that day at Mrs. Trudeau's choir practice. Everybody cheered and gathered around to shake my hand. I was in a real band. Life was beautiful.

CHAPTER SIX

Throughout his teen years, Jon Bon Jovi embraced rock 'n' roll. He was captivated by the success stories in the New Jersey scene and found inspiration from Bruce Springsteen and Southside Johnny and the Asbury Jukes. They were Jon's hometown heroes, and they motivated him to start performing live. He formed a band called Raze and competed in his school's battle of the bands at Sayreville War Memorial High. These contests were big deals in those days as there was very little else a teenager could do to get in front of an audience. The instant opportunities of Star Search, American Idol, The Voice, and X Factor were still decades away. There were hokey talent shows at the YMCA and on local TV, but they rarely allowed rock acts to get involved. Band contests in high school gyms and private parties in friends' basements were the only real outlets for teen rockers too young to get into bars.

Raze failed to garner any attention from the contest. For the next couple of years Jon scratched around the local scene, playing in various outfits and gaining valuable experience.

During my teen years, I worked a few different jobs; a couple of gas stations, and a pizza parlor. Then Mom got me a great job working at the local airport. She flew small aircraft there, having obtained her pilot's license shortly after leaving Floyd. She had graduated into aerobatics with her new boyfriend, stunt flyer Frank Jenkinson.

I flew right hand with her many times, and I welcomed the opportunity to spend time around aircraft. As the ramp rat for Waterloo Wellington Airport, I got to taxi aircraft, drive the fuel tankers, fuel the planes, and do lots of other cool stuff.

One day, a DC-3 landed at the airport. It belonged to KISS. And there they were, walking off the plane as I approached with the fuel truck. It was years before they would unmask and I got to see them in their prime - without make-up! It was awesome. I called Les right away to tell him about it. He was so stoked. It was the first time I felt I had done something he thought was cool.

I hadn't seen Les much lately. Once I quit the military, we spent less time together. We were both on the football team, but I had pretty much stopped showing up. We would run into each other at school and chat less each day. Les warned me not to forsake everything else in favor of music and that I needed more balance in my life. I barely listened. Soon, I wasn't going to school at all and we fell out of touch completely.

Although I loved that airport job and enjoyed having all that responsibility, I was young and easily distracted. I eventually left for a position at Northfield Metal Products, a steel welding and fabrication factory run by a local family called the Doerners. One of the older Doerners was a prominent lawyer in Waterloo and two of the younger Doerner boys, Brent and Brian, were part of a band called Helix – one of Kitchener's most famous musical exports at that time. I jumped at the chance to make some money to buy my own bass guitar.

While working at Northfield, I met Gord Forwell. He was a genuine rock 'n' roll longhair and one of the coolest guys I have ever met. He couldn't play a note, but he knew more about music and artists than anyone. Gord understood rock 'n' roll. He made working at Northfield a breeze for me.

Not long after we met, I started telling Gord about my band, how I wanted to be a singer/songwriter, and that I was learning to play bass guitar. He told me about this guy he knew who was putting a band together who might be looking for a singer and maybe a bass player. I had never considered being in two bands at one time; Gene Simmons only played in KISS, so did Paul, Ace, and Peter. I was afraid that going to the audition meant I had to decide between the two. Finally, I decided I'd go, and if they didn't pick me, I could stay in Black Star and never tell NJ what I'd done.

Gord arranged an audition in Brian Alexanian's basement. Brian Alexanian had the first home studio I'd ever seen. The Alexanians owned a successful carpet business in Kitchener, right next to the armories where I had attended cadets. Brian's studio was decked out with some nice gear. His sister Sue had a band and recorded there all the time. When I arrived at the Alexanian home, Sue greeted me at the door and led me downstairs where a guitar player and drummer were already jamming. The walls were insulated with stuffed burlap and there was a strange sense of claustrophobia as Sue closed the door behind us. Through a small window in the wall, I could see Brian in the adjacent room. He stood behind a large mixing board, with shelves of reel-to-reel tape boxes behind him. The guitar player looked up and motioned to the drummer to stop playing.

"You must be Ted." The guitar player spoke first. "I'm Jim." He smiled and stepped forward to extend his hand. "And that's Mike," he pointed toward the drums. Mike had his drum key in his teeth and was fixing one of his drums. He looked up for a second and nodded. He was a cool looking guy with long hair and a handlebar moustache. He looked like a real '70s rock guy and reminded me of Mick Fleetwood.

Jim, I thought, was a cross between Jeff Beck and John Lennon. My hair was still comparatively short and I felt so out-rocked by these two guys. I was going to have to kick some ass to be taken seriously. Mike finished his repairs and asked me if I knew "Rocky Mountain Way" by Joe Walsh. I had heard the song and knew it best from the Triumph version. I told him I had never sung it before, but I would give it a try.

"I'll start singing and then you come in," Mike said, and Jim played the opening chords. He was the best guitar player I had ever seen in person. Mike came in and he was equally formidable. I was nervous. When the vocal cue came Mike and I started singing together. I wailed the vocal with all my heart, and out of the corner of my eye, I saw Mike start smiling. He let me sing alone from there, and I nailed the verse with everything I had. They carried on until just before the next verse when Mike stopped the song.

"You're hired, man!" He grinned at me and extended his hand between his cymbals. Jim laughed and said, "No doubt, man, that was great!" He shook my hand and I stammered, "Thank you!" I was on top of the world.

"We're getting a bass player next week and we'll rehearse at my place," Jim said.

I was on cloud nine for the next three days. I started thinking about Black Star and being the bass player, and then about Jim and Mike and being their singer. I loved both ideas and I didn't want to give up either. I wanted to be a bass player. I could do that with Black Star. Jim and Mike already had a bass player in mind; I would just stand out front and sing. I wasn't good enough to play guitar alongside Jim. I would be like Mick Jagger or Robert Plant and just sing. That would be cool.

Jim called me every day for the next few days and we met at night in the basement at Gord's parents' house. We listened to music and burned incense. Gord's parents' basement had been named Gord's Bar and Grill, and a sign hung over the bar that said so. The place was stuffed to the brim with records and stereo equipment. Dozens of square plastic milk crates held thousands of LPs that would become my vinyl music professors. Gord had esoteric tastes mixed with rock of all kinds, old and new; he and Jim worshipped Todd Rundgren and I became addicted as well.

It was the beginning of a whole new world in musical discovery. It was in Gord's basement where Jim came up with the name for our new band. Jim was Dutch and had a grandmother who spoke little English. When Jim and his brothers were young, they had once irked her so much that she lashed out in English that they were all "a bunch of hellions." Mike and I loved the name, so Hellion was born.

That Thursday I went to Jim's place, and he brought me down to his basement where Mike was waiting. Mike was out of sorts and was talking to someone on the phone. All the gear was set up and I went over to look at the bass propped up against a large speaker cabinet.

"It's a Kay copy of a Rickenbacker 4001 bass," Jim said. I nodded without a clue. "And that's a Vox Super Beatle." I nodded again, staying silent. I had seen that same bass played by Geddy Lee from Rush when they played our high school. I became an instant fan after that show, and I started listening to his bass lines, along with Gene Simmons, and Greg Godovitz from the Toronto-based trio Goddo. I picked up the bass and marveled at the beautiful feel of the neck.

Mike hung up the phone angrily and announced to the two of us, "He's gotta work and he's not coming into town now until next week." Jim looked thoughtful for a second and then turned to me.

"Can you play bass at all?" I could tell he wanted me to say yes.

"Only a little." I told him, and explained I had just started with Black Star.

"Don't worry," Jim said. "I will teach you how to play. You can cover until the other guy gets here next week."

It was a great opportunity to get some lessons from the most accomplished player I had ever met. I picked along as best I could while we ran a few songs. I had little knowledge on the instrument, but I kept it simple and dropped out when I was unsure. Jim and Mike were confident I could be good enough to cover for now. The new bass player was on the way.

The guy never materialized. Mike and Jim told me the following week I would be the bass player and that was it. Over the next few weeks, Jim gave me a crash course on how to play simple rock bass lines and scales. He drew up some finger charts with scales that became the basis of my bass playing chops. From there, I would build my skills by lifting bass lines off records from pop rock groups like Boston, Styx, Triumph, Rush, Goddo, Max Webster, and of course, KISS.

Jim was an excellent teacher, but there were times when he was also a brutal taskmaster.

On one occasion, Jim was having a dinner party at his house and invited me over to jam before everyone arrived. He sat me down in the basement and told me I had to learn the bass parts for "School," from Supertramp's Crime of the Century album. This was the first time I had listened to this monumental album with the intention of learning the bass lines. That kind of playing was way beyond me. The parts were involved and had a sparse, syncopated feel. To my newbie ears, it was like a complex orchestral arrangement. I looked at Jim in horror. Until now, I'd mostly been learning songs by fumbling around on the bass while records were playing, all the while daydreaming about how one day I would know how to play. Now, Jim expected me to learn parts from players whom I felt were masters of music.

"No dinner for you until you learn the parts." He laughed.

I hoped he was kidding. But he left me there. I struggled in that basement all through dinner and well into that evening until I finally had a rudimentary handle on the song.

Jim was satisfied enough so he fed me. I went home to bed, completely spent from the experience. I will always remember this as the beginning of my understanding of song structure and deconstruction. Drop the needle on the record, listen close, pick up the needle, play it, drop it back down. Begin again, listen close, play, try it... repeat ad nauseum.

It was a long time before I was able to just listen to a song again. Every time I would hear a song on the radio or at a party, I began to hear a collection of parts playing that formed the whole. The bass became separate from the drums, which were separate from the guitars, and again separate from keyboards and vocals. Everything became separate pieces of a gelled ensemble. It was years before I could enjoy songs again without deconstructing them in my head, but not before I went through a spiraling education and musical awakening. My song naiveté, my listener's innocence... it was gone. I had fallen down the rabbit hole.

CHAPTER SEVEN

I desperately wanted to play in the bars. It was where I felt I needed to be. Every band I admired in my piece of the world had played in the barrooms of Southwestern Ontario. Rush, Max Webster, FM, and Saga had all made the jump to larger concert venues, but bands like Crowbar, Major Hoople's Boarding House, Fable Manor, Sphynx, Starchild, and Yukon still haunted the local bars. I wanted to be a part of that scene, but I was still underage.

Then I met Dave Bailey, one of my first mentors in the behind-the-scenes of rock 'n' roll. He took me to one of the Hellfield shows in a tavern in Toronto. They already had one album out and two singles called "Tell Me Are You Listening" and "Too Long." They were genuine rock stars.

Dave had a fake ID and looked a lot older than he was. I had an ID card from militia and a buddy of mine had doctored it, adding a few years. It worked for R-rated movies, but I had never tried it at a tavern. When I handed the bouncer my card, he barely looked at it and waved us in. I did my best to contain my excitement.

Although it was dark and dingy, to me it was the coolest rock palace in the world. The band's equipment was onstage and huge speakers were stacked on each side. The place smelled like cigarette smoke and stale beer. I took in the surroundings while Dave spoke to one of the band's roadies. The guy took us upstairs to meet the band. They were all sitting around chatting, and Dave introduced me to them one by one. They all shook my hand and it was such an incredible thrill to meet some real rock stars.

It was time for them to go on, so Dave and I went back down to get seats in the bar. The stage was blacked out and I could barely make out the band members' silhouettes. Suddenly, the entire room erupted in an explosion of sound and light. The band started with "The Pact," a powerful synthesizer octave–bouncing riff followed by Mitch's screaming vocal, "I AM NOT A - MORTAL MAN!"

The band joined in with a huge background chorus of vocals and a bone-crushing downbeat that rattled the foundation of the small club. The sound was so loud and the lights so bright, they crushed my senses. My pulse raced, and I became aware of the huge grin on my face. The enormous power that emanated from the stage was nothing I had witnessed before. I loved the KISS and Styx concerts, but in those concert settings, I was prepared for what was coming and sat several rows away in a large auditorium. Here, in a small barroom that held maybe 100 people, I was completely engulfed in the sights and sounds of a band that was pounding out pure rock 'n' roll. Never again would I feel that particular kind of adrenaline watching a live act. I fell in love with barroom rock music that night and dreamed of the day it would be me on stage.

My chance came a few weeks later. Jim got a call from a local agent asking us to substitute for a band that had cancelled. The job was ours if we wanted it, but we would have only one week to have three 50-minute sets ready to go. There was no way we could learn that many songs, but Jim figured we could just play as many as we knew and then we could repeat what we needed. We accepted the offer and got to work. We practiced seven days a week until the afternoon of the show. I was so pumped. We had an actual gig in a real bar. I hadn't been this excited since the opening night of Old King Cole.

The gig was in Elmira, a half hour's drive away. It was my first road trip to a gig and I was on the edge of my seat with excitement when we stopped at the back doors of the hotel. The bar manager met us at the door. He was a portly man with a fierce countenance.

"Let me see your ID," he said.

I rifled through my wallet and handed him my trusty military card.

He frowned. "You're 21 years old?"

I nodded and said nothing. He looked me up and down, narrowed his eyes, and relented.

"Fine." He handed me back the fake ID.

"Alright, you guys load in and get set up, no pissing around." He turned to walk away, and then stopped. "Stay away from my waitresses" he warned. "And don't bother my customers."

The place looked like a saloon out of the Old West. Jim snorted, "This isn't even slightly rock 'n' roll." I looked at the wagon wheels on the walls and bales of hay at the side of the stage. I didn't care. This was our big debut! Jim had invited some of his friends and a couple of agents from the local booking agency. They arrived just before show time and added to my growing nervousness. Jim and Mike had experience in bars and were pretty cool about the gig. I sat backstage and ran through some riffs I was having trouble with. Mike practiced with his sticks on the back of a chair and Jim noodled through some scales. We had put together a mix of killer rock songs and were feeling good about the set. When show time came, I walked onstage with the guys and looked out at the crowd. The room was mostly empty.

Hank Williams was cut off mid-song, and the guys at the pool table groaned. The lights snapped on and the few people there stared at us.

"Let's go, boys!" Mike called out and counted in the first song,

"Honky Tonk Women," by the Rolling Stones. We had put what we thought to be all of our country-sounding songs at the beginning of the show in the hopes we could appease the locals. We had a few Lynyrd Skynyrd songs, some ZZ Top, and a Marshall Tucker number. We stacked them back-to-back for the first set. I stared down at the neck of my bass and didn't look up the entire first song. I did my best to concentrate on my parts and not screw up.

No one clapped and no one danced. It was obvious we were a rock band and no amount of Southern Blues was going work. After the first set, the manager came to the front of the stage and told us to come with him.

"Pack up boys," he said. "It ain't working."

I was devastated – fired from my first bar gig.

"Don't get me wrong," he said, as he drew three glasses of draught from the tap on the bar. "You guys are a good band - it ain't nothin' personal. It's just not right for my place." He slid a glass of beer to each of us.

"I spoke to your agent over there and told him you guys are great. I just don't think you belong here." I looked over and saw two middle-aged guys in matching satin jackets at a nearby table. One of the guys motioned Jim to come over. I stayed at the bar with Mike. When Jim came back, he was smiling.

"That's Tim and Brian from Dram Agency," he said, picking up his glass and holding it out to us. "Boys, they are interested in working with us and they want us to go down to their office on Monday." I was over the moon. I thought it was the best news I had heard in my life.

"That's cool," said Mike.

"Yeah, that's cool." I parroted. I tapped my glass to theirs. I didn't know how to feel. I hated getting fired, but I figured if they were cool with all of this, so was I. We finished our drinks and hauled our gear out of the bar.

The bar manager had given Jim $50 and we were well ahead after paying for gas. It was hard to sleep that night. I wrestled with the disappointment of getting canned and the excitement of my first booking agency meeting. It was a weird way to get started. We recounted our adventures the next night at Gord's and he told us that it was the best thing that could have happened.

"You guys are a rock band," he said. "You stick to your guns." He quoted all kinds of examples of bands that had met with rejection when they started out. He told us how Led Zeppelin got their name when someone said their music would go over "like a lead Zeppelin." He recounted other stories he had heard or read about bands struggling and sticking to their guns. It was a big lesson in being resilient and believing in one's self — even if others didn't.

I spent Sunday scheming on how to get out of work Monday so I could go to the meeting with the guys. I could call in sick. It was just one day, and besides, this meeting was way too important.

Early Monday morning, I caught the bus to Jim's house. Mike was already there and we headed down to the Dram offices. Mike and Jim had both been there before, but it was my first time in the offices of an entertainment agency. The reception area was cramped, but well lit. Glossy photos of bands and entertainers lined the walls. The only name I recognized was Helix. The rest were bands that played the local scene.

Jim and Mike knew some of the guys in the posters personally and told me about the bands that were getting lots of gigs in the area. All these bands and variety acts were playing gigs throughout southern Ontario, and some of them had even been out west and to the USA. I looked around and tried to remain calm. A tall, stout man in a brown, collared shirt and silver tie emerged from one of the offices. He waved the three of us in. More pictures adorned the walls of the small, wood-paneled office. Sunlight filtered through clouds of cigarette smoke.

"Who's the young fellow?" he asked as he sat down behind his cluttered desk.

"My name is Ted Moore," I said loud and clear, and extended my hand.

"I'm Brian Daly," he responded with a slight smile. He shook my hand with a clammy, limp grip. His hand was large and I squeezed it tighter until he tightened up his grip. He didn't take his eyes off me. Finally, he loosened his grip and we released hands. My palm was covered in sweat.

The three of us sat down on the overstuffed, fake leather couch at the far end of the office. "Ok, boys," he stared across the room. He flipped through some pages stapled together on his desk. "I want you to have a look at this contract and then sign on the last page. I have to go check on a couple things. I'll be back in a few minutes." He got up, dropped the contract and pen on the coffee table in front of us, and then walked out.

That was it? Did we just get signed? I looked at Jim.

"It's just an agency contract," he said. "Don't get too excited. All it means is they will book us a bunch of gigs and we'll have to pay them commission."

I was still overwhelmed. I listened as best as I could while Jim and Mike went through each page of the agreement. I didn't understand most of it. I just wanted to sign it and get gigs.

When Brian returned, he picked up the signed contract and shook all our hands with the same sweaty, limp grip. He told us about the venues and acts they worked with and how we could get lots of work if we followed their direction. We left feeling pretty good about ourselves.

Nothing came up over the next few weeks, but we concentrated on getting our show ready for when we got the call. I spent less time with Black Star, so NJ's other brother filled in on bass while I rehearsed with Hellion. It was obvious I couldn't manage everything going on in my life. I was 17 and rarely showed up at school anymore. I spent my time at work, rehearsing, or talking about music at Gord's place.

I don't know if the agency ever called; Jim and Mike found places for us to play. We performed a small assortment of gigs around the Kitchener - Waterloo area and gathered a following. Mike landed us a gig at a place in Maryhill, at the Stage Stop Bar in the Trail's End Hotel. We were to play every second Saturday night.

After a few of these Saturdays went by, the locals gathered a committee to stop us. They went to the local paper and claimed we sounded like "a bunch of head hunters that had invaded their neighborhood." Our first press review! I think Mike still has the clipping. (He later named one of his bands The Headhunters.) The locals ended up effectively pleading their case and our gigs were cancelled.

Later that year, we played the Bridgeport Rod and Gun Club. The audience went wild as we rocked the night away. Tragically, some girls from the audience were badly maimed in a car accident after the show. We tried to get back our enthusiasm for the band, but after that night, we lost momentum. Eventually we stopped playing altogether. Hellion was over. Further, Norma Jeanne's brother had taken over on bass and Black Star had moved on without me.

Devastated, I quit school, quit my job, and hitched a ride out to Calgary with a friend who was visiting relatives. That summer I met a guy named Matt Hutton. He had the most bizarre music collection I had ever heard: Spyro Gyra, Triumvirat, Gentle Giant, King Crimson, Vangelis, Brian Eno, Adrian Belew and a lot of other artists I had never heard of. We burned a lot of incense and listened to records.

One day I spotted some suspicious-looking characters cruising through the racks at A&A records, where I had just landed a job. They approached me and we started talking. They said they were looking for a roommate to share expenses in a large house in southwest Calgary. I was wearing out my welcome at Matt's, so I accepted.

The dilapidated old house was near all the music stores, and there were a lot of musicians living in that area. The guys called the house 'The Frankenstein Place' as an ode to The Rocky Horror Picture Show. It had a mannequin on the upstairs balcony named Doris and a host of curious artwork and posters scotch-taped to the cracked walls. The basement was a crumbling cement dungeon with a dirt floor converted into a jam space. Musicians from all over Calgary came to The Frankenstein Place, and we spent hours making plans about forming a band and getting gigs. Most of these plans got lost in clouds of smoke.

Butch Bouchard was the actual renter of the house. He came from Montreal to form a band with some guys who soon gave up on the Calgary scene and went home. I was still licking my wounds from losing Hellion and Black Star, and Butch was bitter and jaded.

Still, we believed we could get a band together and make it work. We auditioned new members; but everyone wanted to party and no one wanted to put in the work. Eventually, Butch gave up and moved back to Quebec. I took over the master bedroom and his share of the rent.

My record store job wasn't paying enough, so I took a second job; I started work as a busboy in downtown cabaret called Lucifers. It was easy money and I got to see a lot of the touring acts that came through Calgary in 1979. It was great, but it reminded me I was without a band of my own.

I tried out for a few local bands: Audio, Mantra, and The Tickets. No one would hire me. For the remainder of the summer, I continued to audition any players that came to The Frankenstein Place to jam. Everyone was reluctant to commit to anything that required real work. I became frustrated and decided I couldn't stay in Calgary any longer. I would to go back to Kitchener and reconnect with Jim. At least he was a serious guy, and maybe we could put something together again. I quit my jobs and used the last of my money to buy a plane ticket home. I told myself not to worry. The future was wide open.

Chapter Eight

I returned to Kitchener in the fall of 1979. I called up Jim and learned he was playing in a country trio with Mike called Six O'clock News. There wasn't a spot for me in the band. However, Jim told me about a friend, Randy Dichnoether, who played keyboards for a touring show band called Teen Angel and the Rockin' Rebels. They were a '50s and '60s band with a doo-wop sound and greaser image. They were looking for a roadie to go on tour with them.

I liked the idea of travelling, and as I didn't really have any other prospects for playing I went to check them out. I had bought a used bass in Calgary I was in the habit of carrying with me everywhere. I took it with me and hitched a ride to the hotel where the band was playing.

Jim's buddy Randy was a stern guy, but not completely unpleasant. He introduced me to Earl Torno, a soundman who worked at the Toronto music store that provided the band's equipment. Earl looked about the same age as me, but was far more experienced when it came to rock 'n' roll. I followed him around and plied him with questions while he was setting up. Earl was keen to share his experiences with gear, bands, and music. We talked throughout the afternoon and I helped with whatever I could. He was easy-going, and I enjoyed his dry humor and quiet sarcasm.

Musicians were milling about onstage when the lead singer, Ron, appeared at the back of the club.

He was a middle-aged man, looking a little bit like a used car salesman, but he seemed in reasonably good shape. He wore a white suit jacket and white dress shoes.

His voice sounded thick and weathered when he called to the stage across the large, empty club.

"How much longer, Gary?"

The band's bass player called back. "We still have to hook up the microphone cables, and no one's even turned on the lights."

"Who's going to hook up the 220?" Ron asked, and looked back toward Earl and me at the soundboard. Earl asked where the power panel was and Ron said he would show us. We followed him toward the kitchen while he laughed as he told us how a guy he knew had hooked up the 220 power and almost electrocuted himself. Apparently, the shock had sent the guy flying and fused his wrench to his hand. I was a little freaked out as Ron pulled off a cover from a large panel on the wall to reveal electrical wiring and connections.

"I shouldn't have to do this stuff," Ron said. "Can one of you guys handle this?" Earl told him he would show me how to do it and I said I would take care of it. He stepped back as Earl drew me to the panel and walked me through the steps of connecting the 220 power wires into the wall connections. He shut off the power and tied in the thick rubber-shielded cable that ran to the stage. I watched closely and finished doing the last connection by myself while Earl and Ron looked on.

"You looking for a job?" Ron asked me.

"Yes Sir!" I blurted out.

Ron laughed. "It's yours if you want it." He explained that the band was heading out on tour through the Maritimes, and although there was not a lot of money, he would see what he could do to pay me a reasonable salary. I accepted the job and shook his hand, thanking him over and over again. I was ecstatic. It was perfect.

For the rest of the afternoon, I wandered around the hotel telling anyone I encountered that I was "with the band." Earl showed me the lighting equipment and gave me a brief run through on how to set up and plug in lights. The entire light show consisted of eight Par 64 fixtures, a bunch of cables, and some large transformer-looking boxes that Earl called dimmer packs. He explained that I would plug the lights into them so I could control them with the light board. Step by step, I followed Earl's instructions. I hung the lights above the stage and tightened the clamps. I ran the cables from the lights to the dimmer packs, ran the light board control line – which Earl called "the snake" – and then hooked up the 220 cable to the dimmer packs. I turned on the power switch and watched as the equipment came to life. I ran back and pushed up one of the sliders on the light board. The stage was washed with light. Earl congratulated me on my work.

Ron was standing by the bar, chewing on a straw and watching. "I don't want any green," he called out. "Green makes people think of Christmas, and Christmas makes people think of spending money." He chuckled. "If I see any green gels in those lights you're fired." I asked Earl what gels were. He opened a small road case under the light board and produced colored sheets of plastic film and a handful of metal frames.

"The gels go in the frames and the frames go in the lights," he said, and I ran with the bundle to the stage to sort it out. I figured it out in a minute or two, and soon red, blue, pink, and yellow lights were streaming across the stage. It was breathtaking, and I had done it all. I was the light man for the band. Earl had the microphones plugged in and began testing the speakers with a microphone plugged directly into the soundboard.

"Check... check... testing one, two, three..." Earl's voice boomed through the loudspeakers. "I'm ready for a sound check," he said. "Let's start with the drums."

The band made their way across the bar to the stage. "Can one of you guys clean up these cables back here?" one of the guys called out toward Earl and me. "There's a bunch of lighting shit all over the place and I'm going to wipe out for sure." I bolted toward the side of the stage and saw the mess of cabling I created during setup.

"It's alright," he smiled as he plugged in his bass. "You have a lot going on today."

"I'll get this cleaned up right away," I said, and set about tidying up the cables. I could hear the drums banging one by one as Earl called for each individual drum in sequence. I couldn't see the drummer clearly, but I could hear the tone of the drums changing in the room as Earl worked his magic at the soundboard. He would adjust each drum until he was satisfied and then move on to the next. When the drums were tuned, he began working with the bass player. I finished tidying up and ran back to the board to watch the rest of sound check. Bass, guitar, keyboards, and saxophone followed in turn.

I studied the process and learned as much as I could, trying to not bother Earl. Ron came up, checked his microphone, and told some jokes. They were crude and corny.

"How about a song?" Earl called to the stage.

"Moe went upstairs," Gary replied, motioning to the drum set. "You'll have to make do with what you got."

Earl sighed and rolled his eyes. "Fine," he said. It shouldn't be a problem. I'll have it all together in the first couple of songs. See you at show time."

The band was going for supper and Ron arranged for Earl and me to be fed too. It was awesome sitting with Earl, eating my free roadie dinner, and talking about rock 'n' roll. Earl told me we would do other shows along our way to the Maritimes. I was incredibly excited, and asked every question I could think of about being on the road. Earl tried to answer as much as possible, but added that Ron had been vague about travel and we would find out more later. Before show time, Earl adjusted the equipment and showed me how to aim the lights. "It's really up to each guy's own tastes" he explained. "You'll figure out what works best for you soon enough."

Around 8 p.m. people began filling up the club. The crowd looked to be in their 30s and 40s. Some looked older. I felt like a kid at a grown-ups' party. Within an hour, the place was almost full and Earl told me it was show time. I watched the band make their way toward the stage. I kept the lights off, preparing to turn them on only when the music began. Ron was not onstage and I searched the room for him.

"Where's Ron?" I asked.

"The band starts first and then he goes on after." he said. "Get ready. They're going to start any second now."

My palms were sweating and my fingers twitched nervously. I was ready to push up the faders at the first note.

The band started playing and I quickly slammed up all the faders on the board so hard that I knocked the light board off the road case it was sitting on. I heard Earl laugh as I scrambled to get the light board back into place, flashing the lights to the music as fast as I could while I resituated the board. It took me a few seconds to regain my composure. After a minute or so, I decided I was doing a good job. It would be cool to do this for a living.

The band was dressed as '50s greasers with their hair combed into ducktails. Their clothes consisted of t-shirts with rolled-up sleeves, penny loafers, and peg leg black slacks. The guy on sax had a pack of cigarettes rolled into one of his shirtsleeves. The bass player, Gary, spoke to the crowd as the rest of the band brought down the volume. I could see the guys in the band were cuing off of Gary while he nodded slowly to the drummer. The drummer brought the level down a little further and they all sat grooving Elvis's CC Rider riff.

Gary welcomed the crowd to the show and started to introduce Ron. Gary's voice got louder and more excited and the band got louder with him. Finally, he roared: "… and from Los Angeles California… Teeeeeen Angel!"

The band played even louder and Ron came running from the wings. I turned up the lights to full blast, a huge grin on my face. Everyone clapped for Ron as he waved to the crowd and grabbed his microphone from the stand. He was wearing a black suede suit jacket and blue jeans that made him look younger and somehow more cool than my first impression of him.

Ron sang CC Rider, and I looked around the large room at the 200 or so faces watching the stage. Everyone was impressed and attentive. Ron boomed through the songs and I sang along.

"His voice is all right," Earl said over the music. "Okay for this kind of stuff."

In my eyes, Ron was larger than life. He was clearly the star of the show.

He talked to the crowd between songs and one song often blended into another. The pace was fast and they hustled from song to song – sometimes with no stops in between. Some of the songs were medleys of several tunes.

As far as I could tell, the band knew the arrangements well, and

I watched as they played their respective parts in the show. Visually, they were quite different looking from one another. Their costumes tied it all together. The drummer was obviously the youngest member of the band. He had a roundish face with just a hint of a moustache and dark hair slicked back behind his ears. Randy also looked young and stood tall behind his small electric piano. He had blonde hair and kind of looked like Squiggy from Laverne and Shirley. He had a definite comical style in his moves and facial expressions. The older guy on sax swayed slowly back and forth, sometimes looking around the stage, smiling, and occasionally nodding toward the audience.

Gary looked older to me as well, but I appreciated how much of the show seemed to be his doing, and guessed he'd been at this for a long time.

As the show went on the guitar player really drew my attention. His name was Rob, and he seemed to be the coolest, most together guy in the band. He gave me the impression he had a real command over his own performance as well as his role in the show; I couldn't help following him with my eyes as he glided back and forth to the microphone to sing. When time came for his guitar solo, he stood at the edge of the stage and looked boldly into the audience. His duck-tailed hair was perfect as was his black sleeveless T-shirt tucked into his black slacks. He was the '50s rebel of the group, and added a Fonzie cool to the band.

They pounded through the set, and I recognized a lot of the material from my K-Tel album of 25 Rock Revival Greats. My cousins and I had played that record over and over, acting out the songs, playing air guitar, drums, and piano.

I sang along and played with the lights until the Elvis riff started up again and Ron left the stage waving and smiling to the crowd. The band continued to play while Gary announced they would be back with the '60s show, and told everyone to stick around until then. The band slammed down the last note of the song, and I shut off the lights in perfect cue.

I waited for the applause to die down and tried to catch my breath. Then I followed Earl as he made his way toward the stage. Gary was talking to Randy and Rob. He had an intense tone to his voice. It threw me back a little and I pretended to look busy while sneaking glimpses at them over my shoulder. He didn't seem angry, but there was something he was trying to get the two players to remember during a specific spot in one of the songs. Something had gone wrong and had apparently been going on for a while. I moved a bit closer as I wrapped cables and adjusted microphone stands.

It was then I got my first real look at the drummer. There was something strange about his look. I strained my eyes to see through the dim lighting of the bar. Then it struck me. He was a girl! Her hair was slicked back into a ponytail and tucked inside her shirt collar and her moustache was penciled in. It was a great disguise. I managed to keep my surprise to myself and listened to the instructions she shared with the guys.

Both Randy and Rob understood what she wanted and agreed they would fix it for the next show. These guys were professionals and I was enamored. I couldn't wait to get out on the road and learn from them. I stepped forward to introduce myself to the drummer.

"I'm Maureen Brown," she said, "But, people just call me Moe." She smiled and her cute face was revealed through the boyish makeup. We talked and discovered we were both from Kitchener and had a few mutual friends. Rob finished re-tuning his guitar and came over to introduce himself. His voice was low and cool – like a radio disc jockey. He asked me if I wanted to go get a drink. I was thrilled and followed him. As he made his way toward the bar, he stopped a few times by people in the crowd. Rob was gracious, but spoke few words aside from "thank you" and some short answers to questions people were asking about the group. He had beer tickets, and got us two glasses of draft from the bar.

"C'mon…" He motioned me to follow and I made my way through the crowd to the doors behind the soundboard that led upstairs.

The Breslau was an old hotel and had vintage hotel rooms that hadn't been redecorated in years. The carpeted stairs creaked under our feet as the canned music from the club faded behind us. Ancient-looking flowered wallpaper lined the walls and I chatted like an excited kid as Rob walked up the stairs in front of me. At the top, there was a room with no door. The band used it as their dressing room. It looked cramped with a half dozen chairs and a cracked mirror.

Rob stopped for a minute to speak through an open door to an adjacent room. I peeked around his shoulder and saw a woman dressed in a sequined bikini sitting on the bed, buttoning up one of her thigh-high black boots. She was an exotic dancer working in another part of the hotel. I had never met a stripper before and this was as close as I had ever been to one. She smiled and spoke with Rob as she adjusted her outfit. I could tell by their conversation they had spoken before.

Rob was now officially the coolest guy on the planet. I was captivated. I was backstage at a show and I was a roadie. I was drinking and hanging out with the Joe Cool guitar player and a real-life stripper. Life had never been better. I couldn't bring myself to say hi to the stripper and I avoided eye contact. She left to do her show and I followed Rob into the band's dressing room.

The room was abuzz with conversation. I asked Rob question after question – I wanted to know everything. The band talked about rehearsal the following day, and I asked if I could attend. No one minded, and I felt like I was a part of the band. I relaxed into the situation, listened to the banter, and watched everyone change costumes for the upcoming set.

Maureen emerged from the bathroom with freshly washed hair. With the moustache gone and her long hair about her shoulders, she was fully transformed back into a girl. She was pretty and I was a little smitten. I was sure she was dating Randy; they spent most of the break in the corner of the room talking quietly to one another.

I went over and introduced myself to the sax player. His name was Roger Cox and he was from Lafayette, Kentucky. I asked him about his home and his saxophone and just about everything else I could think of. He was calm and had an easy manner. Close up, I could see he was probably twice my age, maybe even 45. I hung on his every word. He was a courteous and gracious mentor to an excited kid.

Then Ron walked in the room and everyone was silent.

"How long?" Gary asked from the back of the room where he was wiping down his bass with a towel.

"The guy doesn't know how long he wants the sets!" Ron fumed. "If we go on at half past and do four forties, we can be finished by one." Ron picked up a towel and walked over to the mirror. "I was trying to tell the asshole we only do three shows, so we'll have to wait until the top of the hour. He looked at his watch and shook his head. "If we go on at half past, like he wants, then we only have seven more minutes."

"Screw that..." Gary snorted, and everyone laughed. Rob told me Gary was Dad to the band and usually the one that cracked the whip for set times. However, he was in playful spirits lately; his wife was having their first baby soon.

"Just tell him that we don't know any more songs." Gary smiled at Ron.

Ron was trying to remain serious, but a hint of a smile gave him away. "That's easy for you to say," he said in mock frustration. "You don't have to deal with this guy."

The rest of the band chimed in until it was agreed they would go on later and play three shows instead of four. I was amazed to see them work through it, and I imagined all of my favorite bands did the same thing. I imagined the Beatles talking backstage with John and Paul hashing out details while Ringo and George put in their two bits. I pictured Gene Simmons and Paul Stanley chatting with Ace and Peter in the same way. This was how real bands worked. I watched the easy interplay between them, like a bunch of friends who were also a team. You had your leader and everyone else had his or her part to play. You all figured it out and then you did it.

After a couple more drinks and more talking and laughing, Gary announced there was five minutes left in the break and everyone made the way back to the club. The excitement carried on through the hallways and didn't stop until we reached the club. As soon as the band got into the club they headed for the stage and I returned with Earl to our station.

The second set opened with Gary singing as the audience poured onto the dance floor. He did a nice job on "Love Potion

Number 9," and finished to a big round of applause. The band started up the Elvis riff again and Gary went through a slightly modified rendition of his first set introduction for Ron.

Ron walked onstage, this time in a more casual manner and sporting a different suit jacket. His image had not changed much and the guys in the band were more or less a relaxed version of what they had worn in the previous set. The t-shirts had been replaced by jean jackets and windbreakers while Moe was now very much a girl in lipstick and long, brown hair falling down her shoulders. It was strange and exciting to watch her play. The only other girl drummer I had ever seen was Karen Carpenter. Moe was exact and powerful while Karen was laid back and gentle. Moe attacked the drums with aggression and determination. Her feminine power drew me into her playing, and it was hard not to stare.

The rest of the night was a blur of music, drinks, and fun. It was awesome. I didn't mind that I wasn't playing or singing – it didn't matter. I just couldn't wait to get on the road.

Chapter Nine

My first Teen Angel road gig was in St. Thomas, Ontario. It was a weeklong engagement, as most gigs were back then. We arrived on Sunday, set up, did sound check, and then had supper in the hotel restaurant.

I was so excited to be part of the entourage and I looked forward to whatever adventures the next few months would bring.

Opening night went off without a hitch and everyone felt good about the tour. I remember little from that first week except I was always smiling. I was living the dream. I loved hotels. I loved doing lights. I loved the road. I wanted to do this forever.

As the tour went on, I got a primer on the trials and tribulations of a working road band. Ron had said I could do the hook-up, and then insisted it was still too much responsibility. He wanted to do it himself, citing that he was an electrical expert. I learned he was an expert in thousands of jobs as the tour wore on. When he told his stories, the guys in the band rolled their eyes and feigned sleep.

Expert or not, at our next stop, Ron blew up the club's electrical panel. Rob and I walked in just in time to see Ron knocked flat on the floor. We watched as the screwdriver he was using flew across the room and landed deep into the adjacent wall. Ron's blunder robbed an entire city block of power. Management was livid. Eventually the power was restored, the remaining shows went well that week, but the manager said the power outage had hurt his business. We were told to never come back.

Our next stop was Pointe Claire, Quebec, where our sax player, Roger, quit the band. He hadn't been with them for a long time, but he had created the coolest changes for the band's version of Harlem

Nocturne, and once had stood up for Rob when Ron berated him. Rob told me that Roger had some legal issue going on back home and it had caught up with him in Canada. He left at the end of that week and we never saw him again.

Next, we travelled to Nova Scotia to play the Holiday Inn in Halifax We were set to play four 40-minute shows each night, Monday through Saturday, for a month. At the end of the first week, Gary's wife gave birth and he left after the Saturday show to go home and be a dad.

Everyone panicked. I told Ron I had my bass, and he told me to learn the show and start the following Monday as his MC and relief singer. That was it. My days as light man were over. I was the bass player. I had all Sunday and Monday during the day to learn the entire show.

Okay. Sure. Just pull it off and be the hero of the tour. I tried to remain calm.

I knew most of the stage show by heart, so I focused on learning the music. All the Teen Angel songs were blues-based. Many had the same type of progression that was common for the '50s doo-wop song structure. Ninety percent of the songs were in C, A minor, F, and G. The simplicity of the song structures and chord patterns left me time to concentrate on note value, timing, meter, and listening to the rest of the band. In retrospect, it was a great way to get introduced to playing with a band that was already so together.

Vocals were stacked four, sometimes five, on top of each other and presented a much bigger challenge than just playing bass. I was certain I could pull off Monday night's show. It was a lot of material to learn in a single day, but I was glad I'd watched the show intently during the first few weeks of the tour. Most of the songs and segues were already ingrained in my head. I had memorized all of Gary's intro spiels. The band's choreography was also committed to memory, and I had the '50s dance moves down pat.

When Monday night arrived, I was nervous as hell. Before the show, Moe gave me a pep talk while she styled my hair into a full greaser pompadour.

"Don't worry about anything," she reassured me. "You'll ace this, Sweetie." I could see Randy watching from the corner of the dressing room. He was unimpressed at the attention Moe was paying me. I didn't care. Moe's confidence in me was the boost I needed to help calm my nerves.

"Do the intros and everything just like Gary used to," she told me. "You'll figure out your own style as you go along." I knew I would be ok. I felt more prepared than I had been opening night with Hellion in Elmira. I just had to get past the jitters.

Rob lent me one of his costumes, and he and Moe took turns working on my hair. It took a lot of Brylcreem to press it down flat. Small patches kept springing up into tiny spikes. Rob laughed and told me my new nickname was Spike. When Moe was done, I got up and looked in the mirror. The transformation stunned me. There was a very convincing '50s greaser staring back at me in the mirror. I was Spike. I was ready.

Ron popped his head in the door and did a double take when he saw me. A big smile crossed his face.

"You look great," he said. "Nice job, Moe."

I could tell Ron wasn't really a guy given to handing out compliments. He cleared his throat and the smile disappeared. "Alright, boys... and girls," he glanced around the room. "It's show time." I swallowed a huge gulp of beer and everyone patted me on the back, smiling and giving me encouragement. We grabbed our guitars and headed downstairs. My mind raced. We took our places onstage. Moe never took her eyes off of me. I could feel her sending strength. I looked around to see the same confidence beaming from Rob.

"Ready?" Moe called out. We nodded and she counted us in.

We launched into "Love Potion #9" and I poured my heart and soul into every word and note. My fingers knew where to go and my voice was strong and clear. Moe's drums pounded out the beat and we ripped it with a vengeance. At the end of the song, the audience clapped and cheered. I felt myself loosen up and gain more confidence. The worst was over. We started up the "CC Rider" riff, and I mimicked Gary's intro word for word. Ron came onstage and was smiling more than usual. I looked back at Moe and over at Rob. Everyone was pleased. I was pulling it off.

The rest of the night was a success, save for a few glitches that went unnoticed by the crowd, and we celebrated afterwards. Even Randy congratulated me on a job well done. It was a challenging show to perform – especially since I had to be MC and sing lead vocals while Ron was offstage. There was a myriad of background vocals in the material, and the whole thing kept me busy from the top of the night until the last note of the show.

There were very few times during the night that I was not at the microphone. The years I had spent in choir and glee club had given me great training in isolating my own voice amongst a choral ensemble, and it didn't take long before I was comfortable with the complex harmony structures. Moe, Rob, and Randy were all very capable singers and our harmonies grew stronger throughout that first week. We got together during the day and after the show, gathered around a guitar, and sung parts together – each of us exercising our abilities to improve upon the show, and trying to impress one another with what we could add.

Most off-hours were spent rehearsing. Ron was insistent on large turnovers of material and new songs were always added to the show. The show was never stale and the day was focused around the evening performance. I learned to sleep as much as I could in order to make it through the night.

The Teen Angel show was high-energy and moved at a breakneck pace. There were four, sometimes five, sets each night, with many of the songs running back-to-back.

Moe was adamant about never having dead air. "Never let the audience's attention wander," she said on more than one occasion. "It will look like the band is stuck or not together in some way, and it takes away from the professionalism."

Moe had several little tidbits in her arsenal. Her commitment to excellence, regardless of how she felt about the band and the music that we played, was admirable. At times she was far more drummer than the band needed. She was my first introduction to esoteric musicianship.

She had Billy Cobham stickers on her drum case, and as I'd never heard of him, I asked her about them. She explained he was a jazz drummer from Panama, and then told me about jazz drumming and jazz musicians. There was apparently an unspoken hierarchy, with pop and rock music on a lower rung of the musical ladder-- somewhere below classical, jazz, and blues. Moe's sensibilities were obvious when she talked about jazz. I took every opportunity I could to ask her to show me the patterns and riffs she enjoyed. She had taken the job in Teen Angel because she needed the money. The bluesy nature of the music was less offensive to her advanced musical sensibilities than a spot in a Top 40 rock band.

Moe was a professional, onstage and off. She was very gracious to fans and always had a warm smile for everyone. The last hour before show time, she would get into character and prepare mentally and physically using a practice pad in her room. I would stop by her room every night before the show so she could help me get my game face on.

The show was very much her creation when I joined the band; not Gary's, as I had initially suspected. Moe was a taskmaster at rehearsals and the sets were mostly her construction. She had a great sense of the rise and fall of the set's flow, and I soaked up all her advice. Once she drew a graph on a piece of paper and showed me how a set should work in its most ideal form.

"You've got to come in screaming right off the top," she told me as she drew a rising line on the paper. "Bang, bang, bang – three in a row before you stop," she explained. "Then you come out of the hole with something a little more mid-tempo and give the audience a chance to see some dynamics."

She had a philosophy behind performance that compelled me. Until I met Moe, I just sang and tried not to make mistakes. Moe had a deeper understanding of performance than anyone I had ever known. She engaged me in some deep conversations about music and I was starting to understand her more each day.

The band respected Moe. She called the shots like a drill sergeant. Moe's tone was different with me than with the other guys in the band. She knew how green I was. She felt sorry for me for being thrust into such a demanding role. We both knew I was over my head in this band and she nursed me through the steep learning curve.

I was developing a crush on Maureen. Randy sensed this and it didn't sit well. He was a stoic person offstage, and I'm sure the only reason he was in the band was his relationship with Moe. He and I rarely spoke to one another.

Rob was more receptive and I had never met anyone quite like him. Moe was quite intellectual, but Rob was in a world all of his own. The way he spoke was even more cosmic than Norma Jeanne Laurette.

Rob was the deepest thinker I had ever met. He talked about things that were far beyond my understanding. I often found it hard to fully comprehend what he was saying, but when I did, his advice and observations helped me adapt to life on the road. Rob spoke about the psychology of life, playing, and about the state of being on the road. He called it "psycho-jitsu," pointing out how we made a living by "taking the combined attention of an audience and playing catch with it onstage." He helped with many of the questions and ponderings I had about life, and I began to explore the beginnings of a brand new clarity.

I came of age in Halifax. In four weeks, I learned how to play six nights a week and make it rock every night. One night after a show, still in our greaser gear, we went to Camille's Fish and Chips. Van Halen had performed a concert the same night at the Metro Centre. I looked up in time to see Eddie and Alex Van Halen walk in. Alex picked me out of our group and started play-boxing with me, pantomiming a greaser street fight. Eddie chatted with Rob. I was on the road, and now I was hobnobbing with rock stars.

Our band got better every day, thanks to Moe's strict rehearsals.

The show was polished and people were returning in droves. We were a full-on '50s show and we worked the music with a level of passion the band hadn't seen before. Rob told me that Ron was happier than he had ever been, and it showed in his enthusiasm every night. One night, a woman told Rob and me we looked "just like the men she fell in love with back in her day." She was about 20 years older and her heartfelt words were proof we were on the right track. Many conversations were devoted to better understanding how philosophy defines a show and what it could mean to any given person on any given night. Every aspect of music, our show, and life was up for intense discussion at any time. I loved the routine. Sleep all day and rock all evening, then wax philosophical on everything we could think of until 4 a.m.

One night after the show, I was chatting with a beautiful woman who was 15 years my senior. I was thrilled that an older woman would be interested in me. One thing led to another and we fooled around for a couple of hours in my hotel room. She was a little overzealous and carved her nails deep into my back. After she left, I went down to Moe's room to have her check it out for me. I lifted my shirt for her so she could inspect my back.

"My God!" she shouted. "What kind of animal does something like that?" I was embarrassed and had no idea how to respond. Some of the guys poked their head in the door, but she shooed them away and found some salve for my back. Moe chastised me for my behavior as she put the salve on my wounds. I slept uncomfortably that night and spent the next day feeling sheepish. I was expecting the woman to return for the show that night and was relieved when she didn't.

That evening, a local saxophone player came onstage and

jammed with the band. He was an amazing player and an imposing figure. He was a massive black man with arms thicker than my legs and well over six feet tall. After the show, he sat around with a few of us talking about music and I got the feeling Ron wanted to ask him to join the band.

Drinks flowed and the subject came around to road stories and women. He said he was concerned his wife had cheated on him.

"She'll probably be coming down here to see you guys at some point," he said. "So keep an eye out for her."

He gave us her description and the blood drained from my face. I couldn't look anyone in the eyes. Later that night Ron tore into me.

"I can't ask him to join the band now!" he growled. "If that guy ever finds out you screwed his wife... you're a dead man." He finally calmed down after a bit and told me not to worry about it. Maybe it was funny and not entirely my fault. She never told me she was married and I didn't think to ask. Ron laughed and told me to learn a lesson from it. I told him I would.

Ron and I had a running gag onstage to cover any gaps. I was the "kid" and he was the "old man." One night, my "old man" comment was poorly timed, and I pissed him off for real. I'll never forget the look on his face. He gave me the finger right there onstage. He was serious, and I was in shock.

After the set, I ran up to my room. I liked Ron and I had hurt him with my words. It felt awful. We both got over it, but the lesson would serve me well later as a bandleader regarding crossing the line with playful banter.

On the second week of the gig, I met a girl from Dartmouth named Angie Keefe. She was pretty and I thought she was way out of my league. She was a bit wild and had a Maritime accent that I found appealing. I saw her every night at the show, and we started meeting up during the day. I found out as much as I could about her and waited before we finally spent the night together. After that night, I spent all of my spare time in Halifax with her. At the end of the month, she gave me her phone number and I promised to stay in touch.

I had my first experience with a real recording studio on that trip to Halifax. The band had some money set aside, and Ron used it to record a couple of songs to make a 45 we could sell on the road. The studio was far more advanced than Brian Alexanian's basement and I was thrilled to be a part of the recording process. We performed the songs several times over until we had a drum track the engineer liked. Each of us in turn then recorded our instruments and voices. Finally it was all mixed and mastered and the result was "Money" – a somewhat bastardized version of the Beatles song mixed with Ray Charles' "Tell Me What I Say." The flipside had our version of Neil Sedaka's "Calendar Girl."

The records were pressed within the week and I almost fainted when I got my own copy. I was on a record! Everything I had hoped for was coming true. It was the fall of 1980, and I had only been on the road for a few months. Everything was happening so fast. I was on my way.

The show wrapped in Halifax, and we travelled to Montreal for the next dates. We heard our version of "Money" on the radio on the way there. I floated on a cloud all the way to Montreal.

We played the Yackity Yak in the Hotel De Lasalle at Drummond and Saint Catherine streets for all of November, and then headed for our next gig in Sault St. Marie. After that, we played Arnolds in Ottawa, where Moe and Randy gave their notice. Earl made some calls to a drummer and keyboard player he knew. Dave Cubitt and Bruce Leitl were two of Earl's friends from his first high school band, Act IV, and they had planned to put another band together someday. This was their opportunity to get some road miles together while also helping out.

I wanted to play with Jim and Mike again. Mike was settled in Kitchener and didn't want to go on the road. I did, however, talk Ron into hiring Jim on second guitar by extolling the virtues of his easy temperament and how it would have a calming influence on the band.

Moe and Randy decided to stay on through December to help the new members. Those last few gigs were shaky, and it was my first experience in pretending things was great when they were anything but. Ron's mood was increasingly dark and he rarely spoke to anyone.

When musicians in your band are on their way out the door, the dynamic of the band changes. Everyone is unsettled. Our once solid tribe was cut into two camps, and tempers were frayed. One night, Ron, in a particularly bad mood, belittled Jim over the microphone with a sarcastic rock star comment. I lost my cool and walked off stage in protest. It flew directly in the face of the personal control I had learned in the military.

My discipline was one of the things that Ron had admired in me. I felt this was the biggest statement I could make to him. I had to defend Jim – my friend and mentor. My relationship with Ron never recovered.

That week was disastrous in other ways as well. Our microphones were stolen from the stage. Our crew guys got a lead as to who the thieves were, and they set out to recover the gear; one of our techs got beat up in the process. We got the gear back, but the whole week was a write-off and ended on a very sour note.

We travelled home in silence. I was emotionally exhausted and glad to get back to Kitchener for a hometown gig, and spend Christmas with my family. The band was wounded, but we all had friends and family in town, so we put on a brave face for the crowds.

Ron came in one night before show time and told us we would be flying up north to do a big New Year's show in an auditorium. It lifted everyone's spirits and got us through the rest of that week. The new players weren't ready, so Randy and Moe agreed to do the northern gig; Ron would fly them home afterwards.

It was my first fly-in gig, and I was excited to get on the plane. The weekend turned out to be spectacular. We played a hockey arena in Hay River, North West Territories, in Canada's Arctic Circle. A massive forest fire was raging a few miles outside of the town and there was smoke hanging thick in the air. It was difficult to breathe and there was anxiety amongst the locals who feared the wind might change and bring the fire into town. Nonetheless, the townspeople celebrated our visit by parading us down Main St. in vintage '50s cars. We were in full greaser attire, and I remember freezing in my leather jacket and t-shirt atop a '57 Chevy convertible while clouds of black smoke filled the skies. People gathered on the roadsides, all bundled up, breath steaming, waving and cheering as we drove past. It was both strange and wonderful.

We were having the time of our lives, which distracted the rest of us from what was happening between Ron, Maureen, and Randy. When the gig was over, Ron reneged on his agreements with Moe and Randy and only paid their travel as far as Edmonton. He didn't pay them the full amount for the gig either, and I heard it took several weeks before Moe and Randy made it back to Kitchener. It was the last time I saw either of them.

Chapter Ten

Dave Cubitt and Bruce Leitl started the following week in Edmonton. We played the Renford Inn on Whyte, and I will never forget that horrible night. It wasn't Dave and Bruce that were the problem; they both did well and it was obvious they had done their homework. That night the blame fell squarely on my shoulders.

Earlier that day, I had made a trip to the music store to buy a fretless bass. A great deal of the '50s material we played had that unmistakable hollow thump of an upright bass. I wanted an instrument that would lend authenticity to our repertoire. I knew that there were a few good music stores in Edmonton. The plan was to trade one of my fretted basses and put the balance on credit.

Off I went to tour the local music stores with a couple of the guys and both of my basses. After shopping around, I found a G&L fretless bass that felt incredible. The guy was willing to talk trade and asked to see my basses. He was less than impressed. They were a bit smarmy, as sweat tends to eat away at an instrument over time. I played these guitars six nights a week. There was some corrosion and the finish was quite worn in places. After some pleading and a lot of deliberation, the salesman made me a final offer. He would take both of my fretted basses and two hundred dollars in exchange for the G&L fretless and a case. I looked between my sweat-eaten basses and the beautiful object of my desire. I knew I was unlikely to get a better deal anywhere else. It took me five minutes to decide. I left the store with my new fretless bass.

So now I would be playing opening night on a fretless bass, for the first time ever, with a brand new drummer and keyboard player. It was so rock 'n' roll. The guys in the band thought I was completely nuts and for some reason I thought that meant I had made the right choice.

When we started the show that night, I was the proverbial penguin on roller skates. On a fretless bass, there are only tiny markers where the fret bars would normally be on a fretted bass. They were virtually invisible onstage. I slid around the neck searching for the right notes. On top of that, I had to sing and perform my regular MC duties and bring Ron onstage. It was a recipe for mayhem.

I had to work for every note on the first song. I dug in hard and told myself it could only get better. We finished the Elvis opening and I introduced Ron. We hadn't seen him much that day, and he had muttered once or twice he wasn't feeling well. It was evident something was wrong when he made it to the stage. His voice was hoarse, even for him, and his character was forced and insincere. After a few croaked lines, he went to the drum riser to grab a towel. He held the towel over his mouth and I saw a look of alarm in his eyes.

Rob saw what was happening and entertained the audience with a guitar solo while balancing on side-stage handrails like they were tightropes. I moved towards Ron as discretely as possible. The corners of his mouth were stained red. He showed me the towel; it was streaked with clumped blood. His throat was bleeding and the poor bastard was spitting up red chunks in front of a packed house on opening night. Nice.

I stepped in front of Ron and he gave me the sign to keep things rolling as he disappeared off stage. Now what? How could we do the set without him? I called to Rob for another solo while I got my bearings. There were a bunch of numbers that Rob and I sang in the show, and a fair number of Ron's I knew I could sing. But, they were in Ron's key - much lower than I was comfortable with. There was no way in hell I was going to ask the band to transpose keys on the spot. Not to mention, I wouldn't dare attempt it on a fretless.

Dave and Bruce were doing everything they could to keep their own parts together. What a way to start their first night.

I didn't want to use up all my material in this set and then have to repeat too much later on. I picked through some of Ron's tunes that I figured I could get through with the least amount of trouble. All this stuff was flying around my head as I struggled with the fretless bass. Clearly, the evening was anything but ideal and I braced myself for the nightmare ahead. I grunted through the rest of the material and was relieved when the set was finally over.

As soon as I got offstage, I looked for Ron. He didn't answer his door, and the front desk guy said he thought he saw Ron leaving the hotel with some woman. I stormed back downstairs to the club. We went through the next two sets as best as we could. There were a fair number of slip-ups and some musical bumps and bruises, but we made it through the night.

After the show, the guys congratulated me, but I was thinking of how to finish the week without Ron. He came to my room the next day and said that the doctor had given him some medicine and he was feeling better. He managed to finish out the gig.

That same week I saw my first tribute band. Beatlemania was playing in town and they were staying at our hotel. On the night before their show, they showed up in the cabaret and jammed onstage with us. It was such a thrill for me to meet these guys and have them perform on our equipment. When I handed my bass to the bass player, I felt like I was handing it to the real Paul

McCartney. He was a dead ringer and an exceptional musician. He was a left-handed player – just like Paul, but he played my right-handed fretless bass better than I did. After we jammed, they invited us down to see their afternoon show. It was like I imagined it would have been to actually see the Beatles perform live. These four guys had it nailed down tight. The lighting, stage set, and visuals made the whole thing look like a musical documentary. It stuck in my head for a long time and is still one of the most striking performances I have ever seen. I remember thinking I could do something like that... someday.

We got back to our hotel after the show and got in the elevator. Rob let go the most legendary fart ever. I thought I was going to vomit. We choked and laughed up the two floors to our room. When the doors finally opened, three huge black men were waiting for the elevator. I recognized the guy in the middle as Muddy Waters. He nodded, and in a beautiful, deep drawl said, "Hi boys." Rob and I were speechless and only nodded. As the door closed, we looked at each other in horror. As the elevator descended, we heard that beautiful, deep voice again, "Jesus Christ!" Rob and I fell to the floor laughing.

A few months later, Muddy Waters died. I assured Rob that there was no way he was responsible. I'm not sure if he believed me.

The next week we left Edmonton for the Canadian Forces Base in Moose Jaw, Saskatchewan to play the Officer's Club. It was strange to go on base as a civilian. I prayed things would go well, but they didn't. There were technical problems, the show went on late, and management was pissed. Ron was in a foul mood and the show suffered. Ron blamed the band and decided to fire everyone on the spot and fly home. He screamed at us while we packed up our instruments.

"I'll make sure you little fuckers never work in this business again!"

"How you going to do that, Ron?" I challenged him.

"I'll show you, Jimmy!" he screamed, cocked his big meaty fist, and punched Jim in the side of his head. Glasses went flying as Jim hit the ground. Jim had taken a punch that should have been aimed at me. We were all stunned. We rose to our feet and looked at each other. We all wanted to beat the shit out of him. Then Rob's demeanor changed and he looked directly at me.

"Don't do anything," he said quietly. I was livid, but I trusted Rob's words. He knew this was our chance to get away. Rob whispered in my ear and I went into the office to use the phone. I called the base MPs and they arrived in minutes. They questioned us, charged Ron with assault, and took him away in handcuffs. In the blink of an eye, the Ron Mitchell era of Teen Angel was over.

Earl, Dave, and Bruce wanted to go home. I was already planning out how to proceed without Ron in the band. I went back into the office, called the agency, and told them what had happened. I said I could keep the band up and running and they told me they would talk about booking some more shows under my leadership when I got back to Kitchener. Jim and Rob took a Greyhound back to Kitchener and I went back with Earl, Dave, and Bruce in the U-Haul.

I met with Brian Daly later that week and he agreed to book Teen Angel II. Ron had disappeared off the face of the earth, and Brian was happy we would still make him money. I called Jim, Mike, and Rob along with John Vanderweil who was willing to play keyboards. John had jammed with Hellion and was the guy who

TED MOORE

once showed me how to get a decent bass sound from my amp. The combination of talent was right from the start. We signed a booking agreement with Brian who promised the following year was going to be a busy one.

The next day Brian called to talk about another project he was going to be working on in the New Year. He had been negotiating with a female singer who had once been part of a very successful Canadian recording band. He wanted me to go in as her musical director. He said he would see to it personally that it didn't conflict with my Teen Angel calendar or my recording aspirations. I was flattered, but I didn't give it much thought. I told him I was interested in talking about it when he had more details. I was just happy to have Teen Angel back together.

As the new Teen Angel front man, I had to hand the bass player duties to someone else; the Teen Angel figure needed to be free to roam about the stage. I needed to leave the stage for costume changes, and add variety to the show by featuring other singers, just as Ron had featured me in the MC role.

We discussed either Rob or Jim switching to play bass. I said I would leave the decision up to them. Rob immediately volunteered for the spot, adding, "But only if Jim doesn't want to do it." Jim was more than happy to stay on guitar and Rob was excited about playing bass. He was musically experimental and the adventure of learning new techniques and taking on a new role appealed to him.

Getting out from behind my bass was both liberating and bewildering. I had no idea what to do with my hands while I was singing. At first, I opted for holding my microphone and clutching at my mic stand. It took a few shows of feeling naked before I enjoyed the freedom. It was like learning to perform onstage all over again.

In the fall of 1982, we played Rifters at the Holiday Inn in Sudbury, with the brand new line up. The show was recorded and we were interviewed on a local TV talk show. We went back to all the places we played with Ron and people liked us much more. I started to write songs again and we made plans to record some demos. Morale and expectations grew fast. We bought a big blue bus from Helix and set out, feeling like rock stars, en route to a five week stay in Newfoundland. Along the way we made tour stops at The Brule in Témiscaming, Quebec, The Zoo in Chateauguay, and then The Flagship in Campbellton, New Brunswick.

The week before our tour of Newfoundland, we had a gig back in Halifax. We went to see Alvin Bishop perform at the Misty Moon where Angie worked. She said she missed me and felt bad we had not kept in touch. We spent all our time together that week, and she invited the whole band to her family's place for a traditional Maritime feast of corned beef and cabbage for our last night in town.

After dinner, Angie asked me to her room and opened up her closet. Trophies and ribbons were stuffed on the top shelf marked with engravings: Best Stripper 1980, Wet T-shirt Champion, and a dozen or so others with similar captions. I was completely freaked out. She was a stripper? Stunned and angry, I told her we were finished, stormed out, and walked back to the hotel alone. I couldn't believe it. My angel was a centerfold. When I look back, it seems stupid now, but for some reason it bothered me. Maybe I just felt deceived. I still don't know for sure.

After Halifax, we caught the ferry from Sydney to Port-Au-Basques, Newfoundland and began our tour of the island. Our ferry got stuck in the ice halfway across during a fierce snowstorm. We ran to the top deck to see what had happened. It was the middle of the night and we were surrounded by darkness without stars or moonlight. There were faint streams of light from the windows of the ferry. I strained my eyes and made out giant walls of broken ice piled 20 feet high against the hull of the ship. It was both awesome and frightening at the same time.

We stayed there for two hours until a cutter ship arrived and ploughed the ice. The ferry moved slowly behind the cutter as it continued to ram forward, back up, and ram forward again. The cutter ship's giant spotlight shone out over the black waters of the Atlantic. There was no shore in sight. We got stuck several more times before we made it to the other side. We arrived at Port Aux Basque in the wee hours of the morning, exhausted and a bit traumatized.

We disembarked into the Newfoundland cold and drove toward our first stop – Stephenville. The roads were horrible and the bus kept breaking down. The spark plug cables were fouled with wet snow. The bus would just die and we'd roll down the highway until we stopped and dried everything off.

Once, after drying out the electrics, I cranked the starter while John held open the carburetor and sprayed Quick Start down the opening. A huge flame column shot up, catching John square in the face. I jumped out of the driver's seat, grabbed some snow from the ground, and packed it into his steaming face. I was almost too late. His face survived any burns, but the flames had scorched off his beard, his eyebrows, and his long, curly bangs. It took a month to heal, but fortunately, there were no scars.

When we arrived at the Eldorado in Stephenville, the storm

was so bad and the snow so high that we couldn't start the gig for three more days. Wednesday morning a crew came to dig us out of the band house and we ventured into the daylight for the first time since we arrived. The entire neighborhood was a blanket of white and the bus was nowhere in sight. I went exploring to see if I could find it. I marched to the top of a huge snow bank to get a better view. I heard a clunking sound beneath my feet and cleared the snow beneath me. Several inches down, I discovered the blue roof of our bus. It took us most of the morning to dig it out, but we finally got free and headed to the club to set up our equipment. The bar manager had drinks waiting for us and told us it was the worst weather he had seen in twenty years. We took our gear inside and waited a couple of hours for it to warm up. We had more drinks and got our sound set up by mid-afternoon. We felt good and thought the worst was behind us.

After sound check, Mike and John went to the drug store to get supplies for the week and the rest of us headed back to the band house. Three hours later, we got a call from John. Mike had been detained by store security for shoplifting a mascara pencil. At first I laughed, but John said there was more to the story. Apparently, when the cops arrived they searched Mike and found his stash. Mike was in jail and the bail was set at $500. My heart dropped. We were screwed. It might as well have been $5000.

None of us had any money, so we trudged back to the bar to beg the manager for a pay advance. We hadn't even played the first show. We convinced him that without Mike we couldn't play at all. He relented and gave us the bail money. We paid the bail, but Mike had to spend the night in jail. It had been one helluva week – and it was only Wednesday.

The following night we played the first show and were well-received. The manager said it was a great crowd for a Thursday night, and Friday turned out even better. On Saturday night our soundman, Mark Woefle, got into a conflict with one of the locals. I had lent Mark one of my shiny stage shirts to wear to the club that night so he could look good for a girl he had his eye on. One of the local rednecks made a comment about the shirt and Mark responded by blowing him a kiss. The redneck and his posse went nuts and somehow a huge bar fight began.

Two hundred and fifty angry Maritimers rolled around on the floor beating the crap out of each other and mostly ignored us. It was the weirdest thing. Rob was the scrappiest, and I saw him rolling around with some guy in the middle of the beer and blood soaked dance floor, trying to land some blows. Suddenly, they stopped and looked at each other. They realized they were old friends and immediately stopped fighting and began hugging and shaking hands. It was a strange scene to behold. One by one, everyone stopped fighting, shook hands, and went back to drinking. It was bizarre.

The manager was not impressed. He pulled me into the office and tore a strip off me. To his credit, he paid me the balance of what was due – after the advance for the drummer's bail. We went back to the band house, got as drunk as we could, and raced off to the next gig – a month long engagement in St. Johns at the Strand Cabaret in the Avalon Mall.

Severe drinking, partying, debauchery, and terrible hangovers ensued over the next 30 days. The crowds were sparse in the beginning. The locals initially shunned us as we were Mainlanders. Maritimers aren't tolerant of presumptuous posturing, and we may have come on a bit too strong those first few nights. Still, I worked my butt off for those crowds.

During one drunken evening that first week, I complained to the audience, "You know, it's a real drag when the only people who know you're doing a great job are the people you're working with. I want to thank St. John's for a real bummer."

My sarcastic crack was not well received. I regretted it immediately, and made a genuine and heartfelt apology for my outburst. My sincere gesture wasn't lost on the crowd. Four big, burly Newfies leapt onto the stage, bringing armloads of beer and a round of handshakes. We later found out that these four brothers – Harry, Terry, Larry and Squid (whose real name was Barry), all from Portugal Cove –were well-liked in the area and their gesture made a big impact. The crowd cheered, and soon everyone in the bar was in our corner. Those Portugal Cove brothers saved the gig for us. We all played like demons for the rest of our time there, and the four of them treated us to a Newfie farewell. They fed us moose, rabbit, and Newfie Screetch. They weatherproofed our bus so we could start it easily in the worst weather that Newfoundland could throw at us.

At the end of our last week a severe blizzard hit and the St. John's ferry was not available. We were forced to drive back across Newfoundland in the worst blizzard in over 20 years. The road was like a bob sled track with room only for one vehicle to pass. At one point during the journey, I had to slam the side of the bus into the wall of snow on the side of the road to avoid colliding with an oncoming truck. Lucky for us, he had the presence of mind and quick reflexes to do the same thing, and it saved all of our lives. That truck was the only other vehicle we saw on the seven-hour drive across the island. We were crazy to drive across Newfoundland in that hellacious snowstorm, but we were scheduled to perform Monday night in Kitchener.

We made it back to Kitchener in 24 hours and went onstage at the Breslau Hotel with no sleep. We were tired and we had been through a lot, but morale was high and the adversity had strengthened the band's bond. The show rocked and we had a great week seeing friends and family.

Over the next year, Teen Angel toured non-stop across Manitoba, Saskatchewan, and Alberta. While playing in Brandon, Manitoba, a woman approached us and told us we were using a stolen band name and we had to stop immediately or we would be taken to court. We were all shocked and not quite sure how to react. Rob explained that Ron had once admitted to him that he had stolen the name and that the woman's claims were well-founded. It was one of the reasons Ron wanted to keep the band on the east side of the country. Rob and I explained our situation to the woman, who identified herself as Barbara-Ann, one of the group's founding members. She softened a little as I told her how I had just taken over the band from the original leader and I had no knowledge that it was someone else's band name. I assured her that I would stop using the name immediately and I would have new posters made up for my band with a new name on them. She seemed satisfied with my promises and ended up jamming with us and taking us out to dinner. The whole thing had turned out well, but I went away wondering how many of Ron's other indiscretions might come back to haunt me.

After several months on the prairies, our tour wound down and we headed back to Toronto for a couple of shows. Our prairie tour had been successful, but the relentless pace of six nights a week in the bars had started to show strains on some of the band members – most notably for Rob. As Moe and Randy had joined the band to keep working, Rob had initially taken the Teen Angel gig for much the same reason. He really wanted to play stuff like Jimi Hendrix and Led Zeppelin. He was musically frustrated, and it presented itself in some self-destructive ways. He would empty an entire bottle of Jack Daniels every night, and for a while, still went out and rocked like a madman. Soon the inner turmoil and abuse was obvious. Rob was often late or unavailable for practice, and his performances began to suffer.

Rob had been my friend and mentor for a long time now, and I wanted to stay loyal to him. There were other problems too. John and Mike were less than thrilled with the '50s and '60s stuff and were thinking about doing something else. Everyone was concerned about Rob and some of the guys thought he should be replaced. I told them we could take a vote when we finished the shows in Toronto and then we would get things back on track.

On Sunday afternoon, we pulled away from the hotel and headed downtown. Rob said he wanted to be dropped off in downtown Toronto if we voted him out. The last few days had not gone well and I was sure I knew how things would play out. I parked and called for a vote. It was unanimous – Rob was out.

I'll never forget his face as I cranked opened the bus door in downtown Toronto. What the hell had we done?

We dropped our rental equipment off in Toronto and then made our way back to Kitchener. We had a week to rest until the next round of shows started, and I knew the band could use the break. Two weeks later we headed out on tour again and spent the next eight months playing from coast to coast. I couldn't shake the feeling there was something missing. Rob's departure seemed to have left a hole in the band's spirit.

In the months that followed, morale went downhill. I managed to keep things going for six months, but the end was near. I was tired of fighting to keep guys onboard. Mike and John wanted to stay home and just record and go fishing. During a two-week stand in Kitchener, Mike and John finished up their last days with the band. Our sound man, Mark, called it quits as well.

I called Earl, Dave, and Bruce to help out with the remaining dates that I was obligated to, and so began the short-lived Teen Angel III. It only lasted a few months. One night Earl, Bruce and, Dave came to my room to give notice that they were leaving to form their own band. In a way, I was relieved. It was time for a change. I wanted to write and get back on track. I started thinking about the project Brian Daly had told me about earlier that year. Maybe it was a blessing. I hadn't written a note in months. I was never going to get a record deal if things kept going this way.

Earl and Bruce showed up later in my travels, but I have never seen or heard from Dave. Teen Angel, in all three incarnations, lasted about three years. I experienced a great deal of life during that time and I learned a lot from that band and those people. All in all, it was a lot of fun.

CHAPTER ELEVEN

B rian called the next day to talk about a project he was going to be working on in the New Year. He had been negotiating with a girl named Janet Miller, a singer with a now-defunct recording band that had toured around the world. He wanted me to go in as her musical director. I met with Brian Daly to talk to him about his new project. Janet had been the vocalist for a band that had enjoyed success in the early '70s with a couple of massively popular radio songs. She was beginning her solo career and was looking to put together a touring band. I was to go along as the bass player and musical director.

This offer was huge. Janet was a star and a major player in the Toronto scene. She had history in the Toronto music community, had powerful connections, and had once been married to a famous guitar player. Janet's roommate, Jeff Jones, was the bassist in Rush before Geddy Lee; he went on to play with Red Rider, later joining Tom Cochrane's solo project. Janet knew pretty much everyone who was anyone in Toronto, and I couldn't wait to meet her in person. Brian Daly said Janet liked that I was a songwriter with recording aspirations. This could be my big break.

A soundman was brought in to handle finances. I was to focus on the music. My audition was the following week, and I practiced like a mad man. The audition never happened. One day, Brian just called me up and told me the job was mine.

I stayed in contact with Brian as the players were chosen for the band. Janet had a guy who went by the name 'Hollywood' to play drums, and I got to bring in the guitar player. I called Jim and sold the band hard to him. He was revved up and committed to the project. Janet had a line on a few keyboard players and said that she would have someone soon.

It was a month from the day I was hired that I met Janet Miller. I drove up to Toronto to see her perform. She was on stage and belting out a bluesy tune when I arrived. I was taken by the power of her voice. She was a smaller woman, brunette, with big eyes, perhaps in her early thirties. She was very present onstage and I liked her professional performance style. I thought the band was a bit on the lounge-y side, but Janet had a power in her voice that I knew would rock.

When the set ended, she walked over to my table and extended her hand.

"I recognize you from your pictures," she smiled. "You look better without all that grease in your hair..." I laughed nervously and shook her hand.

"God, it's so good to meet you..." I said, tripping over my feet as I got out of the chair. "I am so excited to play with you and get going with the band. I have been practicing, me and Jim...he so wanted to be here tonight..." I rambled on like an idiot for a few more minutes, and then she asked me to sit so we could talk. We talked about how long it took to find just the right people, and she assured me I would be her right hand man. There was no keyboard player, but she believed the rest of the band should start rehearsing anyway. I agreed. She told me about her rented rehearsal space in Mississauga, and that the band would be partially subsidized with food and accommodations at her house in the city.

This was the big time. It would be so cool to live in Toronto again. The new drummer had a girlfriend and he would stay with her. Jim had a car and a job, and I told Janet he would probably elect to remain in Kitchener and make the commute to Toronto on rehearsal days. I confirmed I could relocate to Toronto as soon as possible. Janet had to go back on stage, but we continued banging out the details between her sets.

We'd been drinking, and at the end of the night, Janet suggested we take a taxi to her house, which she shared with Jeff Jones and his wife. I could stay the night and see where I would be staying for the next month or so. There were a couple of spare beds down in the basement where I spent that first night. I remember drifting off to sleep thinking my future was at hand. I was a little star struck and I couldn't believe my good fortune. Things were happening in a big way.

* * *

Rehearsals started that week with Hollywood on drums, Jim Donkers on guitar, and me on bass. Janet was convinced she would have someone for the keys within another week or two. Pat Benatar's "Hit Me With Your Best Shot" was a huge single at the time, and it was the first song we took into rehearsal. We learned some standard female rock classics like Janis Joplin's "Piece Of My Heart," Jefferson Airplane's "White Rabbit," and a few Fleetwood Mac songs from Rumours. Janet asked me to sing lead for a half dozen numbers during the show and I picked some favorites. The band learned some of the rock stuff I had sung with Hellion and we added some current tunes from Boston, Foreigner, and other charting rock bands.

It was fun living at Janet's and being around her crowd. Jeff Jones was very supportive and didn't seem to mind my incessant questions about the history of the Toronto music scene and all of the things he had done. We were rehearsing at Falcon's Nest rehearsal studios in Mississauga and the place had seen lots of stars come through the door. Kim Mitchell from Toronto legends Max Webster was rehearsing next door to us. Kim and his guys were often in the common areas and I got caught up in the excitement.

One evening I went into the kitchen and made myself a snack. The door swung open and there was Kim Mitchell! I was completely unprepared to stand face to face with one of my idols.

I blurted out "You're Kim Mitchell!" and immediately regretted it.

He must have had a bad day, and was not in the mood for any hero worship. He looked at me with complete disdain. How awkward. He reached into the fridge, grabbed a drink, looked my way one more time, shook his head, and walked out of the room.

In that moment, I became a stupid kid from Kitchener who was in way over his head. I just couldn't help being star struck. The guys from Red Rider had stopped by a few times at the house and I had frozen up each time any of them had come through the door. I could barely speak to Jeff Jones even though he had been so supportive and down to earth with me. It felt obvious I didn't belong here.

I was driving Janet's car one night on the way to rehearsal. I pulled into the studio parking lot and a car came out of a side street and smashed into us. When I told Janet, she hugged me and told me it was okay. Her voice calmed me. I sank into her embrace and my hands slid down her back. What the hell was I doing! I pulled away. What an idiot. I couldn't face her. When I finally looked up, she was smiling.

"Don't worry," she said. "It's fine." I stood there while my stupid boy brain struggled to interpret her response. I said nothing and went downstairs as she called out goodnight. I felt lucky she hadn't fired me on the spot.

In the days that followed, the rehearsals picked up speed. Janet's agent named the band Network. He took control of the group and split some commissions to Brian for his efforts. Brian claimed he was okay with this as Janet's agent had a lot of clout. I figured he knew what he was doing and didn't think much more about it. They were professional agents and I figured I should just trust them.

Both agents agreed the tour should start soon and head west across Canada. Janet found a keyboard player who was finishing up a stint with another band and wouldn't be able to rehearse before the tour. He would use tapes of the songs to learn his parts, and we'd pick him up on the way to the first gig.

Rehearsals continued until the day before we left. That night, we went out to a local bar to see some friends of Janet's play and celebrate our upcoming tour. Everyone, except for me and Janet, were spending the night with loved ones for our last night in town. We got back to the house, drunk and feeling good about ourselves. Jeff and his girlfriend were asleep and Janet and I sat in the dark talking about the tour. Neither of us had spoken about the hugging incident a couple weeks earlier and I wasn't going to say anything unless she did. As the evening drew on and more drinks were poured, we found ourselves talking and laughing downstairs on my bed. A part of me thought this was very wrong.

It was the night before our tour and here I was sitting on my bed with our lead singer. What the hell was I thinking? I'd heard stories from players about how bands had been destroyed because one of the guys had 'slept with the chick singer'. But that wasn't going to be a problem for us. Everything would be fine. There was nothing to worry about. It was harmless...

* * *

The next day, we didn't speak about the night before. I looked over at Janet a few times and caught her looking back. We exchanged smiles and kept busy. I figured we would talk later on down the road. Janet and I got in her car and everyone else piled into the U-Haul. On our way out of town, we stopped in Stouffville, north of Toronto, and picked up Brad Harrington, our new keyboard player. Neither Janet nor anyone else had seen him play, but he came with good recommendations. Brad confirmed he knew the songs, so we piled all of his gear into the truck without further discussion. We were now a full band. With the highest of hopes and the excitement of the unknown, we set out on tour.

***

Our first stop was in Portage La Prairie, Manitoba, at the North 40 Cabaret. We were all nervous; however, the show turned out better than any of us had imagined. The crowd loved us and stayed for the entire evening. There was a huge party upstairs after the show, with girls, booze and incense galore. During the party, I stupidly swallowed some pills some chick popped in my mouth. I remember very little about the evening. The guys in the band said they found me lying half-conscious in the hallway of the hotel; they'd put me in the shower and had tried to straighten me up. When I woke the following afternoon, I remembered next to nothing. Janet had stayed up all night and told me I had rambled on in front of the band about my feelings for her. I apologized profusely. Janet just smiled and told me she felt good about having me with her.

I told myself it was natural for us to feel this close. After all, I was her right hand man and she counted on me to take care of her and the band.

"I will always look out for you and do my very best to not let you down," I told her seriously. "And I also promise to never again swallow anything a strange woman puts in my mouth." She agreed that would be best.

As the weeks went by, I felt the need to be protector and confidant for Janet. Being the only girl in a band was probably a rough go. It's all well and good for a bunch of guys to tough it out eating crap and living in shit, but it was my belief even the strongest of women needed a little special consideration on the road. It was important to me that Janet was protected and felt respected at all times. I tried to make sure she was never alone at parties or walking about the club or the town. I tried to keep the locker room banter down to a minimum when she was within earshot. The guys began to follow my lead, and we all began to keep an eye out for her as best as we could.

One night in Canmore, Alberta, I went to Janet's room to talk about changes in the show. Then I left to go sit with the band and bring them up to speed. An hour later, we heard Janet scream from down the hallway. We jumped up and ran down to her room. The door was ajar, and Janet was standing on top of her bed.

"There's someone in the bathroom!" she screamed.

I opened the door to see a scrawny, half-naked middle aged-man cowering in the corner. He was terrified.

"You're fucking dead!" I heard one of the guys yell behind me. I wanted to jump on the guy and beat the shit out of him, but he looked pathetic and scared to death.

"Stay where you are and don't move, or we'll kill you!" I shouted. The guy began to cry. I could smell the booze on his breath. He begged us not to hurt him. I got one of the guys to phone the police and had the other guys stand guard while I consoled Janet.

"How did he get in here? I asked.

"You didn't close the door all the way!" she screamed. "The bastard just walked right in." She was livid. "When I screamed, the fucker ran into the bathroom." I could see tears welling up in her eyes. My heart sank. I had let this happen. I had left her unguarded. After the police left, we never spoke about it again. On that day, I vowed to never let anything bad happen to her again.

Network went through some member changes in the months that followed. The soundman quit and I took up his duties as band bookkeeper, but I still needed a proper replacement. I called Earl. I knew he was putting his own band together, but I thought he could recommend someone. He said the band wasn't ready yet, and he would love to do sound.

Brad Harrington wasn't the keyboard player we had hoped for, so Earl called Bruce to see if he would be interested in the gig. Bruce said he would love to do it. It was great to have them both back.

It was like old times. To my disappointment, Janet and Jim never saw eye to eye, and I couldn't do anything to change that. Eventually, he gracefully bowed out to spare me the pain of firing my mentor and friend. I reconnected with Rob Juneau and asked him to come join us. He had never held a grudge against me and jumped at the chance to play together again. He learned all of the material in a few short days and was amazing right away.

We replaced Hollywood, our drummer, with some kid that showed up to audition in Hamilton. We kept him for a while, but he was too green and Janet soon asked for a replacement.

Chris "Cozy" Brown was from Scarborough. He joined the band while we were playing a rare home appearance and stayed with us for the remainder of our days. He was a cool, good-looking dude that added character to the band. Every night, we turned out all the lights and he would play his drums with flaming mallets. It was a real showstopper. He only set the stage on fire twice.

The show got better and morale ran high. I was writing again, and we recorded live versions during the day at the club. I gave Janet the tapes and she sent them back to her contacts in Toronto. I would ask each week for feedback, but she never had any concrete answers. She told me the wheels turned slowly and just to keep writing and recording. I left it at that and brought her more songs. We collaborated on a few songs and I enjoyed having someone to bounce ideas off. Rob soon lost interest in the whole thing and told me he was going to pursue a solo project. It was tough to see him leave again, but this time it was of his own choosing and he left on good terms.

John Wittan was Rob's replacement. He played with a band called Secret and was a respected songwriter in the Alberta scene. John was a great addition to the band, and his wife Terri ended up going everywhere with us. It was thought that having wives or girlfriends on the road would be too much of a distraction, but Terri proved to be a great asset to the band. She was great for morale with her always-cheery disposition. She was into numerology and bizarre, cosmic stuff and kept a constant, watchful eye on the band's karma. She told the single guys which girls to stay away from and which ones she thought were cool. She was never wrong, and the guys loved her. On road trips, she would tell us where the moon was in our Zodiac houses and a bunch of other stuff that I really tried to pay attention to. Most of the time, I just smiled and nodded.

John and I wrote some songs together, and he brought some material of his own to the band. It was a prolific period for Network and we stockpiled a lot of material to send to Janet's Toronto contacts. There was still no response though, and I was getting frustrated. I nagged Janet incessantly about her silent connections. Did they like any of the songs? Were her contacts going to help? Janet confided there was little support from her associates and she didn't explain further. They either didn't like our songs, or they'd been stringing us along from the beginning.

We toured on, wrote less, and partied more. The band felt duped into making money for Janet's agent. We felt we would never get off the road. I decided there was no way I could be content spinning my wheels in a Top 40 band. In 18 months, we did three passes back and forth across Canada.

The band was resentful and Janet was disappointed. Our relationship deteriorated. We talked less and argued more. I remembered how painful the breakups with Hellion and Teen Angel were, and I didn't want to go through it again. I had a private meeting with Janet we agreed the best thing was to fold Network and go our separate ways.

The goodbyes were heartbreaking. Most of the members had arranged to join up with other groups, or go home and rest. I set sail for home with Earl and Bruce. There was work to be done.

CHAPTER TWELVE

Earl had received a call earlier that week about a band that was looking for a soundman. His contact said the band was making wholesale changes, and Earl thought there might be opportunities for Bruce and me. He suggested we meet up with the band on our way home and check things out for ourselves. We agreed, and after a couple of calls, Earl got through to Lanny Williamson, the band's manager. He confirmed the band was looking for a keyboard and bass player. They were playing that night in Medicine Hat, Alberta, at The Westlander Hotel. He invited us to come down and do a live audition.

We were half way between Yellowknife and Calgary. Medicine Hat was 12 hours away. Earl told Lanny we would be there. I pointed the U-Haul south, pushing it as hard as I dared. While we mashed our way down the snowy highway, Earl shared what little information he had.

The group was called the Cindy Warren Band. Cindy was a California girl who rarely ventured out of the San Fernando Valley. She was touring Western Canada with her second album and her musicians were bailing on her. Cindy had enjoyed some success in California, singing backup on an Alice Cooper tour and doing hairstyles and makeup for Lionel Ritchie's "All Night Long" music video. Network was in my rear view mirror and I was excited for a chance to play behind a recording artist that was touring an actual LP.

We got to Medicine Hat in time for the second set. The band behind Cindy was a good-looking bunch of guys and they played well together. They were decked out in cool rock outfits and all had California tans. The band had the cool Hollywood rocker chic I had seen in music magazines.

Cindy reminded me of the Joplin-esque Bette Midler from The Rose. She had blonde curly locks and big eyes accented with dark mascara. She had a powerful and well-developed pop/rock singing voice with a somewhat offbeat, Cyndi Lauper quirkiness. Her tone reminded me of Pat Benatar, or maybe Laura Brannigan, cut with a gravelly edge à la Bonnie Tyler. Her energetic spirit and contagious laugh were natural as she joked with the crowd. Her songs and stage manner were sexually charged. Dressed in black leather and spandex, Cindy read from Penthouse Forum to the crowd. Whenever the language got too hot, a band member would make a sound on their instrument to cover the sexually explicit words.

After the set, we went upstairs to talk to Lanny. He opened the door and greeted us with a handshake. Lanny was a middle-aged, regular-looking guy and didn't look much like a rocker. He introduced himself as the band's manager, the soundman, and Cindy's husband. Then he introduced Cindy, who greeted us with a smile.

Lanny and Cindy were professional and easy-going. They explained the line-up changes had to be done quickly. I asked when we could audition and Lanny said it wasn't necessary. He had heard both Bruce and I were capable musicians and meeting the two of us was more important than hearing us jam after a 12 hour drive. I liked him right away and appreciated his straight-forwardness.

Lanny poured us a drink while we talked. Lanny and Cindy were sympathetic as we recounted what we had been through with Network and how management promises had been made and broken. They countered with stories about famous people they knew and contacts they had, and how well placed they were to be successful. They hoped Bruce and I would be interested in contributing as songwriters because they planned to record some new material while they were in Calgary.

"I'm in," I said, and looked at Bruce and Earl. They both agreed, and we toasted the new relationship and stayed until Cindy went down for the show. The three of us were burned out from the drive and elected to get some sleep. Lanny got us complimentary rooms at the hotel and I went to sleep feeling better than I could have imagined. Everything was great. Life was wonderful again.

The next morning, Bruce caught a bus to Calgary to stay with his parents while Earl and I embarked on the long drive home to Toronto. I wanted to get back there as soon as possible, drop the gear and the truck, and fly back to Calgary to start things up with Cindy. I was stoked about the whole thing. This band was going to make my dreams finally happen. I knew it.

I would write songs and we would record them. We would get the record out and do some killer tours. Maybe I'd get signed by her label and get the guys back together. My line up would be Rob, Jim, Mike, and John and we could tour just like the old Teen Angel days. Over that next three days' drive, I mapped out my whole future.

* * *

My mom had moved back to Toronto a few months earlier and was living in an apartment in Etobicoke. I dropped Earl and the rental stuff in Rexdale and decided to spend a few days with my Mom. I told her all about Cindy and the new band, and how I was certain this was my big break. I wanted her to share my excitement. She was distant, but wished me well.

"Is something wrong, Mom?" I asked as I sat down next to her on the couch. I could tell she was searching for the right words.

"I've heard this all before, Teddy." She looked into my eyes with deep concern. I hadn't seen that look since the days when she would drop me off at the TTC subway station. It was unnerving.

"What do you mean, Mom?" I asked, but I knew where this was going.

She cleared her throat and spoke quietly "Every band you've been in has been the one you were sure was going to make it big," she said. The concern faded from her face and was replaced with irritation.

"None of these bands have panned out," she continued. Her voice got louder. "For five years I've been listening to you say how this band or that band was going to be the one. First, it was Black Star, then it was Hellion, and then Teen Angel."

"Mom," I tried to interrupt, but she continued counting on her fingers.

"Then, you were certain Network was going to make it big. And look what happened... nothing."

I didn't know how to respond. What was going on? My mom had supported me without question throughout my life. Her words caught me completely by surprise. I did my best to stay calm and tried to reason with her.

"This time it's different, Mom." I spoke softly and tried to be firm. "She's already recorded two albums, has a record label, and a manager. The whole thing is really together." Her expression softened, but the look of concern returned to her face.

"I'm not telling you to give up, Teddy," She said. "I just want you to be careful." She placed her hand on mine. "You jump in with both feet and you end up getting your heart broken."

I pulled my hand away and sighed. She was winding up for one of her lectures. I wasn't in the mood.

"You're not a kid anymore, Teddy," she continued. "You're 23 years old and perfectly capable of making your own decisions." I rolled my eyes.

"That's right, Mom." I wanted her to stop, but I knew there was more.

"Look," her irritation returned. "You know I want you to follow your dreams and I really do hope this band brings you what you're looking for." I was getting frustrated and she knew it. She grabbed my hand again.

"I want you to temper your judgment about this thing and be careful about your expectations." We both stayed quiet for a minute. I relaxed a little and decided it was best to let her finish. I wasn't going to win. When Mom was serious about something, she was an impenetrable wall. It was best to just let her get it off her chest.

"Remember," she said. "If something seems too good to be true, it probably is."

God, I hated when she did that.

"They know a lot of powerful people, Mom," I stood up. "This is the biggest thing I have ever been a part of in my life." I wanted out of this conversation. There was obviously nothing I could do to make her understand.

"Well then," she remained cool. "All the more reason to tread carefully, isn't it?"

She didn't really expect an answer and I wasn't about to offer one."Ok, Mom," is all I said. I tried to make it sound as dismissive as possible, but she knew she had gotten to me. She always did. She had said what she needed to say and so had I. Anything else I said would have sounded like I was asking for permission. There was no way I was going to let her think that.

I knew she didn't understand how big an opportunity this was for me, but she would understand eventually when I hit the big time and became a star. Cindy Warren was going to take me to the top. Then I would be able to say I told you so. Still, a part of me understood she was just doing what she thought was the right thing to do, to look out for her kid.

She hadn't told me to quit, she didn't suggest I give up music and get a real job. She had just told me to be careful. Fine, I thought. I'll be careful.

I hugged her and told her I loved her. "I'll be fine, Mom. I promise."

I kissed her cheek and she smiled. "I'm proud of you, Teddy," she said. "Never forget that."

The door buzzed. My taxi was there. It was time to go.

"I love you Mom and don't worry, it's all going to work out." She smiled, and I knew we understood each other.

"All right then," she said. "Go and make it happen." It didn't matter how much Mom pissed me off. When I knew she was in my corner, I was charged up and ready to take on the world. I rode the elevator downstairs. God, I couldn't wait to get to Calgary.

I picked up Earl and we were off, Mom's words echoing in my head. Earl and I took turns driving and napping. We talked about Network and Teen Angel, what we thought went wrong, and how this time it was going to be different.

We arrived in Calgary three days later, burned out from the road. It didn't stop us from calling Lanny for a meeting. We met him and Cindy at a downtown restaurant where he laid out the details. Lanny had rented a rehearsal space in downtown Calgary and we would get started the next day. The plan was to rehearse for two weeks and then go on the road for a month to get the show tight. Stefan Poulos was the agent Lanny was booking through in Western Canada. He had rented them space in his Calgary house where they had set up their base of operations. The house was a bit cramped, but there was room for me if I needed it. Bruce's parents lived in Calgary, and Earl would stay with him. I went straight to bed when we got to Lanny and Cindy's, and slept for 14 hours.

Bruce, Earl, and the new players were already at the rehearsal space when I got there. The drummer was Dave Herron. He was from Guelph, Ontario, a little town a few miles outside of Kitchener. He was a skinny longhair who reminded me of the guys I knew back home. I felt comfortable with him from the start.

The guitar player was Ron Champagne, a local favorite in the Calgary scene. He had long blonde hair, chiseled features, and piercing blue eyes. He had a great look and was dressed in a black leather jacket that looked European and expensive. He was an imposing figure, but amiable, and he spoke easily with everyone. Until recently, he'd been with a popular Calgary band called The Unusuals. Cindy saw him performing one night and sold him on joining her band. Ron had a peculiar eccentricity and I loved his dry sense of humor.

Everybody hit it off and we set up our gear to jam. The band was killer right from the first note. After rehearsal we all went to some clubs and partied into the wee hours.

Over the next two weeks, we worked a bunch of new songs into the show that Cindy wanted to learn. Everyone was happy to let me direct the rehearsals and keep everyone on track; I was comfortable with the role, and Cindy and Lanny valued my leadership.

The look of the band was important to Cindy. She wanted everyone in the band to have a Hollywood rocker look. She colored everyone's hair blonde, took us shopping for cool clothes, and we went to the tanning salon every day. We pored through her rock magazines and studied L.A. rock couture; she and Lanny wanted us to look like an authentic Hollywood metal band, and that's what we became. She would tell us about the scene in Hollywood, what everyone did, and how they behaved. It served to get us focused into her headspace about the ideology behind how she wanted to be perceived.

She directed us to pay special attention to one of the newest and most successful bands to surface out of L.A, a heavy rock outfit called Mötley Crüe. Cindy wanted that same sexy, hard rock image to be the touring face for her new album, Trouble. Her first album, I'd Do It, had a light California pop flavor to it. Cindy opted for more edge on Trouble. The songs were Hollywood pop/rock with a heavy guitar edge, themed with sexually suggestive lyrics and drug-related undertones. I learned the songs and delved into this new world. It was a bit of a culture shock, but I soon felt we were cosmopolitan and hip.

I liked the idea of being contemporary and edgy. Cindy was happy with the band's look and even more so of how we'd developed into a hard-hitting and aggressive sounding outfit. The songs from Trouble sounded great, and the ones she elected to re-work from I'd Do It, turned out well.

Cindy was still searching for something that could help us find our own niche in the new MTV-driven hard rock marketplace.

Every night after rehearsal we would gather around the TV and talk about the new wave of glam rock bands dominating music videos of 1983.

One night we watched The Police perform "Synchronicity II." The song was a hard-driving departure for the Police and featured a sort of Mad Max post-apocalyptic costume image for the band. In the video, they stood atop a mountain of post-apocalyptic rubble while the wind blew their hair and attire adding a cool frenetic energy and intensity. We were hooked and agreed that would be our look.

Over the next week, we created costumes, set decorations, and soon had a solid arsenal of Apocalyptic Rock accouterments. We designed torn fishnet and rag-adorned shirts. Our pants were leather chaps, faux burned with spray paint and had ragged scissor cuts. We wore army belts and gas masks around our waists. Our bleached hair was huge and methodically disheveled.

There was a backdrop curtain of scorched army net webbing and foam crumble bricks. Our stage had the same post-nuke look as our attire. Cindy found a mannequin to place in front of Dave's drum set and dressed it in torched army fatigues and a gas mask. Our look was complete and the set list was killer. We were ready to make our debut.

Our first gig was north of Edmonton, Alberta at a small club in St. Albert. Lanny decided it was best to keep out of the major centers and test market the band on a small town crowd. We blew people's minds. We brought 1983 MTV Heavy Metal Hollywood to rural Alberta. The rednecks scowled and the girls swooned. More people came out in droves. By the weekend, the place had a line-up down the block.

For the next six weeks, it was the same everywhere we played. We hit those northern communities like a glam storm and gathered scores of new fans in our wake. The band was tight and we knew we had hit on something huge.

My writing changed overnight. With Cindy's influence and our new song list I was in full creative mode, and I began writing monster rock metal and riff rock pieces that mirrored our edgy image and direction. Cindy loved them. She was ecstatic to know that there would be a steady supply of new material and she talked about plans for recording her next album. I was thrilled.

Cindy and I talked about the process she'd gone through on her previous albums: what had gone right, what had gone awry. I felt a genuine trust form between us. She said she appreciated having a writer with my drive and enthusiasm, and someone who could keep the band sharp and get things done. Lanny took me aside one day and told me he appreciated Cindy and me getting closer. He encouraged me to collaborate with her on some new material, and said he would book some recording time after the first leg of the tour if we had a song or two ready to go. I made it my priority to hash out ideas with Cindy every chance I could get, and we developed a good routine on the road.

Our reputation grew quickly, and by January of '84 we became a mainstay in the rock palaces of the Alberta scene along with acts like Steeler, Guy Jones, Click, and Nick Danger. One of our biggest recurring gigs was at Lucifer's in Calgary, the same place I'd once worked as a bus boy. During the '80s, Western Canadian bars-goers were in love with heavy music. There were dozens of clubs throughout BC, Alberta, Saskatchewan, and Manitoba where good hard rock bands could play. We toured non-stop throughout the summer of '84.

We travelled to Vancouver and played Outlaws. Our opening night was simulcast on 99.3 CFOX. It was my first trip to the West Coast. The week went by all too quickly and I saw very little of Vancouver. I instantly fell in love with the mountains and the ocean, and I swore I would live there some day.

Whenever we played in Calgary, I stayed with Lanny and Cindy at Stephan's house. He was a short, burly, hippie guy with a round face that reminded me of David Crosby. He had a sharp, cynical sense of humor and made no bones about wanting to score big with a hit act and move back to his native San Francisco. I liked Stephan and we became good friends. Lanny was quiet at home, but he was always pleased and supportive about my growing professional relationship with Cindy. By the end of that year, we had grown inseparable.

Cindy was a beautiful woman inside and out. I was enamored with her and she knew it. She was always honest with me and I felt I could trust her. She became less and less guarded around me and I remembered how Janet had done the same. I didn't mind the role of surrogate girlfriend. She had some skeletons in her closet and would talk to me about them, usually after a few drinks. I enjoyed being there for her and it made the band feel good too. I had Cindy's ear and yet I was still one of the guys. It was a good arrangement.

One night Cindy told me she had heard from Lionel Richie's manager. Lionel was playing Calgary with Tina Turner and he asked Cindy if she wanted to come down and visit backstage for a while. She agreed and arranged to have an extra pass waiting for me. I was ecstatic. When the night of the concert arrived, we dressed in our best rock star clothes and went to the arena. The show was amazing, but all I could think about was meeting these two huge stars.

At the end of the show we were escorted backstage. Several journalists and photographers were complaining that no interviews had been granted. Lionel's manager spotted Cindy and ushered us through a crowd of angry press folks. Some of them took pictures of us and I could hear them asking who we were. We entered the room and Lionel greeted Cindy with a hug and shook my hand. It was awesome. I chatted with Lionel and told him how much I admired his song writing. He was wonderful and made me feel at ease. There was nothing presumptuous about him and we soon fell into an easy conversation. He appeared interested in my writing with Cindy and shared stories about his days with The Commodores and now, as a solo artist. He told me that he would usually write several songs for each record, but kept a small bag of hits he could draw from to sprinkle into each successive album. He had no reservations about sharing his insights into the craft, and I soaked up every word. I never got to talk to Tina Turner, but that night was still my most amazing celebrity encounter. Here was Lionel Richie, one of the biggest music stars in the world, encouraging my questions. I had so much respect for the man. He was a gracious star. I knew this was how I wanted to be with my fans. That night, I floated home on a cloud and I swore I would always make people feel the way that Lionel Richie made me feel that night.

* * *

Band morale was high and productivity followed suit. I kept writing and included Cindy in the process. She brought cool musical ideas to me and we started to put together some great songs. One of the first songs I wrote with her was "Trust Me." It had a hard driving guitar riff with a simple, tongue-in-cheek lyric that was an ode to Cindy's more cynical nature:

You say you've seen one, you seen 'em all,

And all of their lines are the same.

But, you'll still give in, then watch me grin.

You know that it's part of the game

Why don't you place your trust in me?

What have you got to lose? Trust me

The song was perfectly suited to the glam image we had created for ourselves. Our sound and look were entirely cohesive. We were perfect for the hard rock scene of '84 and we could compare ourselves to any number of the bands making hit records at that time. My only fear was the whole thing might soon become all too cliché. How long could glam last?

During that summer in '84, I was sitting in my hotel room after a show in North Battleford, Saskatchewan, watching MTV and getting inspiration from the hard rock bands ruling the charts. A video came on for a song called "Runaway" by a group called Bon Jovi. It opened with a ball of flame burning through a nuclear fallout newspaper clipping. The flames dissolved revealing a wild-eyed teenage girl squaring off against her frightened parents while everyone floated on a sea of dry-ice fog. When the musicians appeared onscreen, I remember thinking how the band looked so similar to ours. Complete with spandex, leather, handkerchiefs, and backcombed poodle cuts, Bon Jovi were poster-boys for what had now become '80s modus operandi. Musically, the chorus was catchy, and there was certainly no denying the guys in the band were all good-looking. I cavalierly dismissed them as yet another generic glam contender. I scoffed they would soon get lost in the mix as another Mötley Crüe, Ratt, or Poison clone just like the other hair bands cluttering the MTV's hard rock hit parade.

That night I decided we needed an exit strategy. I went to talk with Cindy. She had seen the Bon Jovi video too and we agreed it was time for us to move on.

"We don't want to disappear in a cloud of hairspray like those Bon Jovi guys," I declared. We needed a new look and a new sound. It was time to write new songs. I had written in the hard rock genre for most of the year and we recorded some great demos, but nothing had fired Lanny up to book studio time. He knew the whole hair band phase was going to run its course. Cindy and I approached him with the idea of finding a new direction, and he was relieved and excited.

"Where do you want to go with this?" he asked.

"Well," I replied. "There's a new techno movement gaining popularity. It may be where the radio market is going."

Bands like Flock of Seagulls, Culture Club, and The Thompson Twins brought a second-generation new wave movement to the UK dance clubs and it was taking hold in North America. Most of the stuff was kitschy and vanilla, but at least it was a starting point.

I knew Bruce would be an asset as we moved in a new direction. He was a great piano and organ player, and lately he was exploring the new digital synthesizers. He had some expensive new keyboards, a Yamaha DX7, and a Korg DW 8000, and on occasion, we had holed ourselves up in his basement studio in Calgary to goof around with them. Bruce had a classical yet trippy bent to his writing style. I found myself enjoying it more and more. I loved Bruce's bizarre melody lines and the intricacy of his orchestral style of arrangement. His penchant for creating cool sounds and sci-fi string pads appealed to my Trekkie side. I began to envision little mini-epics as parts of what might be great techno fodder for a futuristic concept album.

We bounced a few rough ideas off Lanny and Cindy. They were skeptical but positive. We assured them we could find ways to use the techno stuff in a pop sensibility. We were in Calgary for two weeks, which gave us ample time to write a couple of songs in the new vein. Lanny and Cindy could decide then if it was a direction worth considering.

Bruce and I set up shop in his basement and began writing the future for the Cindy Warren Band. Bruce was not a lyricist, but he sang well and had good melody line ideas. It was a good partnership. I wrote lyrics to Bruce's techno riffs, syncopated synth drum patterns, and expansive layers of otherworldly keyboard sounds.

The first song Bruce and I wrote together came quickly, and within the first week, we had "Feel It" recorded on his Tascam 4-track. The song featured a funk bass line and dance groove that served as a hypnotic base for Bruce's keys. He had created some lush keyboard tracks and dreamy synth sounds, and I ghosted a falsetto vocal for Cindy to work with. It was a complete reversal of everything I had written over the past year and the novelty had me and Bruce pumped.

We were like two excited kids when we played the tape for Lanny and Cindy. By the time the chorus hit they were sold. It was pure future pop. They told us to go ahead and put together a couple more. So we did. Bruce and I picked up speed, and we found ourselves working comfortably in the genre. By the end of the week, we had three more songs, including one that would become the title track for the album Roomful of Strangers.

Both musically and philosophically, we believed in the new direction; we couldn't wait to include the songs in the show. We had a contemporary saleable direction to follow and we vowed to leave the glam phase behind us as soon as possible. As the two kinds of songs didn't mix together we resigned ourselves to not include both in the show.

We began recording the Roomful of Strangers album in August of 1984 at Smooth Rock Studios in Calgary. We spent 12 to 15 hours a day in the studio. It was a lot of fun initially, but the novelty soon wore off and eventually became much like any other tedious job that I just wanted to finish. I looked forward to playing shows and getting out of the studio for a while; I would return to the studio with renewed vigor that lasted for a week or so until I wanted to get back onstage again. Bruce and Earl absolutely loved the studio. I found it fatiguing and monotonous.

Over the fall and winter of 1984, we balanced our recording time with playing shows in the old hard rock format. We kept our new image, songs, and direction a secret. Just as we had done for the glam rock phase of the band, we created costumes and set designs to complement our new image and sound. It was all very sci-fi and hi-tech. There were PVC grates and hosing for our stage setup, which looked like something from an Alien movie. I bought a headset microphone, a blue flight suit, and white dryer hoses that would serve as space age leg warmers. I purchased a silver headless Riverhead bass that looked like a space ship. The rest of the band followed suit with costumes and gear of their own. The hard rock Cindy Warren Band played its final show the week before Christmas in 1984.

On New Year's Eve, we debuted the new Cindy Warren Band. Many fans were shocked and I know we lost some of them that night. New fans came on board and some old ones made the transition with us. Our sound and the look were contemporary and focused. We were a cross between Missing Persons, Animotion, and Berlin. There was no mistaking our intended marketplace and we felt strong about our chances to score a deal with the new songs.

We demoed some of the material with mixes from the studio sessions and Lanny sent the cassettes to a few labels. He sent packages to anyone that would take his calls. No one was biting. Then he and Stephan took matters into their own hands. They formed Haute Rock Records, to target techno-pop record buyers like those who listened to Depeche Mode, Tears for Fears, Howard Jones, and the Thompson Twins. They picked up another artist and started planning their empire. We didn't care too much about all of that. We were just thrilled we'd be able to press our LP.

The album was mixed and mastered over the next eight weeks. Haute Rock arranged a small manufacturing deal with CBS. Roomful of Strangers was released in March of 1985. We had the record release party in Calgary accompanied by a fanfare of press and local celebrities. Calgary radio started playing the record and Stephan began booking a Western Canadian tour.

It was awesome to hear myself on the radio for the second time. The song that got the most airplay was one I'd written, called "Remember Tonight." It had bigger drums and guitars than the rest of the songs, but I gave it enough future pop formula that Lanny and Stephan let it get recorded.

Alberta, Saskatchewan, and Manitoba radio stations play-listed

Remember Tonight that summer and I received my first royalty advance. Song writing had finally made me money. I was over the moon. This wasn't like the Teen Angel 45, getting played once or twice, this was going to be a hit!

Remember Tonight started charting, but the album never got the distribution or airplay it needed and it soon fell into that big black hole of near misses. Haute Rock had no mechanism for working the radio stations, they had no money to pay a radio tracker, and they hadn't clarified with CBS any tangible terms for distribution of the record. The strength of the material got the record some airplay, but there was no machinery behind it to take it to the next level. Lanny and Stephan tried to rework the distribution deal, but came up empty-handed. Remember Tonight hovered in the Canadian Top 100 for a short time and disappeared.

The demand for the band slowed and our show price went down. Gigs got worse and morale began to slide. Lanny was frustrated and it put a strain on his relationships with everyone, including Cindy. They separated and Cindy decided to move back to California with a guy she'd met on tour. We played a few painful last dates and then parted ways in the summer of '85. Once again, I was without a band. My mother's words came back to haunt me, and I knew I couldn't go home. I was heartbroken. I had no band, very little money, and an uncertain future. But I had some songs and the will to keep going. I just needed to keep writing and find a way to shop some demos. I went home to Stephan's house and started making plans.

CHAPTER THIRTEEN

I set up a reel to reel and a small mixing board in my bedroom, and began recording drum machine rhythms and guitar/bass demo tracks. I started writing material that appealed to my own tastes, far removed from the techno material on Roomful of Strangers. I wrote whatever came out of my head for the sole purpose of writing.

The songs had a Middle America flavor with flecks of John Cougar, Tom Petty, and Bruce Springsteen. Another influence had crept into my writing. I had seen the movie Eddie and The Cruisers and it made a deep impression on me. The sound of the songs and those characters appealed to my days with Teen Angel. The Cruisers had a driving rock sensibility that I loved. I wanted to put a band together like that someday. I could picture a cool sax player like Wendell and a female background singer like Joann. It would be awesome.

The current music scene was still hair metal and techno pop, and I was tired of it. I figured bands like Bon Jovi were a dime a dozen. They'd released 7800° Fahrenheit in March of '85 but it wasn't going anywhere. I was certain pop music was changing. It was only a matter of time before the hair band phenomena died and I wasn't going to go down with it.

This new Cruisers dream caught fire for me. I had a plan; now I needed to get it off the ground. I approached Stephan with the concept.

"I have an idea that could open some doors for both of us," I said as I laid out the whole Cruisers/middle America concept for him. He nodded, and soon he was grinning from ear to ear. I brought him into my room and played him a brand new song I had just finished called "Hard Line." It had a driving, steady beat with a cool sax hook, and featured a full-on Springsteen/Cruisers type vocal. The lyrics were blue collar and direct:

I get home from work and the sun starts crawling down

I grab my guitar and hitch a ride into town

They say you've got to stay hungry

Been so long, I forgot what that means

There's got to be an easier way

Than to follow your dreams

I know they say it's a hard line

But, it's a harder line to leave

It wasn't Shakespeare, but it worked. Stephan was blown away. He hugged me and told me we were going to be rich. I believed him.

We sat there like excited kids and I played him a half dozen more songs I'd been working on. He was completely sold and told me he wouldn't rest until we had a record deal. It was a meeting of the minds. I knew I'd enlisted the right guy. We could accomplish anything together.

The next day Stephan wasted no time. He made calls to record companies to see who would be willing to receive a cassette. He called the local studios to get time to record. One of the studios said there was well-known producer in town that we should try to meet. Stephan made more calls and got us an appointment to see Mark Goodman.

Mark had enjoyed Grammy success with a gospel group called the Blackwood Brothers a few years earlier and was now in Calgary teaching at the Columbia Recording Academy. He had lived in Decatur, Illinois just outside Chicago, and had moved to Calgary a year earlier. The word on the grapevine was he was looking for projects to produce. Before he would meet with us he wanted to hear my songs. I did a few touch-ups, finished some vocals, and before the day was out I had mixed down six songs to a cassette. Stephan raced the tape down to the studio. I barely slept that night.

At nine o'clock the next morning the phone rang. Stephan took the call, and then knocked on my door. He wore a Cheshire cat grin.

"Goodman loved it, man! He loved it!" He laughed and handed me a glass of orange juice. "He wants to meet with us at lunchtime."

I was dumbfounded. The project was two days old and we had interest from a big-time producer. It was absolutely beautiful. We drove downtown to Columbia Studios while Stephan laid out how to deal with things. He would act as manager and I was happy with that. I had no idea how to talk to a big producer and I was relieved to have Stephan negotiating for me.

The studio was on the top floor of a commercial complex and occupied the entire floor. We found Mark in the control room of the studio complex talking to a group of students huddled around the mixing console. He looked like Kenny Rogers with darker hair and beard, and his voice had a Southern drawl. He excused himself from the class when he saw us peek in the door. Mark was easy going and we had a great first meeting. He had also seen Eddie and The Cruisers and thought I had nailed the spirit in my recordings. He agreed to help me record songs and put together a better sounding demo tape. Then he and Stephan would shop it to his record company friends in America.

"It's not about getting a record deal," he told me. "It's about getting a good one – one that is right for you." Between Mark and

Stephan, I felt things were really going to happen fast and in a big way. Mark was also doing jingle projects on the side and started bringing me in to play bass and sing on radio spots so that I could make money to live. We saw each other almost daily and became good friends.

It took two months to record a dozen songs. Now we had a demo to shop. We got our first bite a few weeks later. Arista had offered $30,000 USD for me to be a staff writer. Clive Davis was looking for songs for some of his label artists and he was especially excited about a new R&B artist from New Jersey named Whitney Houston.

Before I had the chance to jump up and scream in exultation, Stephan and Mark told me they'd turned the deal down to wait for a full recording deal with a much bigger advance.

I couldn't believe it. I was outraged that I hadn't been consulted.

"I would love to be an in-house writer!" I argued. "I could write songs for all the artists they had on their roster. They'd love my work and I could get a record deal for myself." I pleaded with them for over an hour.

"I'm sorry Ted," Mark finally said. "The deal is dead. The best move is to wait for a better deal."

"You're going to get a great record deal," said Stephan. "You'd be a fool to take this little deal. Who the hell is Whitney Houston? She'll probably never amount to anything anyways."

"We're just trying to protect you from wasting your talent," Mark added.

To me it wasn't a waste – it was a huge opportunity. They assured me they were "older and wiser and had been in the business so many more years – they knew what was best for me." I insisted they call Arista and salvage the deal. I knew they were wrong. They told me if I forced the issue, I would be on my own. They'd drop me.

The idea of losing them scared the hell out of me. I needed their help. They had a way to talk to record companies and that's what interested me. I was told record execs didn't deal directly with the artist and I needed representation. Besides, I didn't know the first thing about negotiating a record contract. I relented and put my faith in their judgment.

Months went by without any offers. I asked about Arista again; but they refused to call. I asked for the number and the contact but they wouldn't give it to me. If I pushed any further the whole thing could blow up. Our lives were completely intertwined at this point. Stephan and Mark kept me working so I could pay my room and board at Stephan's. I worked as an agent building and booking bands for Stephan, and I sang and played bass on jingles for Mark.

Mark finally called Arista, but the deal was gone. Clive Davis wouldn't return his calls. Someone else at the label told him they weren't signing any more writers that year and we should try again in the spring. That was the beginning of the end of my relationship with Mark Goodman.

He called me less and less for jingle projects. Stephan was in California to attend to a family emergency. I was still working Stephan's agency business and one of the bands, Asylum, still needed a lead singer.

Lorri Vonne was a local musician known for her ability to sing "guy metal" songs. She had huge '80s rock hair, heavy metal leathers, and lots of makeup. After a brief meeting she agreed to rehearse with Asylum. She hit it off with the guys right away and the band soon had a rocking set list. When Stephan got back at the end of the month, Asylum was ready to go and we sent them out on the road. I repeated the process a couple more times for Stephan, building two more bands for the regional Top 40 circuit, and soon we had a business that paid the rent and gave me lots of spare time to write and demo.

During the weeks of building Asylum, I talked to Lorri about my songs and the band I wanted to build around them. She was also a fan of the Eddie and the Cruisers movie and we watched it together one night, chatting about the characters and what we thought their back-stories were and so on. We started seeing each other when Lorri wasn't on the road.

Asylum played for a few months and then a couple of the members gave notice they were leaving. It was tough to lose the agency income from Asylum. I decided to put something together of my own, get back out, and sing again. I figured I could use the opportunity to make more money and get some players that might work for my dream band.

I wanted to put Lorri into my project rather than in another band, so I built a band for a house gig on 11th Avenue in Calgary. A lot of clubs and cafes had opened there and the strip became known as Electric Avenue. I had a friend who worked as a dishwasher at one of these new venues called Dillinger's. Nightclub veteran Guy Jones had done the grand opening there, so I knew it was a good venue with a decent budget.

I didn't want to sidestep Stephan, so I had him solicit the club; he negotiated a decent deal on a month-by-month basis. I met with the club owner and pitched him my idea. The movie The Big Chill had made a successful run through the theatres recently and given new life to a lot of old Motown songs. I thought a Motown theme would be a great set list for Dillinger's, and I managed to sell the owner on the idea. Over the next four weeks, I put together a killer line-up that would come to be known as The Cool Front.

Earlier that summer I'd met a guitar player in Lillo's music store in Calgary. His name was Edwin Daniel Kazmir, but everyone called him Fast Eddie. He was a local hero of sorts and was with a successful club act called The Tickets. They had Rolling Stones, Brit-rock look and a set list to match. Fast Eddie was an energetic guy with a fast-paced, dry humor and quick intellect. His manner was true to his name. He was a little older than me and had been touring the clubs for many years with the Tickets and the first version of the band, known as Elder Dark. Fast Eddie was a mainstay in the Calgary scene. He had carved a good reputation for himself as a wicked guitar player and had done fill-ins with lots of bands. I told him I was doing demos and it interested him. I asked him to come down to the studio and play some lead tracks to a song I was recording, and he agreed. He was amazing. I knew he was the perfect guy right away.

We partied together that night and pantomimed the entire first Montrose album together in front of party guests with air guitars. I hadn't rocked with anyone like that since my KISS days with Les Starkey. I wanted this guy in my life.

While I was putting my Motown band together, Eddie joined up and said goodbye to his other projects. Now we were three. With Lorri and Eddie's help, I got a drummer, Ken Smith, and a tenor sax player named Ron Leppard. Ron brought in a trumpet player named Tony, who in turn brought in an alto sax player named Freddie. I wanted to put Bruce Leitl into the lineup, but he was working on another project and couldn't commit.

Fast Eddie recruited a guy named Sean Burke-Gaffney to play keys. We put together a great show of songs by The Supremes, Aretha Franklin, The Ronnettes, The Temptations, the Four Tops, and other gems from the '60s and early '70s Motown. Eddie and I became fast friends while Lorri and I became inseparable. Everything was falling into place. We had the Cool Front to make money, and worked on songs and recordings during the day. Lorri made extra money doing whatever jingles Mark was still sending our way, and I got Eddie involved as well.

One day Eddie came in all excited about a name for our Eddie and The Cruisers style original band. He had seen a Jack Nicholson movie the night before called The Border, and we took the idea to Mark. He and Stephan had been shopping all of my songs as Ted Moore. They loved The Border, but could we please make it Ted Moore and the Border? I liked that it was similar to Eddie and The Cruisers, but I was self-conscious about having my own name hanging out there like that. It was unnerving. I figured once we had a deal we could call the band whatever we wanted to.

We spent most of 1985 writing songs for Ted Moore and The Border while we made money as The Cool Front. Things were on track, and I hoped that Mark and I might recover from the Arista fiasco.

In early 1986, things fell apart for Mark at Columbia and he told me he was going to head back to Chicago. Shortly after, the Dillinger's house gig ended as well. The club went into receivership, the owner had fled, and we got stiffed for the last week's money. I went to court with my local Musician's union-assigned aid to no avail – there was no one to sue.

Stephan called me the next morning and told me Mark had moved back to the States. He had left a message with Stephan saying he was sorry that he had turned down the Arista offer against my wishes and that he knew I would find something else someday. I never heard from Mark again.

The jingles and recording time for my project was gone. The Dillinger's house gig was gone. Stephan was frustrated and decided to move back to San Francisco as soon as he could. I would have to find a new place to live. He gave me a number to an agency that might be able to book some long road dates for the Cool Front and that would give me some money and time to find a place to live. I thanked him for his efforts and wished him all the best. A week later Stephan was gone. I'd lost my manager, my business partner, and my good friend. Once again, it was time to regroup and come up with a new plan. This time I wasn't completely alone. I still had a band.

Chapter Fourteen

I called the number Stephan gave me. It was an agency in Edmonton called Studio City. I didn't have a contact, so I talked to the receptionist about my band. She said they probably wouldn't have a lot of interest for a nine-piece Motown band. They were more into booking hard rock and Top 40 bands on the circuit. She wasn't unpleasant, in fact, she sounded willing to help. She said I should get a photo and a heavier song list and send the materials in. Someone would call me back. In the meantime, I was broke and homeless and I told her so. She said she would talk to someone at the office and see if they could get us a couple of shows to make some food money.

I went to Fast Eddie's place and we started calling the guys in the band. It was over a month since the last Dillinger's gig and people had started to scatter. Our keyboard player and two of the horn players found other gigs and couldn't commit. I gave Bruce a call and he said he could fill in for a couple of shows here and there.

I put together a new promo shot with Eddie, Lorri, Bruce, Ken, Ron, and me. I called the agency every day from Eddie's place where he let me stay until we could hit the road. An agent from Studio City named Atilla Ambrus called and said he would book some shows for the band.

The first gig was in a couple of weeks. Bruce was no longer available. Eddie had heard about a keyboard player he'd met at Lillo's music. His name was John Bright, he was new in town and he was a good piano player. The first thing I noticed when we met him at the music store was the guy looked younger than the legal drinking age. He had moved out from Peterborough, Ontario where he had grown tired of the limited local scene. He was a decent guy and played well. I hired him right there in the music store.

I got a lead on another sax player and met him the following night at a local gig. He was a huge black guy named Ray Myers and he reminded me of Clarence Clemons. Ray was showy and had lots of charisma. He was a monster on the saxophone. He played baritone sax, and it would work well with Ron on tenor sax. We had a full band again.

Our first gig fell through, but another band had been fired half way through a two-week gig in High River, just outside Calgary. We were asked to replace them. I took the gig and off we went with the unrehearsed keyboards and saxophones. We jammed through lots of stuff and everyone got tight real quick. That served as our agency proving ground, and the gigs came in steadily through the winter of 1985 and into the spring of 1986. I took the band off the road for a week while Lorri and I moved in to a new apartment. I was feeling creatively productive again.

"This line-up is perfect for my original project," I told Lorri. Having a band was a big part of the strength I drew on to keep moving forward. There was something tribal and empowering about having a secure group and writing specifically for musicians you played with all of the time. I just needed to keep us together, keep touring, making money, and recording songs. The rest would come along.

I worked my songs into the Cool Front show until more than half of the show was original material and the rest was an assortment of Motown tunes and classic rock. I wrote songs and rehearsed wherever and whenever we could while on the road. I had a new poster made with the name Ted Moore and the Border and the show became progressively more in tune with the Eddie and the

Cruisers styling I was looking for. We added some Bob Seger, Bruce Springsteen, Tom Petty, and John Cougar songs to the line-up and they complimented my original songs well. Material was coming to me quickly and I catalogued a fair number of new songs.

I needed a way to get some more studio time and demo them. Every studio in town I approached wanted cash up front. The thought of us getting straight jobs vs. touring came up in conversation. We knew straight jobs would change our ability to tour the band for weeks at a time, and that if we turned down road gigs, agents would put us to the bottom of their lists. But if straight jobs could help us get seed money for recording, and we could play local shows now and then, maybe it would work out better.

I listened to arguments from every member of the band. We talked about possible partnerships and incorporations for sharing the recording expenses, but ultimately, no one wanted to share the risks. When I asked everyone how they felt about chipping in their straight job money for the band's recordings time, everyone got quiet.

"They're your songs, Ted," Ray spoke up. "You need to find the studio time to record them." Ray was very matter-of-fact when he spoke and I could tell the others agreed. I was the songwriter and the bandleader and it was up to me to fund my recordings and figure out how to do it.

I agreed to run the group and take care of the finances. Everyone was free to contribute songs and the group would have a voice in deciding whose songs to record next.

We agreed that the person whose song became a hit would be the one to make the most money. This way everyone had a sizeable stake. Now I needed to figure out how we were going to raise some money.

I went home that night and watched Eddie and the Cruisers again, letting my mind drift through the options. I had no financier and I didn't have an American Express Gold Card. How was I to get recording time for a new band that had no money? Without a rich relative or working a straight job, I was left with few options other than to raise money by touring.

No problem. I was happy when I toured. I wanted to perform. I wanted to be a rock star. Rock stars don't have straight jobs – they play music. I needed to get this band out on the road and get it seen by as many people as I could.

Mom always told me that if you work hard at something, and truly believe in what you are doing, your dreams will come true. I believed her. I wanted to travel the world, have millions of people love me, and make millions of dollars. A bit naïve perhaps, but lots of people had done it before me. It was my turn.

The Beatles started from humble beginnings and they became the biggest band in the world. They were just four working class guys that were discovered playing in clubs. That was another reason I needed to get my band out on the road. The more we played the more chance we would have to be discovered. I was going to make it and that was all there was to it. Nothing would keep me from trying.

That Bon Jovi guy had made it big. His band was ripping up the charts with their new smash album, Slippery When Wet, and they were headlining tours all around the world. Jon Bon Jovi's success story was now a matter of public record. He got a job as a gopher at New York's Power Station Recording Studios. He traded work at the studio for recording hours and got some of the great musicians coming through to lend their time. One of the songs they recorded was "Runaway." The labels all passed.

Then in 1983, radio station WAPP 98.3 in New York assembled a compilation of songs from regional acts for an album called New York Rocks 1983. Jon got a DJ at the station to play "Runaway." The regional spins exploded into national rotation until Jon had a turntable hit. The labels came running and he was eventually signed to Polygram. After years of playing regional club shows around New Jersey while he wrote songs and shopped demos, his career was finally in full swing. Now on his third album, he was a millionaire and fully capable of supporting himself with music. His money struggles were over. At 25 years old, Jon Bon Jovi had achieved his lifelong dreams of musical success.

I had no problem admitting to myself, or anyone else, that I wanted to make money in the music business. I needed to get recorded, do an album, and get a song on the radio. Things would start from there and maybe I could force the labels to take notice just like Jon Bon Jovi had. I had made up my mind. I would tour the band, make money for demos to shop, and find a way to get on the radio and get discovered.

The next morning, I called everyone and told them they could let go of their apartments and jobs. We were going to hit the road and make a living as a touring band. Then we would record the demo and get a deal. It was as simple as that. I'd created a Top 40 cover song band with my recording band players and we'd go on the road to play the clubs to generate recording money.

The northern communities were replete with engagements that lasted for weeks, sometimes months, at a time. I sought them out on a regular basis. A long, stationary gig would give the band plenty of time to rehearse and write new material. It was a win-win situation, or so I believed. With the best of intentions we packed up the band and headed north for a few months of writing and rehearsing. The plan was to return home with new, well-rehearsed songs, carrying a pile of money.

The flaws to my plan were obvious after the first couple of northern trips. Aside from the party distractions, the trips to get there were often fraught with problems. In order to maximize profits, I elected to drive 1,200 miles rather than pay for expensive flights. The nasty northern roads put serious wear on our vehicles, and on many occasions, I spent a lot of money on repairs.

On our second trip to Yellowknife, I found myself lying in the snow, in -35°F weather, under our van trying to diagnose why the vehicle would run but would not drive forward without stalling. The fuel pump had frozen solid and we had to be towed to the nearest town where the oh-so-friendly-locals made repairs and gave us the nasty bill. We were running out of money already due to the inflated fuel prices. I wrote a post-dated check. The first week's gig money was now earmarked for vehicle repair. I had no other choice but to keep the band on tour. I booked more shows, stayed up North for longer periods, and told myself it was a means to an end. I just had to keep touring and make money.

CHAPTER FIFTEEN

Touring can be a brutal and lonely existence. It is a ludicrous circus, and not for the faint of heart or the weak of spirit. When a tour schedule extends into months, sometimes years, it can be a recipe for disaster. For many players, the pace is too much to handle.

During most of the '70s and '80s, bands played six nights a week. The '80s were a good time to be in a travelling bar band. There was a multitude of agents and gigs; enough to keep a band working for an entire year. Gigs ran Monday to Saturday, with Sunday the designated travel day. The next stop could be an hour away, but usually it was several hours before we reached the next gig.

Canada is a large country and bands were accustomed to long drives between gigs. If an agent didn't get us a connecting date, we'd take whatever came our way, just so the band could eat. Ten to fourteen-hour drives were a regular occurrence. Twenty and thirty hour drives were not unheard of.

Road burn sets in at different times for everyone. Keeping an eye on the brass ring is tough to do while sitting in a drafty hotel room in the frozen north on week three of a two-month stint.

For the most part, I loved touring. We'd pull into town, set up, perform, tear down, pack up, and move on. There is a sense of constancy – a perpetual motion that brings fun to everyone, town by town. Arriving in a new town was like an invasion. Our gang brought good times and was given the same in return. I loved having a group of musicians sharing the same experience together. We celebrated and commiserated the adventures of road life in a rock 'n' roll band. We'd swap stories, share conquests and missteps, and witness each other's experiences. We hatched plans for new additions to the sets, how to improve what we had and retool the weak areas. Our bond was a safety net for lonely times.

Time is different on the road. Weeks and months flew by without notice. During any given gig week, the routine was more or less the same. After the show we would listen to a recording of the evening's performance, have some drinks, and burn some incense. Guests would show up and parties lasted until sunrise. We slept most of the day and then got up and met in the coffee shop for something to eat. After that we'd rehearse, or go and explore the town

Sundays were travel and down-time days. I spent many a Sunday night twiddling my thumbs trying to figure out what to do. Sometimes I appreciated the alone time, but invariably I would wander down to someone's room just to sit with them and watch TV.

A well-travelled musician is easy to spot. They are comfortable in their own skin and they have an independence born out of necessity. A seasoned road vet doesn't brag about conquests and is often reticent to divulge certain information. Tour veterans, more often than not, display a general calm, devoid of boastful bravado. Many an evening I listened to drunken road rookies brag about their sexual escapades and road warrior stories, only to later see them hurling in the kitchen sink and then crying on some chick's lap.

Then there are the ones who become jaundiced towards the whole experience. Night after night, city after city, the decadence, debauchery, and excesses of life on the road with a rock 'n' roll band take their toll. Many will tell you they simply "grew out of it." As for me, I would take my band to the ends of the earth if I had to. We would play to as many people as possible, build a fan base, and get discovered.

* * *

The northern gigs were reasonably productive. We were now Ted Moore and The Border and the song list was half original material and half blue-collar cover songs. The Eddie and the Cruisers spirit of the group was not lost on the audiences, and we began to gather a loyal following throughout the Prairies and the North. The audiences loved us, club operators were happy, and agents were getting good reports.

We weren't a typical hard rock band, and quickly found a niche for ourselves. We had a rock edge, but there was sax and keys throughout the songs. I was a cross between Eddie Wilson and Eddie Money and the whole show had a New York / New Jersey flavor. As we had an arsenal of original songs, we filled a variety of opening slots for larger concert acts. We opened for Prism, Trooper, Harlequin, Alannah Myles, and The Powder Blues Band. With such a variety of middle of the road songs, we became the band that could open for just about anyone.

On November 25, 1986, we opened for Roy Orbison at The Jubilee Auditorium in Calgary. We played to a packed house for 35 minutes. The set sat well with Roy's crowd. We performed "Stop in the Name of Love," so Lorri would be featured, and the rest of the numbers were mine. We performed "Fast Times," "Suzie's Getting Older," and "Hard Line." I had just written a new song called "Alone Without You" and we debuted it at the show. It was the highlight of the set. There was thunderous applause, and I knew we'd accomplished something special.

Roy Orbison came on and moved the audience in a way I had never seen before. His voice was pure and beautiful and his band was outstanding. I stood in the wings and studied him. I learned more that night than ever before in my career. He received three encores and a standing ovation that lasted five minutes. After the show, Roy invited me and Fast Eddie back to his dressing room.

"I loved the songs, guys," he nodded to me. "And you," he added, looking at Eddie, "Are an amazing guitar player. You boys have a real future."

We sat around for an hour while he talked about the music business, Elvis Presley, and life in Texas. I was mesmerized.

"Send a tape of your songs to my management company," he said as we were leaving. "I'll pass along a good word for you."

I thanked him and floated home.

I sent the cassette as Roy had asked. A few weeks later, his manager responded they liked the songs and would contact me again. I never heard back from them, but I was grateful for Roy's help and appreciated that his manager at least replied.

I had actually opened for Roy Orbison. He had liked my songs and then referred me to his manager. That was amazing to me. When Roy died shortly afterward, I mourned the loss of a great entertainer and one of the nicest people I have ever met.

CHAPTER SIXTEEN

We hit the road and played constantly for the first half of 1987. Whenever we were in Calgary, I spent whatever money I saved and recorded more demo tapes. The Calgary label offices weren't signing anyone, and recommended I move to Vancouver or Toronto to get right under the labels' noses. They gave me a contact number in Vancouver.

The next day I made a call to Sam Feldman and Associates. I talked to a guy named Lenny Goddard about gig potential for Ted Moore and the Border in Vancouver, and he said he'd send someone out to see the band. The following week, in Wetaskiwin, Alberta, a guy named Michael 'Casey' Boyle came to see the band. He loved the show and signed Ted Moore and the Border to the Feldman roster that night.

Casey said that he would shop the tapes if I agreed to sign on with his management company and pay an additional 10%. With Feldman's commission, that would be a whopping 25 points! I was assured we would have a deal in no time and so I signed. I believed Casey was just the kind of guy that we needed and I resolved to move to Vancouver as soon as possible.

It would mean a lot of people and a lot of stuff had to be moved and I dug into the details. Eddie decided to keep a small place in Calgary for his girlfriend. John's girlfriend, Anne, had come out from Peterborough and she would stay in Calgary until John could send for her. The rest of us would put our stuff in storage and find apartments in Vancouver.

The move to Vancouver was a big undertaking and not everyone was up to it. Ray, our sax player, opted to stay in Calgary. Our latest drummer, Mark Reid, and his girlfriend had just had a baby, and he decided he would take this opportunity to get off the road and stay in Calgary with his family. I called Casey to feel out the player situation in Vancouver, telling him I would need a couple of replacements. He told me he knew lots of drummers in Vancouver and he would find one for me in no time. He also felt one sax player was a better move as everyone would make more money. I agreed and trusted a new drummer would be easy to find in a metropolis like Vancouver.

In July of 1987, we packed up and moved to Vancouver. The mountains and coast were breathtaking and Vancouver felt more alive at night than any place I had ever been. There was so much happening. Vancouver was a backdrop for so many films and TV it was known as Hollywood North. The club scene was bursting with music everywhere.

There was a wonderful spirit to the town and the people I met at our first couple of gigs struck me as so serene. They were more laid back than Albertans and much more laid back than the people I knew in Toronto.

I remember my dad talking about Vancouver when I was a kid. He and some of his buddies described a city full of 'hippies and draft dodgers'. They said everyone in Vancouver was a surfer or a stoner. To me, Vancouver seemed like heaven.

There were record companies, producers, and a killer live scene in the clubs. It was perfect.

I would submit demos, get the band up and running with a new drummer, and play some label showcases in a few key venues. With Feldman and Associates I could still tour the band in case things didn't pan out right away with the labels. Potential existed all around me and my hopes were high.

The version of Ted Moore and the Border that entered the Vancouver music scene in 1987 was lean and mean. We had Detroit soul, a New Jersey sensibility, and a Middle-America heartbeat. The show was three-quarters original, and we surrounded our original songs with Bruce Springsteen, John Cougar, and Tom Petty covers. Several people thought our original songs were album cuts from those artists. We often opened the second set with Eddie and the Cruisers' "On the Dark Side", and it became a calling card for the group. We were different enough from most of the local bands and it made for a smooth integration into the Vancouver scene. The other bands were friendly to us as we weren't stepping on anyone's toes. Our song list, our look, and our demeanor were fresh enough that we stood out, yet we still blended in.

I began to see and meet many of the bands and artists working the local clubs. Some of the bands I already knew from the Calgary scene, but there were a whole host of new bands that dominated the Vancouver in-town scene:

Paradox, Shama, The Edge, Pretty Boy Floyd, Chrissy Steele, Raymond May, Frenzy, Young Guns, K. Lee Reich, Lovehunter, The Restless, Wildchild, Giant, Witchhazel, Boyz Room, Vertigo, Metropolis, Mad Max, Cinderella Rockerfella, Long Train, Neverland, 911, Bazooka Joe, 3D, Sparkling Apple, and others could be seen on any given night in a dozen or more venues in and around Vancouver.

The clubs had great stages and production, and the bands looked and sounded great. The big downtown rock rooms were the Body Shop, Vancouver's Tonight, Outlaws (which later became The Metro), Richards on Richards, and Club Soda. In the surrounding boroughs there was California Dreaming in New Westminster, Frank's Place in Richmond, Shooters in Newton, Champagnes in Surrey, and The North Burnaby Inn, Club Kaos and The Caribou in Coquitlam.

Ted Moore and The Border soon became a target for some diverse open spots our first year in Vancouver. A massive venue had been built a year earlier for Expo 86 called the 86 Street Pavilion, and it was now serving as a giant nightclub and show palace. We became a regular fixture for opening spots there. The place was often packed with up to 1,000 people. We opened for Bachman Turner Overdrive one night, and I got to meet two of my heroes, Bryan Adams, and Headpins' singer Darby Mills. I have played many places in Vancouver since, but I think 86 Street will always be among my favorite Vancouver venues.

Over the next six months, we played non-stop, and by the winter of 1987 it was obvious the band was established in Vancouver. Eddie and John decided it was time to let go of their Calgary apartments. John, Eddie, and I made the trip out to Calgary in the band's 5-ton truck. As much stuff as my truck could hold, it wouldn't fit everything. We decided to make two trips.

The first trip went smoothly and I got us back to Vancouver in record time. As soon as we had dropped off Eddie and the first load, I packed John and Anne into the truck and headed back to Calgary. I had been up for 24 hours now and I knew I was too tired to go any further. John volunteered to drive the rest of the way, but I was hesitant, as I'd never had much luck with other people driving my vehicles. But I was too spent to continue so John took the wheel and I went up on the bunk behind the driver's seat to get some rest.

Within less than an hour, I awoke to a loud banging and the

sounds of John cursing. I jumped from the bunk as we came to a stop and went outside to have a look under the smoking hood.

My heart dropped. The motor was blown. It was so bad the oil dipstick had been driven out of its sheath and was wagging around, mocking me, amidst the smoking ruins of my truck's engine.

Night had set in, snow was falling, and the Coquihalla summit was a few miles up the mountain. In jeans, a t-shirt, a jean jacket, and cowboy boots, I walked to the summit to see if I could find a house or roadside rest stop to use the telephone to call for help. There was nothing for miles, but I knew the tollbooth was at the bottom of the summit. I closed up the collar of my jean jacket and walked the barren, snowy highway five miles down to use the tollbooth phone.

Coquihalla Towing picked me up and we went back up the summit to the truck, where John and Anne were huddled under blankets in the bunk. The driver got my truck on the hook and towed me to their base at a horse ranch. I arranged for John and Anne to get a ride to the bus station where they could wait in Vancouver until the truck was fixed. I stayed with the truck and began making calls until Casey finally found a replacement engine.

I spent the next three days living in the mechanic's bunkhouse while they replaced the engine in my truck. It was beautiful on the Coquihalla summit and I explored as much as I could. On the third day, I went out with one of the lead hands to look for one of his horses. After a couple hours, we found the animal tangled and bleeding in barbed wire. The blonde hair of his mane was clumped with blood from the open wounds at his neck. He was suffering badly. Without a word, the ranch hand went into the back of the truck and got his shotgun. He aimed and fired at the dying animal.

The sound of the blast echoed through the mountainside and then everything was quiet.

On the morning of the fourth day, the truck was fixed and I set back for Vancouver to pick up John and Anne. I watched the ranch disappear in my rear view mirror and tried to put the past few days in perspective. We were all okay. I'd survived walking the Coquihalla in winter and I'd watched a man shoot a horse. It had all been quite surreal.

* * *

Casey made good on his promise of finding me a drummer. Brian Lousley was the drummer for a successful Canadian band called Stonebolt. Brian was great, but it was understood from the start that he could only stay on temporarily to help us out, as he was a very busy session guy around Vancouver. He stayed a few months while we searched for someone permanent.

Eric was a friend that our bass player, Brian Louden, had brought in. He was a good guy and decent player, but he left for Eugene, Oregon, to start a business.

Next was Pat Barrett, followed by Rick Fedyk; both of whom were valuable commodities around town and they too left.

The right guy would come along. I rolled drummer substitutes through the line-up while I concentrated on recording new songs. Casey arranged some studio time with a guy named Craig Waddell. He was an amiable fellow and agreed to record and engineer if I could make payments. So the tour-record-shop demo cycle began again.

Casey had a lawyer named Andrew Atkins from Russell & Dumoulin shop my existing tapes to the local labels and to some in California. He met with some guys and they encouraged him to keep submitting tapes. They were interested – they just didn't hear a hit. I took the news as inspiration to keep writing.

Casey kept the band working six nights a week and was spending most of his time on our calendar, so I tried not to bug him too much about why he couldn't get the record companies to budge. What was wrong with the songs? What was missing? I kept asking for details that could give me direction, but he had little to offer. The guys in the band didn't write and I felt the pressure.

Doubt crept in, so I took a step back and viewed my songs against the current backdrop of the radio marketplace. Maybe I needed to change what I wrote. I chased my tail for the next few months and took it out on my guitar. I banged out every kind of song and tried different voices, lyrics, and melodies. I got some books on song craft and the music biz and tried to improve as a songwriter.

I was starting to feel desperate. I had spent years shopping demos with no bites. What was wrong? Did I need help? I had no co-writer, no sounding board. Maybe I was writing blind. Was it my song structures? Were the hooks not good enough?

Or maybe my sound was just not in-vogue enough for what was going on? I knew my songs sounded different than other original bands around Vancouver.

On my nights off I would watch them play. I paid special attention to the ones who were recording and shopping originals. Many were in the glam rock vein and they were staying there for a while yet.

My songs were more roots-based--maybe that's why the record companies weren't biting. There was already a John Cougar, a Bruce

Springsteen, a Tom Petty, Eddie and The Cruisers, and maybe the labels were looking for the hair-band-quick-sell that '80s hard rock lent itself to so well. Those Bon Jovi guys had carved a place for themselves and their fans stayed with them, even though 7800° Fahrenheit had fallen victim to the sophomore jinx.

In the video Bon Jovi: The Hits, The Legend, Bon Jovi's road manager claimed the failure of the album had been such that they were "in serious danger of being dropped by the record company." I thought about this. Many bands often fell into the one-hit-wonder category, or fallen prey to the sophomore jinx, but at least they had touched the brass ring. I wasn't even close.

Years later, studio engineer and producer Ray Roper enlightened me on what it was like for someone to enjoy great success to then lose that momentum. Ray was part of a monstrously successful pop group during the '70s called Stonebolt, which still tours today. They had a huge hit with their single, "I Will Still Love You," from their self-titled debut album. The resultant popularity had them opening for Burton Cummings and Pablo Cruise and host of other '70s arena rock groups. The band's second album yielded another hit, "Lovestruck," but with the death of Neil Bogart, president of Casablanca Records (the bands mothership label), the single literally disappeared from the charts almost overnight. The band then found themselves searching for another label and signed with RCA Canada but never enjoyed the success of their previous US label, Parachute Records.

One night, Ray and I were sitting around in the studio listening to playbacks of a session we were working on. I motioned to the gold record on his wall and told him how much I envied him for his accomplishments. I believed it was better to at least have had it even for a short period of time than never. Ray's feelings on the matter were quite the opposite, he said sometimes it was worse to have it taken away.

For someone like myself who had never been on the world stage, I believed I would have gladly traded away my obscurity for even a small, fleeting taste of success. Nonetheless, I tried to put myself in his place while he spoke, but I had no real way of knowing. I could only empathize.

Bon Jovi may have been hit with the sophomore jinx, but they'd kept going. Their most recent album, New Jersey, had been like a Slippery When Wet Volume II. The band rocketed around the world and the airwaves, repeating the same fervor that Slippery When Wet had generated. Bon Jovi was one of the most successful acts of '80s, and they just kept getting bigger.

I started paying more attention to the Bon Jovi story. They had become a big part of the Vancouver scene. I would see Jon and some of the guys occasionally around town getting out of a limo and going into a club. I envied their success. They were jet setting around the world, playing huge concerts. They spent weeks in Vancouver recording with heavyweights like Bruce Fairburn and Bob Rock. It was frustrating to have them so physically close and realizing how far away I was from their achievements.

During their Vancouver stays Bon Jovi lived in a condo on West Fourth. Their outrageous parties were legendary. Their lair was fairly well-known in the Vancouver downtown rock 'n' roll circles, and I was often tempted to go there and see if I could talk to Jon or even one of the guys. I decided against it. I wanted to do this on my own.

I continued to have Casey work the group to keep money

coming in, and he talked less and less about recording while pushing me to play as many dates as there were weeks in the year. During that first year in Vancouver, we worked every week, with the majority of dates in Vancouver, interrupted briefly by road stints to Northern BC and Alberta.

Lorri was tired of being on the road. The pressures of constant touring, combined with frustrations of trying to get the band signed had the two of us at odds more and more each day. Thankfully, we both recognized the signs and we agreed we needed time apart. Her parents lived outside of Vancouver and she would stay with them for a while. I weighed the pros and cons of having another female singer in the band. There was a general feeling that our image with a girl backup singer and saxophone player had once served us well, but it had run its course. The guys admitted they felt a bit campy compared to the polished, contemporary look of the other bands in the Vancouver scene.

Later that week I got a call from my sax player. He was leaving the band to take care of personal affairs. I took it as a sign and decided the future was unfolding as it should. The band would go on sans female backup singer or sax player – at least in the live show. The guys were excited and our metamorphosis happened quickly.

The Middle-America flavor was there, but all traces of Motown were gone. In its place we added some hard rock numbers, à la Aerosmith and the like. We replaced the sax-dependent tunes with more keyboard-driven numbers to feature John. The overall look of the band changed and my suit jackets and ties were replaced with leather, chaps, and Harley shirts to add to the overall toughness of the group's image.

Our new hard-edged look was well received and our local

following expanded to a hard rock crowd and a rowdier response. The name of the band seemed less appropriate now with the new sound and look, and the guys suggested we shorten it to The Ted Moore Band. I was proud to have my name on it.

Celebrities, local rockers, strippers, and drug dealers started to come out to our shows more often and we felt we had become a bona fide Vancouver band. I met a lot of wild and crazy people and became a regular player in the local scene. The band was doing well and we had integrated ourselves nicely as part of the in-town barrage of rock 'n' roll groups that you could see on any given night around the Lower Mainland.

It was a crazy time to be a club band in Vancouver. There were never-ending parties and the drugs and booze flowed freely. I started exclusively dating strippers and waitresses. My breakup with Lorri had been difficult, but I began to enjoy being an unattached rock singer living in Vancouver. I moved through a fair number of dancers and waitresses and enjoyed the non-committal mutualism of these relationships. Then there was the cocaine.

At the time, cocaine was something I had little or no experience with. It had always been marijuana and booze at parties and I was surprised how much of the white stuff flowed through the Vancouver bar scene.

It was tough to find anyone who wasn't doing it. Most of the parties I attended were huge snowstorms.

I remember my first experience of sitting in a room full of cokeheads and seeing how different the mood was in comparison to pot parties. There was no inane giggling and voracious pig-outs. People on cocaine talk a lot about everything and nothing. Everyone was really happy, yet serious, and every exchange was oh-so-visceral-and-intense. Even the most mundane conversation was astounding and the bullshit flew at light speed. I sipped my drink and listened in on each conversation, a piece at a time, and started learning the patterns of coke-talk. Most of it revolved around sex and was often times a prelude to sneaking into the washroom for a private counsel. It didn't take me more than a couple of these parties to realize it was Vancouver's drug of choice.

The waitresses, DJs, and bartenders would sneak backstage or into the bathroom to powder their noses and stay lively, while many club managers packed their noses in the back offices. The bands were merely background to the snow parties, and more often than not the musicians were high as well. Strippers came in late after their shows and more dealers would show up. Then there were the never-ending invites to after-parties. It was sex, drugs, and rock 'n' roll in its most decadent form. Money and booze flowed, cocaine was available everywhere, at any time of the day or night. Everyone slept with everyone else and the party raged free and wild throughout the city. The streets were paved with gold and white. Sex, drugs, and rock 'n' roll were here to stay and we were having the time of our lives.

But just south of the border, in a place called Seattle, something was brewing that would spoil the party forever.

1962
Me and my mom in front of our one room house in North Bay.
The house was built from railroad ties in 1914.

Uncle Art – This photo was taken shortly before he died.
He is the reason I become a musician.
I will always be grateful to have known him.

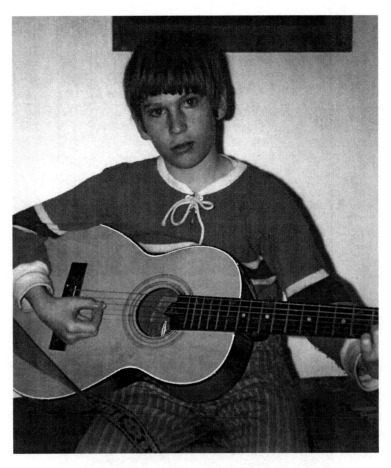

Christmas 1968
My first guitar, and still my favorite Christmas present ever.

1981 Earl Torno
Everything I know about musical gear started with Earl.
He set the bar for every technician I would work with in my career.

1982 Rob Juneau – Taught me the Zen of performing
– and a great many things about life.

1980 – My first record! "Money"/"Calendar Girl"

1981 Maureen "Moe" Brown – Taught me how to run a professional show. I still use many of her ideas when building set lists and working a crowd. One of the most amazing drummers I have ever played with in my life.

1982 – Me in Teen Angel, dressed for the '70's set. By this point, we had several costume changes and each set featured a different musical decade. Nice hotel room – I think this is in Hamilton, Ontario at The Jockey Club.

1984 Cindy Warren – Cindy was an awesome performer. Stylish and dramatic she designed wild outfits for everyone in the band.

1984 – Me onstage with Cindy Warren Band.
The outfits were difficult to get on, but we looked so cool. It often
took me over an hour just to get ready for the show.

1985 – Cindy Warren II – We ditched the glam metal image and
switched to Techno Pop almost overnight.
L to R: Dave Nay, Me, Bruce Leitl, Cindy, Dave Herron.

Halloween 1986 – The Cool Front
L to R: Lorri Vonne, Fast Eddie, Bruce Leitl, Daryl Kuss, Me
(dressed up as Jon Bon Jovi), Ken Smith, Ray Myers.

Early 1987 – "Teddy and the Cruisers" The first official promo shot for Ted Moore And The Border. L to R: Ray Myers, Lorri Vonne, John Bright, Me, Ken Wilgosh, Fast Eddie

1989 – The Ted Moor Band during our heyday in Vancouver
L to R: Fast Eddy, Doug Grant, Me, Tim Rath, John Bright.

1990
The trip home from Colorado riding my Dad's Harley.

1992
The Boneshakers L to R: Fast Eddie, Me, Darry Major

1995 Locomotive Dream – My last original music project.
L to R: Tim Rath, Fast Eddie, Me, John Bright, Doug Grant.

2002 - Me and Lhesa. The medieval wedding was Lhesa's concept from start to finish. We had everyone in attendance wearing period costumes. The ceremony was like an afternoon at Camelot.

susanfosterphoto.com

2013 – Blaze of Glory on stage aboard the Jewel of the Seas
L to R: Doug Grant, Randy Robertson, Kevin Williams, Me, Mike Champigny

Chapter Seventeen

A new music movement flowed over the border and into the Vancouver music scene. Nirvana, Pearl Jam, Soundgarden, and Alice In Chains skyrocketed up the charts. What had started as a neo-punk alternative movement from a group of Seattle bands called the Deep Six had moved into the mainstream. They favored low-tech, stripped down musical sensibilities that flew directly in the face of the bombastic, hair-band rock that dominated the '80s. Guitar sounds were grainy and organic; vocals sparse, stoic, and unaccompanied. Bands were less polished and musicians dressed in plaid shirts, baggy pants and over-sized cargo shorts. The world of glam was about to crumble.

Grunge had arrived.

The term Indie came into existence to describe some of the new independent, unsigned bands that populated the alternative original scene that invaded the Pacific Northwest. Low-budget indie bands were playing four and five at a time in the big clubs. The Top 40 infrastructure couldn't compete. Some indie bands paid to play and club owners jumped on the cheap entertainment. It was the death knell for the bloated, over the top, hard rock scene.

Many club bands dropped out of sight overnight. Venues started dropping our dates. We got in-town gigs maybe once a month, which drastically reduced our income. In response, I decided it was time to put the band on the road in Alberta and Saskatchewan where they still favored hard rock.

Before I committed I needed to revisit the topic with my band about getting straight jobs. It was shot down unanimously. We would tour and do whatever in-town shows we could get in between. There would be no straight jobs. I had made money on the side doing movie extra work, but it was completely flexible and I could choose to do as much or as little as I liked.

We hit the road and when we returned three months later, it was evident the once vibrant mood of the Vancouver music scene had perished under the weight of grunge and indie angst. It was a dark time and most of the bands and people I knew had scattered to the winds. Whenever I came home we partied, but it was mostly pity parties; bitching about how grunge ruined everything. The road trips were brutal and taking a toll on the band. Touring costs were expensive. We were only making enough money to survive and there was little, if anything, left for recording. We were miserable and our spirit deteriorated. I spent most of my time partying and drinking and my outlook became dark. I was bitter and disengaged from any hopeful vision of the future.

It was around this time I met my first wife. I was sitting in a bar commiserating with some fellow musicians over the state of things when I saw a young woman staring at me. I fell in lust. She was slender, with blonde hair, blue eyes, and large breasts. We exchanged glances over the course of the evening and I knew she was interested. I was half in the bag by this point, so I went to talk to her. If she could put together a couple of lucid sentences, she would be perfect. I stumbled over to her and we exchanged some banal chat about the club and the crowd. It was nicely hopeless. The drunker I got, the smarter she got. That was good enough for me.

I hadn't even begun to run out of stupid yet, and so three months later I married her. She was a child of an alcoholic parent and came with all of the accompanying issues. We were perfectly miserable and self-destructive together. We argued most of the time and it soon became obvious to both of us we'd made a big mistake.

In the fall of '89 the band went out on a 13-week tour. When I got home, my wife was six weeks pregnant. I did the math, went to the Law Faculty at the university, and got a divorce for $140. This was the easiest part of my relationship with her. When we split up we divided everything 50/50. She got all of the stuff – I got all the bills.

The divorce sent me into a depression that lasted for most of 1990. I drank and partied most of that year away and most of my memories are blurry. What I do remember is being bitter, angry, and miserable.

My professional relationships were disintegrating too. The Ted Moore Band was in trouble. I was still going through drummer after drummer. Then Brian Louden, our bass player, went back to school.

I saw the familiar writing on the wall that signaled the end of a band.

It wasn't just the grunge invasion: the tours were more brutal each time we went out, and tensions were growing over a number of issues. Substance abuse, career dissatisfaction, jealousy, women, and money can breakup even the strongest band.

Ours was no exception. Things were falling apart, and rebuilding wasn't on my radar. Feelings of defeat, coupled with a lot of drinking and partying took its toll on my spirit and my creativity. By the fall of 1990, gigs were almost non-existent. Even dates on the prairies were becoming scarce.

Our tours were only a couple of weeks out and then we were home again, out of work. There were barely any paying gigs in town; indie bands were playing for free or next to nothing, and I was almost broke.

I took a job as a DJ at Club Soda and watched the grunge movement approach its zenith. Nightclubs closed down and the once vibrant Vancouver rock venues lost their crowds. Rock 'n' roll regulars weren't interested in the stream of garage-band shoe-gazers parading through, stacked five and six each night. I did my best to embrace the new culture. I saw a lot of Seattle bands and regional copycat grunge hopefuls bang out their angst-riddled neo-punk ethos to an often-empty room.

Quite simply – they weren't any fun. The audiences were mostly composed of band girlfriends and skid row punk types, none of whom had much money to drink. Club Soda, along with many of the venues that had caved to the new format, lost money. My job was short-lived.

I got another DJ gig working at RJ Christies. The room was a decent venue with a good-sized stage and became one of the last bastions for Top 40 rock acts. It was fun to see them and the crowds again and for a while, it reminded me how cool things had been.

What I made at RJ Christies wasn't enough to keep an apartment; I put all of my stuff in storage, bought an old Chevy van, and lived in it.

I would park wherever I could and occasionally go to someone's house for a shower and do my laundry. I slid further down than I could have ever imagined.

The loss of my musical livelihood, my lack of creativity, and my divorce had driven me into a deep depression. I responded by staying as incoherent as possible and frequented local soup kitchens for infrequent meals. I lost weight, and whatever rare bits of writing I did was dark and brooding:

"Shame"

I was a victim; you were a victim suffering
Intent on breathing life into a future smothering
We watched the '90s spinning 'round and 'round
It wouldn't stop for me; it couldn't stop for you
I tried to save you from the tower
The dragon swallowed you, devoured the best of you

The songs I was writing, "Shame," "Help Me," and "Suffertown," were a collection of deeply cynical lyrics of hopelessness, despair, and resignation. It was obvious I was in a bad place. I knew it and my band knew it. There was one ray of light during this time. I met a guy who became my favorite drummer in the world.

Ray Roper and his band, The Edge, were playing one night at RJ Christies. I talked to the band's drummer after the show and told him about my constant drummer woes. He was an extraordinary drummer and one of the nicest people I had ever met. His name was Doug Grant and he'd been playing the Vancouver scene since the late '70s. I had a promo tab that allowed me to drink any concoction in the bar for one dollar and I decided to use it to get Doug drunk and talk him into joining my band. Between the two of us we drank about 50 bucks worth of promo drinks. Although most of that night was quite blurry, I was successful in selling myself to Doug, and he agreed to join me somewhere in the middle of it all. He must have seen something in me. I am still not sure of what that whole conversation must have been like from his perspective, but it worked and several years (and drinks) later, he's still my drummer.

With Doug on drums, all we needed was a bass player. As local bands came through RJ Christies, I kept an eye out for any guy that might be a good fit. Neverland had a female singer named Shelly who could belt out rock and blues like a hurricane. The band's bass player, Tim Rath was a technical player and had a cool rock image. He was in great shape and spent most of the night shirtless. I called Doug down to take a listen and he agreed he might be the guy we were looking for. With Doug's help I cornered the shirtless bass player and we convinced him to join up.

It was ironic that I was able to forge these new relationships when my other relationships were falling apart. I knew Eddie and John were worried about my excessive partying and often commented that the lyrics I was churning out were alarming. Over the years, my relationship with Eddie had grown strained. For the first five years, he and I were on the same wavelength when it came to the musical direction of the group. He was very much a blues-rock traditionalist with a huge passion for roots rock. As I moved further into more esoteric areas with my lyrics and musical thinking, he was less than enamored. My lyrics were darker, but they were more sophisticated too. I wrote whatever came to me and explored as much as I could. Eddie wanted nothing to do with most modern music and felt much of what the radio played was crap. I was frustrated by the grunge invasion, but still believed it had merit. I thought if we added sprinklings of these new elements into our own music it would work. Eddie and I would go around in circles and these discussions sometimes became heated. At some point, he stopped listening and I stopped talking.

By now, we argued constantly at rehearsals and even when we had a gig. One night at Club Kaos, Eddie and I got into an argument backstage between sets. It was about music and then turned to old issues that were never resolved. It escalated into a shoving match and the guys had to split us apart. Everyone was freaked out, and no one spoke to anyone for the rest of the night. I could see what was happening and I knew I had to change something and fast. My deteriorating relationship with Eddie was affecting the band's morale and I could see the guys were afraid the whole project would blow up at any minute. I convinced myself it was because we were all under financial strain. We got a few recurring gigs in Vancouver and on Vancouver Island and things brightened somewhat.

I found more work as a movie and TV extra. I got bit parts in The Trial Of The Incredible Hulk, Bird On A Wire, and in Pabst Beer and Canada Coolers commercials. It was enough to get a roof over my head, and I rented a small, cheap house in a nasty section of town.

I hired a new manager and gave him my demos. He peddled them around town for a few months and came up with a bite from a local company called Nettwerk Records. When he called, I was ecstatic. Before I could ask for any details, he cut me off, saying he had turned the offer down. I tried to keep my cool but he insisted, stating his high-powered business associates and his lawyer told him it was a bad move to sign with such a small label. I told him I wanted to take the deal and that I had been burned before. He grew impatient and said he wouldn't do it.

"They're too small time," he snapped. "And the only thing they have on their roster is some folksy nobody named Sarah McLachlan. You'll thank me later, Ted."

In my desperate state I wanted to take whatever I could get, but I didn't want to lose my new manager and his connections. So I told him to do what he thought was best for me. Six months later, with no offers on the horizon, we parted ways.

My communication with the band and everyone else became non-existent. In the summer of '91 I was wasted most of the time. Gigs were scarce again and my money problems returned. The movie work stopped coming and any jobs I found in the classifieds were snapped up by people far more qualified and experienced than I was. I finally went to Social Services to get rent money and I returned to the soup kitchens to eat. I was angry and embittered and I rarely went anywhere unless it was to find food or collect my welfare check.

From my crappy little house, I saw hookers, junkies, and police go by in a steady stream. When I felt social, I would invite the neighborhood druggies and hookers in to party until dawn. They made drug deals and stored stolen merchandise there. I didn't care.

At times my house was full of people lying about passed out or puking, and I didn't know any of them. Friends would call my phone over and over trying to reach me and eventually come by and pound on the door. I'd be hiding in the basement, completely annihilated. I heard the band guys, peelers, and druggies all screaming at me to come to the door. I just played dead, sometimes for days on end.

One day I realized I hadn't left the house in over two weeks. I was curled up in a ball on my basement floor bemoaning all that was my misery. I didn't want to see anyone, I didn't want to go anywhere. I was done with everything and everybody. I just wished the world would go away and leave me alone. I wanted out.

I was only looking backward now, instead of forward. I thought of all of the bands I had played with, hoping how each one would make my dreams of stardom become reality. I pictured all of the musicians I had played with, the girls I had known, the clubs I played, a family I had missed for most of my adult life, the father I hadn't seen in 30 years.

Each person and place became little vignettes in my mind, playing over and over, swirling and intertwining against a distorted backdrop of the roads I had travelled.

They were roads paved with disappointment and failure. I had to put an end to this stupid, meaningless existence. I thought about that horse on the summit. It had been quick and painless – the horse hadn't felt a thing. I thought of Mom and my brothers. I thought of who would find me. It would be two weeks until the landlord came for rent. I thought about the funeral. I could picture my mom looking down at me, her hand stroking mine, tears streaming down her face.

"I'm sorry, Mom" my voice croaked, hoarse and weary against the cracked cement walls of the darkened basement. I knew it was time to go. I had done all that I could. The game had been played and lost. I was circling the drain and I just wanted to pull the plug. For a second, I tried to think of something better. I couldn't imagine how things could be any worse.

And then the phone rang.

Chapter Eighteen

Sometimes when a phone rings, you just know you have to answer it. So I did. I shook myself out of my delusional state and crawled up the stairs.

"Hello?" My voice was weak and cracked. I wiped the tears from my eyes and tried to focus on the voice on the other end.

"Hi Teddy – it's Mom." Her voice was gentle and I got the sense something bad was coming. "Mom?" I cleared my voice and tried to sound as straight as I could. "What's up?" I asked.

"Oh, Teddy," she paused for a second. "Your father died."

I was confused. Was it Floyd or my biological father? She had said father, not dad. "You mean Ted?" I asked.

"Yes," she said. "He died of a heart attack this morning and someone has to go down to Boulder, to take care of things with the funeral home."

"Oh God," was all I could muster.

"I can't go," she said, before I had a chance to say any more. Her voice was stressed. "There is no one on his side of the family that can make the trip." Her voice softened again, "Teddy… you're going to have to go down there and take care of things."

I waited for a second to let the whole thing sink in.

Jesus.

I'd have to take care of things? What did that mean? What could I do to help someone else? I couldn't even help myself.

"What do you need me to do Mom?" I asked.

"You need to go and make arrangements for the body and the funeral Teddy," she paused. "And to settle his affairs. There may be a Will, but, as far as I remember, he always wanted to be cremated.

"You will have to take care of this, Teddy," she was quiet, but firm. "He's your father."

The reality of what had happened suddenly hit me. My father was dead. I would never see him again. My granny had kept in touch with Ted and would tell me things about him whenever I saw her. I had known for years that he had settled in Colorado and he was playing music. I flashed on all of the times I had imagined going down to Boulder for my surprise reunion with my dad. I'd walk into a little bar where he was doing a weekend jam or something and I get up on stage to sing with the band. After the song, I'd reveal my identity to him. It would be a wonderful surprise and we would rejoice in the reunion.

That was never going to happen now. I had let the opportunity pass me by. I had planned it for years, but I figured I had all the time in the world.

"Okay, Mom." I spoke up and tried to sound confident, or at the very least, alert. "I'll take care of things." She gave me the information and told me I could get a deal from the airline for an aggrieved traveler. Her practical nature was always comforting to me and I could tell she was trying to keep me calm. I told her I loved her and said I would call when I got back.

My plans to escape my shitty little life had to wait. I had to tidy up the end of my father's first. Besides, I could check out anytime. If things got too out of hand at any point down the road, it was one sure-fire way I knew to leave all my worries behind forever.

I put it aside and formulated how to take care of my dead father. I looked on my kitchen calendar and took note of the date: November 1st – my dad died on November 1st.

"November first!" I hollered. "Shit! I've got a gig tonight!"

I had completely forgotten I had booked a one-nighter a month before. It was an opening slot behind some recording band, I couldn't remember who, and the gig was one of our now rare performances. I had to get ready and leave soon.

I tried to put thoughts of my dad aside as I stumbled into the shower. I made the water as hot as I could stand it and struggled to clear my head. The details of how the next week would play out were still an unknown. I had the gig tonight and I could borrow some money for a plane ticket and leave the next day for Boulder. That's all I knew.

I got out of the shower and the phone was ringing again. It was Doug reminding me about the gig. He seemed happy that I was reasonably together and getting ready for the show. I decided not to tell anyone about Ted and to try and make this rare show a decent night for everyone. As soon as I hung up, it rang again. It was Floyd. He said Mom had called him and told him about Ted.

"I'm so sorry for your loss," he said. "I just wanted you to know that I've always felt like I was your Dad. I know this man, your birth dad, was a stranger to you, but still this must be a tough thing to go through."

I listened to him talk. He was compassionate and offered to give me some money to help cover the costs of going there and straightening things out. I was amazed. My stepdad was helping me settle the estate of my birth dad. I was overwhelmed by the gesture. I wanted to be able to tell him I was okay, I was self-sufficient, and I could do this on my own. But I couldn't, so I graciously accepted his offer.

That night I got as drunk as possible and then flew to Denver the next morning, hung over and drained. By the time I landed I was anxious, tired, and scared of how this whole trip was going to unfold. A man greeted me the moment I walked off the plane and called out to me.

"Jesus, you look like your dad." He looked in his early '50s, streaks of grey running through his hair and handlebar moustache. He was like a modern day cowboy in his Stetson, faded denim jacket and blue jeans. He shook my hand with a firm grip.

"I'm Jack," he said and mustered a faint smile. "I'm real sorry about your dad, Teddy – he was my best friend." His face was worn, yet strong and the sadness in his eyes seemed out of place.

"Thank you," I said. "It's good to meet you, Jack." I gave him a smile and we walked toward the luggage carousel. Jack told me where I would be staying for the few days it would take to get Dad's affairs in order. The whole thing was like a strange dream as I drifted through the airport hallways. He chatted nervously about the local weather and other minor events. Jack was careful to avoid any details of my dad's death and I figured he was saving the nitty-gritty until later.

I appreciated that.

Jack Ray was a genuine and personable guy. He told me he and Ted had been friends for years. They'd played in a band together for most of that time. Jack's wife, Kathy, sang with them as well. They did local shows around the area on the weekends. We jumped in Jack's old pickup and drove northwest for a little over an hour as I took in the awesome sights of northern Colorado. The terrain was rugged and the mountains more jagged and wild than in Vancouver.

Jack had a place in Jamestown, northwest of Boulder, on the edge of Rocky Mountain National Park. It was a spacious hobby ranch on a hillside and his back yard spilled out onto the rocky parkland. It was a beautiful and serene place and it was easy for me to see why Ted had settled here. I imagined living there, raising a family, and spending the rest of my days a happy man. Jack pointed out Ted's pickup in the driveway and then to the Harley parked on the deck.

"That's your dad's bike," he said as we came to a stop at the top of the driveway. "Over there in the drive shed he's got some tools and there's more at the shop downtown where he worked."

Dad had a '66 Cadillac he was fixing up over at a yard across town. Jack said he would take me there in the morning. Tonight we would sit around with some of Ted's old friends.

"Everybody's pretty excited to meet you," Jack told me. "Jesus, you really do look like your old man," he said again, grinning. "You're really going to freak them out."

We looked at each other for a second and then laughed. It was the first time I'd laughed in a long while. Jack took me into the house and introduced me to Kathy. She was a few years younger than Jack and had a pretty face with big blue eyes that betrayed she'd been crying.

"Nice to meet you, Ted," she said as she shook my hand. She stared at me with her eyes wide. "Geez, you look like your dad." A faint smile crossed her face. Jack laughed and grabbed my luggage.

"Damndest thing... isn't it? C'mon, follow me Teddy and I'll show you to your room." He led me upstairs to a bedroom with a large bay window revealing a panoramic view of the mountainside.

"Ted stayed in here sometimes," Jack spoke as I looked out the window.

"But he'd been staying with a girl in town for a while now and spent most of his nights there." I turned toward him, his expression darkened.

"He came over yesterday morning and said he wasn't feeling well." His voice became quieter still. "We took him to the hospital and his heart just stopped beating. Doc cracked his chest open and massaged it by hand. It was the damndest thing…"

He looked away, staring out the window. "It just stopped beating…" His voice was wavering.

I thanked him for sharing what had happened.

I settled in to the place and had something to eat while Jack and Kathy told me about the man I never really knew. Ted had some small success as a bassist and acoustic guitar player in the local pub scene and had a contract to fix the fire engines and police cars for the City of Boulder.

"He was a real renaissance man, your Dad," Jack said. "Everyone really liked him around here. You should be really proud." I told him I was really looking forward to meeting some of his friends that night.

The whole trip had been a bit overwhelming. I was also still a bit hung over from the show and I appreciated when Kathy came in to suggest I might want to catch a nap before supper.

I slept for a few hours and woke to the sounds of laughter and music coming from the living room. I walked in to see a dozen or so people gathered about the room talking, laughing and singing old country songs. I walked in and everyone stopped immediately. For a second, they just stared.

"Jesus, you look like your Dad!" some guy called out. Two or three others chimed in and we all had a good laugh. I began to meet and shake hands with the men and women who were all of the most important people in Ted's life. They welcomed me like a lost son

188

and told me stories about my father. It was a wonderful evening. We all talked, sang, laughed, and cried until the late in the evening.

The next morning I went to the crematorium. They had put Ted in a temporary casket and brought him into a room so I could spend a few moments with the father I barely knew. I sat down next to his body and stared into the face of the man who helped to give me my life. A life I had resolved to throw away less than 48 hours ago.

His face was my face, but twenty years older. I gently ran my finger down the bridge of his nose. It was cold, but the contours felt like my own. I had never liked my nose; it had always been one of the things I'd have liked to change about my face. In that moment, I was proud to have it.

I hadn't seen him in over 30 years and my memories were vague at best. But he was my father. I would take care of him and put in order all that he left behind. There had been no Will, and I would have to decide how to handle all of Ted's final affairs. I could do that later.

There was so much I wished I'd told him when he was alive. I wanted to share my adventures with him, the places I'd been, the people I'd met, and the musician I'd become. I wanted him to be proud of me. I thought of the last couple of years of my life. I was glad he hadn't seen that. I felt tears roll down my cheeks. The realization of what was happening overwhelmed me. We would never meet again. I waited too long – he waited too long. I felt it was just another in a series of failures in my life. I had let this happen. I had let us slip away.

"I'm so sorry, Dad," I spoke aloud. "I tried, I really, really tried." I fell across his cold body and sobbed against his chest. I did my best to choke back the tears and speak as though he could hear me.

"I'm so sorry I didn't come to see you, Dad. I love your home here. Jack and Kate and all of your friends are so amazing." I wiped my eyes. "Everyone here loved you so much. You did real good, Dad. Everyone will miss you so much."

I told him about meeting Roy Orbison and Lionel Richie. I told him about the ferry getting stuck in Newfoundland. I told him about life on the road, the musicians, and all the pretty girls. I told him about the good things I remembered about my life. I smiled and even laughed a little when I told him the story about Muddy Waters and Rob's epic fart in the elevator. "Ask Muddy waters about it when you see him, Dad!" I laughed at the thought of the two of them discussing it in heaven. I could picture Muddy Waters describing it to my dad in that deep voice. "Man, it was legendary!"

I wondered how much my Granny had told Ted about me. Mom told me he should have come to see me and she was angry that he hadn't. I'd never held it against him, and I didn't now. We just hadn't found a way or the time to make it happen. Maybe neither of us was to blame, and yet, we both were. It didn't matter now. I touched his nose once more and kissed his cheek.

I arranged to have him cremated and went back to Jack's house. All of Ted's friends came by again to say their goodbyes. I promised I would return soon to collect my dad's belongings and we would get together. Jack said he would keep all of Ted's things secure until my return and that no one would disturb them.

The only items Jack asked to keep for himself were my father's guns. Kathy had told me how the two men enjoyed shooting out in the back hills and how Jack had always loved Ted's antique black powder pistols. I gave them to him. The next morning I collected my dad's ashes and flew back to Vancouver.

On the flight home all I could think of was the missed opportunities to reconnect with my father. In some way, I guess we had. Still, I wished I could have seen him alive, just one more time. I still do.

When I got back to Vancouver, any thoughts I had about ending it all had vanished. I ran through the words I said to my father at the mortuary and repeated them to myself. I thought about how his friends would miss him so much, and how that was the best advice I could have received. Who was I to end the life my parents gave me? What right did I have to put those who cared for me through the nightmare? No way, I could never, would never do it. I wasn't going anywhere until it was the right time.

It felt as though a huge weight had been lifted from me. I was renewed, invigorated, and looked towards the future with hope and optimism. I went home planning the changes I would make. It felt like a brand new beginning. Death sometimes does that for you.

Chapter Nineteen

The first thing I had to do was put some distance between me and the house in East Van. I called the landlord and told him I was moving out. I packed a suitcase full of clothes, my guitars, Ted's ashes, and caught a flight to Toronto.

I spent Christmas of 1991 with Mom and my brothers in Kitchener. I drove around to places that were landmarks in my life. I visited Les Starkey, Norma Jeanne, and the guys from Teen Angel. I went past the armories, walked up and down King Street, and within a few days, my head had cleared from the dark times that had brought me so close to the edge.

I made the drive to North Bay to deliver Ted's ashes to his sister, my Aunt Celina. She arranged for some cousins and other family to meet me. It was a nice, if not surreal, reunion. I had never met many of these people and the rest I barely remembered. They welcomed me like lost family and we spent two days remembering Ted through photos and stories. Aunt Celina arranged to bury Ted's ashes beside his father, and I felt a sense of closure in bringing him on this long trip home.

I began to think how Ted's death had saved my life. The long journey to bring him home would never square the debt. I had been given a second chance for a good life. I told Mom I was staying in Kitchener. To my surprise, she wouldn't hear of it.

"Teddy, you know I would love to have you here and see you all of the time," she said. "But you don't belong here anymore."

I was shocked. There was no sadness in her eyes or trace of regret for what she had said.

"But, I could find a job, Mom" I told her. "I went to see friends last night and it was really nice. I could see myself staying here." She rolled her eyes and sighed.

"For how long, Teddy?" There was a tone of impatience in her voice. "How long would it be until your mind starts to wander?"

I started to argue, but she continued. "And what if you did settled down in Kitchener, got a job, maybe even started a family – then what?"

I pictured it in my mind. A family, a decent job, and close to all of my childhood friends. It felt like the right thing to do, but here was my mother telling me it wasn't. I was confused. What mother wouldn't want her child to have a nice, normal life, fall in love and live close to her?

"Don't you want me to be happy, Mom?" I asked.

"Oh, you can stop that right now!" She rolled her eyes and looked right through me. "Teddy," her voice softer now, "you've been running away since you were three. You've been running towards some dream, some adventure, and that adventure sure as hell isn't in Kitchener working at some 9-5 job."

I didn't know how to respond. I sat down beside her.

"And what happens to that family you've built when your wandering spirit takes hold of you again? What happens to them Teddy?"

She didn't wait for me to answer and continued. "I went down that road. I tried the home and hearth, coffee with a neighbor in the morning, making beds and dinner and I didn't find what I was looking for."

It was unsettling to have her talk like this. She'd always been my mom and now she was speaking to me like a friend, telling me things she knew I'd have trouble hearing. I thought of how she and

I had been alone for all of those years and how her independence had been our savior. I supposed it would have been much easier for her to find a husband and settle down to make a nice, stable home for us. And yet, she forged ahead, with me in tow, working hard to better herself with little help from anyone.

"There's a lot of things I regret from those days, Teddy, but I never regret pursuing my dreams." Her voice was firm and I could see how resolute she was.

Since I was a little kid, I had watched her leave to go to work and I never once felt that she had abandoned me in any way. I knew she was doing everything in her power to better her situation so she could, in turn, better mine. Even at that age, I had understood. I was proud of her. I knew she hadn't been completely comfortable in her relationship with Floyd and with her role as a stay-at-home Mom and homemaker. She was always working on some project, setting goals for herself. But, she had been a great mom to Christian and Patrick, and as far as I knew, a loving wife to my stepdad. She also had a quest for adventure and I guess she had always kept domesticity at arm's length, knowing that someday she could very well find herself alone again. And she was not the kind of person to be caught off guard or unprepared.

I began to understand why she didn't want to me to settle back in Kitchener. It was hiding. I had been through a lot in my life, especially the past couple years, and I had come home to lick my wounds.

" I get really lonely sometimes, Mom," I turned to her and extended my hand. "Don't you ever get lonely?" She squeezed my hand and forced a faint smile.

"Teddy, we are all alone. It is part of the truth of our existence."

Her eyes were full, but not a single teardrop fell from them. I nodded. "But I will always be here for you," she said wiping her eyes. "And if you ever need me I am just a phone call away." I hugged her and she held me tight.

"Don't hide here," she whispered. "And don't give up." She pulled away and looked straight into my eyes. "Never give up." Her voice was firm, all traces of tears gone. "Finish what you started," she said. "Pursue your dreams with all you have. And if things don't work out exactly the way you planned, at least you will never have to live with the regret that you didn't try."

We spent the rest of that night watching TV and talking. It was good to be with Mom and spend time with Christian and Patrick. I had seen my friends, I had visited old neighborhoods and my birthplace, and I had brought my dad home. In the morning, I would catch a flight back to Vancouver. It was time to get back to work.

* * *

I flew back to Vancouver on New Year's Day, 1992. I had no idea where I was going to live or how I would get things started again. Throughout the four-hour flight, I wracked my brain trying to figure out my next move. I was in my early thirties and had thus far failed to make my big break in music. There was so much to figure out, but first, I needed a place to live.

I spent the first couple of weeks living in my van until I got a check from welfare. I took the money and found an apartment in Maple Ridge, a bedroom community about 30 minutes from Vancouver. I told myself that putting distance between me and downtown was important. I cut ties with my party friends and withdrew from the scene completely. For the first month, I only went out to get food. The apartment was in a ghetto section of Maple Ridge. I kept my curtains closed and slept 12 to 14 hours most days.

I began to notice the comings and goings of my neighbors at all hours of the day and night. It turns out I had moved right into the middle of Maple Ridge's biggest drug trafficking zone. I could hear deals going down, fights, and screaming at all hours. I remember sitting in my apartment one day shaking my head and laughing; of all the places I could have moved to straighten myself out...

One evening, I heard a drug deal going down in the hallway. I recognized one of the voices. I peeked through the peephole and saw a stripper I had been seeing when I lived in East Vancouver. Her name was Keisha. The last time I saw her was the day her parents tracked her down to my little east end house and pounded on my door. I will never forget the horrified looks on their faces as I led them through piles of garbage and passed-out bodies to the back bedroom where their daughter was recovering from a three-day bender. They looked at me like I was Beelzebub himself. I thought that would be the last I saw of her, and that she'd been sent to some recovery center where she would get better and go on to live a straight life. Nope. Here she was scoring some blow right outside my door.

Without thinking, I opened the door and greeted her. We chatted and she told me how she had gone to rehab and stayed straight for a couple of months. She said she was only doing a little bit now and then and how she could handle it better now. I told her I was clean and how getting away from the city had been so good

for me. She came in to talk and within a week had moved in. By the
end of the month we were both out of control, and worse than ever.
We tried to get it together. We moved to a better section of Maple
Ridge, but our problems followed us. I knew there was no way that
I was going to get out of this mess as long as I stayed with her.

I needed to get away and now was a good time to go to Colorado
to get my dad's stuff. It would be a huge undertaking and I knew
I would need some help and some money to pull it off. Fast Eddie
agreed to go on the trip and suggested we bring along his friend
Darrell to help. Darrell agreed to advance me the money for the trip
with his credit card and we could drive down there in his van. To
pay him back, I would join Eddie's three-piece pub band called The
Boneshakers. Eddie would deduct regular payments from my wages
and pay Darrell back.

In the summer of 1992, we set out for Colorado in Darrell's
van on a pilgrimage to recover my dead father's belongings. The trip
had an ominous purpose, yet we managed to make it an adventure.
It was great seeing Jack and Kathy again. We had a great couple
of days of visiting while we got the Cadillac and Harley ready for
travel. I prepared US Customs paperwork and tied up the rest of my
dad's loose ends.

On the trip back, I rode the Harley, Eddie drove the Cadillac,
and Darrell had my dad's tools and personal effects in his van. It
was a thousand mile journey home. The July sun scorched us, but
the first day's ride through Colorado and Wyoming was awesome. It
was breath-taking to see the county from the seat of my new bike. I
had ridden motorcycles all my life, but holding onto the handlebars
at 70 miles per hour for 12 hours a day tested my limits. At night,
the rain felt like needles piercing my face as I blasted through the

darkness following the taillights of the Cadillac. Darrell and Eddie were keeping a breakneck pace and I kept my mind busy to remain alert.

The reality of why we had all gone to Colorado hit hard as we travelled back home. The three of us hadn't spoken much during the fuel stops and at meal times and the exchanges were mostly about obligations that were waiting at home. Darrell needed to get back to manage his business and I think Eddie just wanted to put the whole thing behind him. The trip had bothered him and his usual stalwart nature was showing signs of stress and melancholy.

Eddie's dad had died a few years earlier and this trip had stirred some memories. He and his dad hadn't seen each other in quite a while and Eddie had gotten the news of his death right before a show, just as I had.

The similarities in our two situations hadn't escaped our notice. He commented on it during a food stop in Cheyenne. Ever since I had known Fast Eddie he hadn't talked about feelings. He gave the impression he was a rock, and I think he liked having that role. I was always the one to find emotional context in a situation; he would act as balance. Over the past year our arguments had brought deeper feelings out and they had caught me by surprise.

It was a big deal for me when Eddie agreed to go on the trip. In the past year, we'd fought a lot and I pulled away from him. We hadn't really spoke in the few months prior and I think both of us recognized this trip as an opportunity to put some bad blood behind us. Having him here with me now meant the world to me. I counted on him so much over the years, and he had always been a strong ally to have on our grueling adventures on the road.

But, Eddie's mood grew darker as we made our way home.

Darrell and I kept up the chatter when we stopped to eat, while Eddie would sit quietly staring out the window. It was a strange role-reversal to be keeping things upbeat while he was feeling down. I thought about all the times he had done it for me and my heart went out to him. I figured that once we got home and everybody had some decent sleep, Eddie would be his old self again. We just needed to put the last 400 miles behind us.

We began day three of our journey after a four-hour sleep at a cheap motel. It wasn't near enough, but I jumped back on my bike and hit the highway behind Darrell and Eddie. It was hot and I tried to enjoy the ride, but by early afternoon, I felt serious signs of road fatigue.

I was dizzy, swerved in my lane, and felt my hands loosen on the grips. I told myself it would pass and I could make it the last 200 miles, but it got worse. When we hit the Washington border I had to stop the caravan. Stopping for sleep was not an option as Darrell was due back the next morning for an important meeting. We hashed things out, and we decided I would drive the Cadillac and Eddie would ride the Harley. Eddie had ridden dirt bikes when he was younger and figured he would be okay. My mind raced back to all of the bad experiences I had when others had driven my vehicles, but I had no choice. It was too dangerous to hold onto the grips anymore and driving the car was the best option. The bike was vintage and had a right foot shifter, but after a few miles Eddie had the hang of it. I felt better in the car and kept myself awake with the radio blasting.

About an hour later, I lost sight of Eddie in my rear view mirror. I flashed my lights for Darrell to pull over. We turned around to see what had happened. A couple of miles back, halfway up a long hill, Eddie was on the side of the road waving his arms. Smoke was seeping from the bike and my heart sank. The engine was blown. The bike was now 600 pounds of dead weight.

I couldn't be angry with Eddie. He had ridden the bike for my benefit, come on this trip for my benefit, and he brought Darrell along for my benefit. In reality, I couldn't have done it without him. There was no use for blame. It happened and now we had to get home.

Darrell went into Yakima and came back towing a small trailer. We loaded up the dead bike, Eddie jumped in the Caddy with me, and we drove the last few hours home. On the way, Eddy spoke very little. I tried to let him know I wasn't angry. The bike breaking down was simply due to the long trip. He stared out the window without saying a word. When Eddie finally broke his silence, he spoke in a voice I had never heard in all the years I had known him.

"My spirit is broken." His voice cracked and his eyes were full.

I didn't know how to respond. I just sat there. It was unnerving to see him this way. He had no more to say and I figured it best to just let him deal with it. We drove the last hour in silence and I dropped him off at home. Neither of us said a word.

The trip had taken the wind out of us, but there were still a couple details remaining. Darrell referred me to a guy in Maple Ridge where I could store Ted's tools and his Cadillac. The guy also had a shop where I could work on the bike. He looked a bit shady but Darrell vouched for him and that was good enough for me. We dropped everything off and I walked home.

I needed to get some sleep and thankfully, the house was empty. Keisha left me a note saying she had gone to work. She was dancing at some club in Vancouver and wouldn't be back until early in the morning. There were signs she'd been getting high a lot over the past week. The place was a mess. I looked around for a minute. I had to get out of there.

I packed my clothes into a couple of garbage bags and made a run for it. I went back to Darrell's buddy's storage place and slept on the shop floor beside my bike. It was damp and dirty, but I didn't care. I was alive, I had a place to sleep, and I had escaped a bad relationship. Things were looking up.

Chapter Twenty

I stayed in the shop, going out during the day only to look for food. At the end of the month, Keisha had stopped looking for me and moved out of the house. The landlord locked it up and seized whatever items I had left behind. I didn't care. I didn't want to go back anyway, and whatever possessions I cared about were with me. I picked up some casual work at a local mill and registered with the welfare and temporary labor offices in Maple Ridge.

Finally, I had enough money to move - this time to a cheap warehouse stall in an industrial section of Maple Ridge. There was room for the Cadillac, the Harley, and my dad's tools. There was an office upstairs I could use to sleep in. It was actually a pretty cool setup. I got a phone hooked up and called Fast Eddie. The Boneshakers had gigs coming up and I told him I was ready to go. It was good to hear his voice again; he sounded better. Playing gigs together would be just what we needed.

The Boneshakers worked every weekend. During the week, I worked on the Cadillac and planned how to get the Harley back on the road. The bike needed parts and I just didn't have enough money. Most of my Boneshakers pay was going to Darrell for the trip, and what was left bought me food and rent. I was just getting by.

Time was slipping past and I didn't know how to rekindle my music career. I hadn't written a song in almost a year and the guys from my band had joined other projects. Maybe my rock 'n' roll days had ended. It was a frightening prospect and I decided, just for now, that I would concentrate on getting mobile.

I traded some parts from the Harley for a rough-running

Triumph, with the understanding I could buy the parts back. I took the Triumph to a bike shop in Hammond where I met a guy named Randy and he introduced me to some new friends. They were all heavy partiers and I soon found myself joining in. At first, it was just the odd occasion, and before I knew it, I was drinking all the time again. The weekend gigs with the Boneshakers also had become complete booze fests and I was rarely straight anymore.

1992 went flying by. By the spring of '93, I was frustrated with everything. I wasn't writing, my original band was gone, things were messed up, and my career looked dead in the water. The only time I was 'happy' was when I was drinking, so I stayed drunk. I was, in fact, miserable to be around. The torch that Ted had lit for me seemed so dim against the darkness of my moods. I was pissed about everything. Playing classic rock to drunks in the barrooms didn't inspire me. It was just a means to pay the bills and an easy excuse to get wasted. Eddie and I shared our frustrations and talked about how we needed to get something tangible going again. Most of it was drunken rambling and we'd usually get into an argument. I felt more and more hopeless about my situation and started to care less and less. I wasn't suicidal; I was indifferent and irreverent. I partied harder and slept with more women. I don't remember much about that time of my life. Sometimes I'll run into someone and they'll tell me about some god-awful shit storm I'd been involved in back then. I have to take their word for it.

I had to change something. Music wasn't working out. I knew my situation wasn't unique. There were lots of other people in the world that spent their lives training for a career that didn't pan out. Others spent years doing one thing and then changed careers overnight. But how could I pick something else when I had only ever wanted one thing?

I reached back into my past – back into my earliest memories to try and discover if I was ever passionate about anything else other than music. Maybe I could pursue acting full-time; even at my age, I imagined, it was possible. I could take lessons, get speaking parts, and forge a career as a middle-aged character actor. But what if I spent years trying, and found myself right back here again? Did I want to take that risk? No way. To hell with the entertainment business! I resented my failed journey, anyway. For the first time in my life, I actually considered I might never be a star. I had no idea what I was going to do.

One day at the bike shop, I found Randy kneeling over some guy who appeared to have passed out on the floor. "Call an ambulance!" Randy yelled. His face was streaked with tears and he was desperately blowing into the guy's mouth trying to resuscitate him. I ran into the office and called 911. When I got back Randy was on top of the guy and performing CPR. But his efforts were in vain. I watched as the shadow of death crept over the guy's face and his pallor changed right before my eyes. He was gone. The paramedics arrived a short time later, but there was nothing left for them to do. They confirmed he was dead and called the police. I gave my statement and went home. I called Randy a few days later and he told me it had been a heroin overdose. I wish I could have done something. It was a terrible feeling of helplessness, not being able to save someone, and it was something I never wanted to experience again.

I went down to the Red Cross and took a First Aid course. While I was there I got into a conversation with another student. She was going into teaching and taking this course as a requirement for an Early Childhood Education (ECE) degree. She had thought about becoming a teacher for as long as she could remember. She had seen an Arnold Schwarzenegger movie called Kindergarten Cop and it had cemented the idea in her head. It intrigued me that she was so excited about teaching. I had thought about being a teacher when I was little; but I figured every kid went through that stage. The more she talked about it, the more I began to like the idea of being a teacher. I decided to investigate the possibility and see what kind of education I needed. I went to the local college and got some literature and course catalogues, and I rented Kindergarten Cop. When I was returning the video to the store I recognized a man standing near the checkout counter. It was Attila Ambrus, the agent who worked for Studio City in Edmonton, and booked dates for the Cool Front. He recognized me, and we started chatting about the old days and reminiscing about the way things were before grunge had "wiped out the '80s."

Attila asked me what I had been up to. I kept things light and upbeat, and told him I'd been writing, played on weekends, and was still searching for that ever-elusive record deal. He said he'd made some good contacts in Europe and he would take my demos with him on his next trip. We talked for over an hour. Attila was hoping to sign artists and build Attila The Hun Artist Management Company. I figured I didn't have anything to lose by getting the guy to shop my stuff and told him I would come down to his office with a tape.

The following day I drove to the address he gave me. He worked out of his house and had made a somewhat professional-looking office in his living room. My tape included "Suffertown," "Shame," and "Help Me," along with some older Ted Moore and The Border songs. He listened to half of "Suffertown" and turned the tape off. "This sounds fantastic," he told me. "If the other material is as good, I think we have a pretty good chance of getting you some interest."

I was thrilled. I told him there was other stuff on there that was just as good, maybe even better. He asked about the band and I lied a little bit, saying yes, we were still together.

He was pleased and said he would get me signed. He would shop the tape to his contacts when he travelled to Europe in a couple months. He asked me to sign a short agreement stating he would have right of refusal to manage the band if he got us a deal, and I told him it was no problem. I figured if nothing happened with the tapes I would be no worse off than I was, and if something did happen, I wouldn't mind working with him. It seemed like a good idea, so I signed.

I tried not to think about it too much and went back to my research about becoming a teacher. Fast Eddie was furious when he found out I was considering another career path. We argued for hours. He thought the idea of me going back to school was a "complete and utter waste of time" and that I should concentrate my efforts on getting the band back together. I told him about Attila and that he was shopping the songs. That lightened the mood a bit and I remained careful not to talk about school anymore.

I called up the guys to ask for a rehearsal so Attila could see how strong the band was live. Eddie had Fast Eddie's Guitar Hospital, Tim had taken a job in shipping and receiving at a large warehouse, John was the superintendent of an apartment building, and Doug was playing drums for Canadian pop legends Doug and the Slugs. Everybody made time to get back together and play.

The first rehearsal was absolute magic. The guys had the

material well prepared and we rocked through the songs as if we'd never been apart. We talked and laughed like old friends, and left that night feeling excited about getting a deal in Europe. I arranged for a meeting at a coffee shop so the guys could talk with Attila. They were all comfortable with him managing the band. He came to rehearsal the following day and was blown away by the powerful performance. We felt things were getting back on track and a solid schedule of rehearsal followed over the next few weeks. My spirits lifted and I drank a lot less. I began to write again.

In December of '93, I wrote six new songs and we rehearsed the new material with a sense of hope and spirit that I hadn't felt in a long time. I gave the new songs to Attila, and he added them to the tapes and sent out the packages on New Year's Day, 1994.

He called me the next week with an offer from a record company out of Germany called Long Island Records. They absolutely loved "Suffertown" and wanted to release it as a single. I told the guys at rehearsal that night. Everyone was overjoyed with the news, but I felt something wasn't quite right. A part of me had somewhat already resigned from the music business and I was still dealing with the painful decision to let go of my dreams of rock stardom. I didn't want to get too excited about it and I was being careful to temper my enthusiasm. The guys sensed my apprehension, but we talked through it and I went home that night with a renewed, if tentative, sense of hope.

Signing the Long Island contract was a monumental moment. As I went through it line by line with Attila he complained and we argued about the small advance of $6,000 USD.

"Forget it Attila!" I was not losing another deal because I didn't move on it. "I'm going to sign this deal."

"What about a counter offer," he pleaded.

"No!" I told him. "I've been stung before because I didn't go with my gut feelings. I won't go through that again. I'm taking the deal. End of discussion." I signed on the dotted line. "Besides, we can always turn this deal into something bigger," I said. "At least it's a foot in the door."

He listened to my arguments, and although he didn't agree completely, he eventually relented.

Only one thing remained – the name of the band. The name Ted Moore Band no longer appealed to me. During rehearsal, we kicked around a bunch of different names and we landed on Black and White as an interim solution. But, I wanted a name that would reflect the new songs and the deeper, introspective nature of the project. The Long Island deal had been drawn in my name, but the label needed the name of the band in the agreement. After a night of burning incense, I decided upon Locomotive Dream. Even after the incense wore off it still sounded cool, so that was more reason to keep it.

In summer of '94, we became Locomotive Dream. The signed contract was sent to Germany and Attila found us a producer and a studio so we could record the album. We found a young up-and-coming producer named Mark Hensley who was willing to work for a percentage of album profits, and no cash up front. We could spend the $6, 000 solely on the record. Attila struck a deal with Greenhouse Studios in Vancouver and we would start recording soon. To help keep the money coming in, Attila booked me and Eddie to play for one of his other artists - Noah Shilkin.

Noah was a singer-songwriter from New Zealand who garnered some local success playing in a band with one of the Finn brothers before they found their fortune with Crowded House. Noah's songs had a cool, eclectic, folksy thing going on that had a sort of Smiths/Morrissey vibe to it. He was making a new start in Canada when he and Attila met and decided to join forces. The Noah rehearsals paid well and the songs were an interesting departure from what Locomotive Dream was doing. In the meantime, I answered an audition call and got the gig as a bass player for Hardacker. Legendary producer Bob Rock had offered his involvement to the Hardacker project, as his brother-in-law, Mike Gillies, was playing second guitar in the band. It was great to spend time with Bob, meet famous rock stars, and stay at his amazing house. Bob's gold and platinum albums filled an entire section. It was an exciting connection. Hardacker was a great band with cool songs and I really liked all the guys. They understood that I had my own project and that I was temporary until they could find someone permanent. It was a great arrangement and we were having a blast.

Fast Eddie was livid. He begrudgingly understood the Noah project was necessary to keep money coming in for us, but felt any other moves I made outside of Locomotive Dream could only serve as a distraction and liability for our band. I tried to explain the value of my networking efforts, but he wouldn't hear any of it. I told Eddie that Locomotive Dream was my main priority and that when the time came I would leave Hardacker. This seemed to assuage Eddie's fears, but I knew things were never going to heal for us. The Boneshakers gigs started becoming more stressful and the two of us were bickering constantly.

In early 1995, when the time came to begin recording the Locomotive Dream album, I told Hardacker I was leaving. It was hard for me to say goodbye to such a remarkable group of people. Hardacker's lead guitar player, Eric Rowlett, had been an acquaintance of mine during the '80s and we became close friends. I ended up being the best man at his wedding to another '80s friend of mine, Laura who had worked at the Strathcona hotel in Victoria – a venue I had played many times. The times spent with Hardacker, both on and off stage, were some of my favorite experiences.

Things were dark in the Locomotive Dream camp. The recordings weren't giving us the results we were looking for and everyone felt the intense pressure to finish the album on time and within budget. First takes were often kept as finals and songs were rushed to completion. The producer showed little interest in the project. Eddie and I were barely speaking and the rest of the band watched, helpless to intervene.

One of the brighter moments came at the end of the sessions. We were fortunate to have Steve Brown come in and mix our record while he was visiting Canada. Steve had worked with Elton John and The Cult and we were all excited to have such a big name and all his experience involved with our album. Steve's mixes helped to shape the final product and we soon had the album finished, on time and within budget. We sent the masters to Long Island. They manufactured and produced some nice artwork for the CD and sent us some copies. I held one in my hands. It was awesome; 11 songs all penned by me, pressed, and packaged by a real record company, and ready for international distribution. There had been discussions with the label about me doing some interviews for the media in Western Europe and we would follow up with a full European tour in fall of 1995. Attila made phone calls to Long Island to set things up while the band rehearsed the studio versions of the songs.

After a couple of weeks, Attila called me to say Long Island hadn't returned his calls. He finally received word from one of the execs that our contact man in the company had died. The Locomotive Dream campaign, along with any other projects he was working on, died with him. We were released from our deal. Attila pleaded our case without success. The other guys at Long Island had other projects they were working on and didn't want any more acts. Attila tried shopping the masters elsewhere, but no one was interested.

The Noah project had released a 4-song EP and Attila failed to get any interest for it either. His other bands had broken up and he was in a financial crisis. He tried to get things going with a couple of young country artists and brought me in to do some writing, but nothing materialized. He had no funding for recording and he'd worn out his welcome with all the studios in town. One day I called his office to find his phone had been disconnected. I went to his house. Attila was gone.

Bob Rock moved to Hawaii and took Murray and Mike with him. Within the space of a year I had gone from four bands on the go with more than one bright future at hand, to having only Boneshakers gigs once or twice a month.

The Long Island tragedy had crushed Locomotive Dream. We tried to regroup under the name Jobella, rearranging a fresh slant on the tunes and trying to keep a positive outlook, but again the writing was on the wall. I couldn't keep up the brave face any longer. My determination was gone.

Jesus, I had finally signed the band to a real record deal and then it was gone. Just like that. It only took a few weeks for the band to splinter and communication to stop. By Christmas of 1995, there was no contact at all. Locomotive Dream was history.

I had lots of time on my hands, so I started going through my options again. I decided some dreams were just not realistic. I could cross off being captain of a Starship. I had wanted to be a professional hockey player, but no one makes the NHL draft at 35.

I looked again at the course catalogues and tuition guide from the university. It was going to cost me tens of thousands of dollars and four years to get an undergraduate degree and then I would have to spend two more years and a few thousand more dollars at Teacher's College. It was overwhelming. I didn't even know if I could go back to school at my age and do well enough to graduate.

I decided to put teaching on the back burner and first concentrate on making enough money to eat and pay rent. I had no training for anything that paid well, and minimum wage jobs were even scarce. I signed up with a casual labor agency and walked around to all the construction sites I could find asking for work. Occasionally, I would play weekend stints with the Boneshakers during which Eddie and I rarely spoke. There were some really bad weekends.

Months flew by and I fell back into the same cycle of pickling myself in pity. All I could think of was how I was going to exist in a world outside of rock 'n' roll. The real world was completely foreign to me. I was terrified of it. How could I even talk to normal people? I had lived in a bubble of performing, parties, and travel. I lived in hotel rooms, chatted with fans and groupies, and had relationships with women that never lasted longer than a few hours. I figured anyone from the real world was going to spot me coming a mile away.

But I had met some normal people during my rock 'n' roll days, hadn't I? I thought about all the people who had come to the shows over the years. Not the drunks who spent six nights a week in the bar; but the ones who had just come for an evening out to get away from their regular routines and see a band play. I had met people that weren't staggering drunk, who spoke of jobs, family, and other regular stuff like flea markets and lawn fertilizer. It wasn't being around normal people that bothered me – I just didn't know if I could become one.

Mike Cressey was a guy who came out to see the Boneshakers on a fairly regular basis. He wasn't a drinker, or a stoner; he was a music lover and he really enjoyed live music. He was a well-travelled music aficionado and had some pretty cool stories about his musical experiences – not the least of which was seeing the Beatles perform live at Empire Stadium in Vancouver in 1964. Mike was a normal guy, by my standards, and I found myself drawn to his company. His easy-going manner and sobriety was a refreshing respite from the chaos and absurdity of the world I had lived in for decades. He had been a bus driver in Vancouver, had a wife and kids, and lived in the suburbs. It was the life I had forsaken for a chance at stardom.

In a way, I envied him. Sure, his life wasn't perfect. There were marital troubles, his kids were sometimes frustrating, but all of his problems looked simpler to me, and more importantly, real. I perceived it as traditional, not like mine at all. I enjoyed hearing his refreshing version of life and I told him so. We became friends, and he started visiting me at Boneshaker gigs on a regular basis. I looked forward to seeing him whenever he would visit, and we would exchange stories about our lives. It worked well for both of us. We each had a peek into someone else's life, voyeurs into lives we could only imagine for ourselves.

Mike's kids were of legal drinking age and he promised to bring them down to see the band. He joked that if I really wanted to meet some normal people, his kids were as normal as you could get.

"You'll recognize them right away," he laughed. "They'll stick out like a sore thumb."

A couple of weeks later I was playing at the Freeworld nightclub in Langley when Mike came up between sets and asked me to come meet his kids. I scanned the room and spotted them instantly. Mike was right; they stood out. We walked over to greet them. Mike introduced me to his son Jim, and his daughter Lhesa. Although they were 19 and 20, they looked much younger. I felt like a haggard old degenerate standing next to them and found myself apologizing for the bar room. Jim was an aspiring guitar player and said bar rooms didn't bother him. He was thinking about joining a band someday and would probably see quite a few of them if he decided to pursue that career. I thought about saying something then held my tongue. I had no right to piss on someone else's dreams just because my experiences had left me so bitter.

Lhesa was a young looking 20 year old and quite opposite to the strippers, groupies, and bar chicks I'd met over the last twenty years. She looked entirely out of place in the bar. She was pretty – there was no doubt about that. She had big, beautiful eyes that matched her long mane of deep, red curly hair. I found her very attractive, but I had no delusions. She was a fresh-faced suburban chick and way out of my league. A girl like her would go on to marry a stockbroker or a jock and have two or three kids and live in a suburban castle somewhere on a nice, sunny street. Nonetheless, for the rest of the evening, I couldn't stop staring at her. In any version of reality I could think of, I would be lucky to even deliver this chick's mail.

Still, she seemed reasonably interested in what I had to say and we talked a fair amount during the evening.

I went back to the warehouse that night unable to get Lhesa off of my mind. I thought about the life I had missed out on; suburbia, little league, PTA meetings and white picket fences. I caught myself imagining what it would be like to live that life.

But wait … was I out of my mind? Would I really choose the suburban ideal over rock and roll? Not a chance. I was just pining for another life because my rock star dreams were passing me by. Besides, even if I wanted the straight life, who the hell was going to want a guy like me? I was a used-up bar star – damaged goods. No decent woman would want me. I was certain of that.

Lhesa came out to see The Boneshakers a few times, and then her visits became a regular occurrence. She was coming out on her own, without her dad or her brother. What was this chick up to? Was she slumming it? Every ounce of restraint I had went into not asking her why she kept coming out to see the band. Maybe she just liked rock 'n' roll. Maybe she thought we were amusing. Maybe we were just different than what she had known in her life and she was broadening her perspectives.

Whatever the case, I enjoyed seeing her and started looking forward to it. My anticipation was such that I would curb my drinking on those nights so I could stay lucid and enjoy her company. When I went out of town with the band I was becoming less interested in pursuing my baser instincts. It was weird and wonderful.

Lhesa had become a panacea for me. I was cleaning up my act so I could look less run down and present some semblance of normalcy. One night she told me she wouldn't be back the following night. I figured I would take the opportunity to get a little off of the hook and have a few drinks with the guys. Around midnight Lhesa walked in. I was happy to see her, but also self-conscious that I had been drinking. I had enough liquid courage and asked her to come out to the van and have some whisky.

"Sure…" she said. "I don't think I want any whisky, but I will come out and chat." I was surprised and hid my astonishment at her response. It must have been the combination of my elation and the buzz from the drinks, but I actually found myself considering for a moment that this girl might somehow be interested in me. It seemed improbable and yet there she was – following me out to the parking lot. Was she nuts? My better judgement told me to stay away from this girl; I had no business even hanging out with such an innocent creature as this and even less right to take her out to the van. I was nervous and found myself drinking in large gulps to find my comfort zone.

The combination of the booze and fascination got the better of me. I began formulating a plan on how to steal a kiss. Jesus, the whole thing felt so wrong. By now, I was past the point of making logical decisions. She looked beautiful and showed interest in all the crap that came out of my mouth.

In a moment of drunken bravado, I went for it. She leaned in and kissed me back. My mind screamed for me to stop. Her lips were soft and chaste and I sunk deep into the kiss. It was one of the most erotic experiences I ever had in my life. This beautiful young woman was kissing me – hard. All of the sexual experiences I'd ever had suddenly paled in comparison. Her little tongue pushed into my mouth and my body burned.

I was going to hell. I was certain of it. I had no business being here. The only thing that could save my wretched soul was to stop and tell her to get out and run away.

After a moment of bliss, I pulled away slowly and hung my head. I couldn't look at her. I had no words. When I finally had the courage to look up, she was smiling. It was a peaceful smile that showed no signs of remorse or regret. She wasn't ashamed. The only one suffering here was me. I wanted to do it again. My mind swirled, trying to think of something to say – anything that might ease the tension. I had nothing.

I cleared my throat. "We should go back inside. The next set is starting soon."

She smiled sweetly, "Okay."

Her voice was like music. It was lilting and soft without a care in the world. My God, she was an angel. What the hell was she doing with an animal like me?

We started back and she said she was going home. I said goodbye and watched her walk to her car. I went into the bar and felt strangely out of place. One kiss had turned my world upside down. I could taste that kiss in my mouth for the rest of the night.

Chapter Twenty-One

In the summer of '96 I saw Lhesa on a regular basis and found myself missing her when she wasn't around. This was a first for me. I was in uncharted waters. In recent years, my relationships with women had been somewhat disposable. It kept any potential for true romance at arm's length. Could I even make a relationship work, let alone make it last? The track record for entertainers and marriage wasn't good--most didn't last. There were some exceptions, but they were few and far between. Jon Bon Jovi made his marriage last. He met Dorothea Hurley in high school and they were still together. Jon and Dorothea had gone through rough times and I remember reading somewhere they had broken up for a time. Jon had dated actress Diane Lane, but his separation from Dorothea was short-lived. They got back together and are still together.

Maybe it could work for me too. Just being around Lhesa made me look at life differently. She talked about things that were foreign to me. She kept in touch with people she'd gone to school with and had friends in her neighborhood. There were few people in my past that I ever talked to. I had reconnected with Les Starkey and we spoke now and then. Other than that, I couldn't really remember anyone that I had gone to school with, let alone kept in touch with.

Being with Lhesa inspired thoughts about where things could go from here. I knew whatever line of work or career I was going to go after would require education and training. There would be tuition, rent, utilities, food, and other expenses. Then there was the fact that I'd ruined a lot of brain cells over the years. I wondered if I had enough left to be a student.

At the end of 1996, Lhesa asked me to move in with her. We

were in love and I knew I wanted to spend as much time with her as I could. Financially, the timing was right. The money I saved could go towards education. I agreed. The whole thing felt right.

My dark days seemed behind me now. Everything good revolved around Lhesa. I left the warehouse, got rid of some crap I'd been hording and put the rest in storage. With a suitcase full of clothes and some toiletries, I moved in with Lhesa into her dad's house. Mike had been my friend for a while now and we got along well. It was strange at first. He knew me well enough long before I met Lhesa. He also saw that I made his daughter happy. I knew his friends gave him a hard time for letting Lhesa date a much older man, let alone having him move into his house with her. He never once let on that he doubted my relationship with Lhesa or me. Mike had suffered a bad heart attack earlier that year and his years in the work force had ended. He really enjoyed having me around the house to help with things, and we grew closer over the following months.

With a secure place to live and a supportive environment, I felt empowered and confident. The community college ran some tests to determine whether I could go straight into university or if I would need upgrading. I passed the university entrance requirements with flying colors – except for math. The saying "use it or lose it" was true in my case. I had to repeat Grade 12 mathematics before I could take first year university math. That was fine by me. After all I'd been through, I was happy I still had enough brains left to do anything scholastic.

Now I needed a job. With Mike and Lhesa's help, we put together a resume that highlighted my leadership skills. I printed off a bunch of copies and applied for several jobs. By the spring of '97, I had a part-time job as a fleet supervisor at an RV dealership. It was great to be working, even if the money I made was meager.

I applied to Kwantlen Polytechnic University and was elated when I was accepted. There was information about Canada Student Loans attached to the package and I filled out the forms and sent them off right away. A few weeks later, I was granted a loan to cover tuition and provide some additional monies for living expenses. Everything was going my way. Now I had to figure out how to keep money rolling in until school started.

My job at the RV dealership was spotty and my shifts sparse. I took the occasional gig with a Top 40 group called The Papa Woody Band. Papa was a guy from one of Atilla's bands, and we had spoken a few times during the recording of the Locomotive Dream album. He was working on a solo recording project and used his Top 40 gigs to fund it. He didn't want to play all of the time and this worked for me. Gigs were easy and presented none of the old band issues that plagued me with my bands. It was nice to have someone else handle all the headaches of booking and running the tours. I just sang for the pure joy of entertaining. We had a great summer rocking around British Columbia and Alberta.

I started university in September '97. It wasn't easy, but I powered through and managed to win three scholarships which helped augment the student loans. Lhesa was going to school too, and it was a great to have someone to study with and share the experience.

That Christmas, we got a special gift, we found out Lhesa was pregnant. Every first-time father out there has a story about how they felt when they were informed they were going to be a dad. It was the happiest and scariest moment I had ever experienced. Lhesa and I stayed up all night making plans. We decided one of us had to leave school at some point and the other would finish up and get a good career started. We weighed the options and decided I would keep going and she would go back to school at some point in the future. I could enter Teacher's College after my undergrad was complete and start a career in teaching by the time our child was 5. To support ourselves, my student loans would help a little, but Lhesa said she would go back to work after maternity leave. We were nervous, but hopeful.

On August 18, 1998, Hannah Marguerite Moore came into the world. She was a beautiful, healthy baby girl. Nothing in my life had ever felt this good. I held that little baby in my arms and I was on top of the world. I was never so proud as the day I saw Hannah for the first time.

In January of '99, I began the application process to Teacher's College. I loved university life. I was surrounded by brilliant minds and my grades were excellent. I maintained solid A and A+ grades and stayed on the Dean's Honor Roll for the remainder of my undergraduate degree program. Scholarships kept rolling in and it looked like I had found my true calling.

I was a dad, a student, a teacher candidate, and had successfully escaped the sordid world of rock 'n' roll. I had made it. The time to second-guess myself was over. Things had gone the way they did for a reason. If I'd had a big hit record and gone on marathon tours like Jon Bon Jovi I likely wouldn't have met Lhesa and had my beautiful daughter. I couldn't bear the thought of a life without them. This was what I was meant to do. I was going to be a great teacher and a great dad. My life was set.

CHAPTER TWENTY-TWO

The next two years passed quickly, and I graduated with a Bachelor's Degree in Geography and English. I began the Professional Development Program for teachers at the Faculty of Education and worked even harder. Lhesa had finished her schooling and landed a job as Nursing Unit Coordinator at the local hospital. Money was coming in, and we were on the way to establishing decent careers. We had recently moved in with Lhesa's mother, Donna, and she was so supportive. She made me feel absolutely welcomed and part of her family. I can't imagine how Lhesa and I would have ever gotten through those days without her. She helped us get on our feet and get started as a family of our own. I will always be grateful.

I began a teaching practicum in a Grade 7 class and found I had a knack for reaching tween kids – especially ones with behavioral problems. Sometimes when things got hairy in class, I would bring out my guitar and play a song until everyone was singing along. I treated the kids like a stubborn audience and found different ways to keep them engaged.

Several kids told me I looked and sounded "just like Bon Jovi." Initially, I laughed it off. I had received these comments back when I played in the bars, and I could sort of see the resemblance. But what surprised me was these eleven year-olds knew who Jon Bon Jovi was.

Bon Jovi had recently released the Crush album after a six year hiatus and the band was finding resurgence in the marketplace. The new record had a darker, more contemporary tone to it and the single, "It's My Life," found a whole new legion of fans drafted into the already powerful Bon Jovi army. It was cool these Grade 7 kids were excited about a band that had members as old as some of their parents. I bought a copy of Crush and played it in class during free time. I utilized the novelty of their perceived resemblance between me and Jon to further engage the kids, and encouraged their excitement about music and the arts.

I had an arsenal of traditional teaching tools and years of life experience. Using them together gave me some remarkable results with the kids. It did not escape the notice of my colleagues and superiors. I received positive comments from the kids' parents and the school administrators. I was thrilled that the life skills I'd acquired managing rock 'n' roll bands were paying off in the real world. The discipline I'd developed in the military had pushed me through university and studying, and my well-oiled memory for music and lyrics gave me a distinct advantage as well. I made peace with all that had happened, and didn't happen, in my rock 'n' roll years. Things worked out the way they did and I was grateful to the Universe, and Lhesa, for setting me on the right path.

We'd been together for seven years, we were growing as people and as a couple; a family. The talk of more children and the picket fence kept creeping into our thoughts and conversations. One day Lhesa sat me down and told me we were getting married. The date was set, arrangements made, all I had to do was show up.

"Okay." I told her. "That sounds great." It made sense to me.

She orchestrated an amazing medieval wedding and on April 19, 2002 I was dressed in full knight's regalia standing in front of an entire congregation with a minister, friends, and families all dressed in 13th century garb. It was an amazing day.

We went to Manzanillo, Mexico, for our honeymoon and stayed in an all-inclusive resort. We checked in at the hotel, I dropped off our luggage in our room, and the phone rang. It was the front desk. They needed a Canadian to participate in a big relay down on the beach. I said I would love to help, and went right down to the ocean shoreline where four lines of contestants were receiving the instructions. As I approached, the announcer called out through his megaphone.

"Señor Bon Jovi has come to help the Canadians to veectory," he shouted in a thick Spanish accent. "Let's have a beeg welcome for Señor Bon Jovi!" Everyone cheered and clapped. I laughed and raised my arms high in salute. I could see Lhesa shaking her head and smiling from the crowd. One of the Canadians shouted, "Okay, Bon Jovi, you're the anchor!" I nodded and took my place at the end of the line. Four teams: Canadians, Americans, Europeans, and Mexicans, were to race to settle which country had the best beach athletes at the resort. Everyone cheered at the sidelines in support of their respective countrymen.

The starting gun went off and one by one, the runners bolted the 100 yards down the beach, ran circles around a half-buried tequila bottle ten times, and ran backwards to rejoin their teams. After spinning around that damned bottle ten times everyone was so dizzy, running backwards was a huge challenge. Everyone fell over themselves on the way back, and it was obvious some had more tequila in them than others.

By the time it was my turn we were behind by a fair margin. When my teammate tagged me I ran with everything I had down to the bottle, I closed my eyes, spun around ten times, and then started running backwards. I kept my knees as high as I could to avoid tripping over myself. I glanced to my left and right. I was about to overtaken my opponents. I poured it on and saw two guys fall into a heap and the third guy slowed down. The crowd went crazy. We had come from behind and won the race.

The announcer screamed, "Three cheers for Señor Bon Jovi and heeeeees fellow Canadians!" My team lifted me up on their shoulders and everyone exchanged high fives. It was so cool and a great way to start our Mexican vacation.

In the days that followed, everywhere I went I was greeted with "Hey, Señor Bon Jovi!" The resort guests, the staff, even the locals in the nearby town caught on and soon I was Señor Bon Jovi wherever we ventured. I must admit I enjoyed the attention of being compared to the famous rock star.

Lhesa was having a great time too and getting a lot of attention as the only red head at the resort. The locals were especially intrigued by her long red locks. They grabbed her out of the crowd one night and dragged her onstage for a competition. To Lhesa's horror, it was a beer-chugging contest. Lhesa had never been a big drinker, by any stretch of imagination. Now it was too late to back down as she was put on the spot in front of the crowd. To her credit, she did her utmost to help her team, but they lost and by the end, Lhesa was a mess. It was a long and difficult night and in the morning she was positively green.

By mid-afternoon I summoned the hotel doctor. After examination, he determined that she was indeed hungover; however, she also had strep throat. He gave her some medication and prescribed bed rest, small sips of bottled water, and no alcohol for a couple of days. She spent most of that day in the room and I alternated swimming in the ocean and checking on her progress.

Lhesa grew bored and later that night suggested we go down to the central complex for the Karaoke contest. I had never seen Karaoke and thought it would be fun. Lhesa bundled up and we went downstairs. Everyone was gathered in the large central area of the resort. It was a beautiful, warm evening. Moonlight and torches lit up the entire courtyard. Dozens of staff members took turns playing air guitar while locals and tourists sang karaoke versions of classic rock and pop songs and some traditional Spanish numbers. I was about to sit down when someone called out, "Señor Bon Jovi sing a song!"

The announcer caught wind of it and began shouting over the microphone "Si, Señor Bon Jovi, Si, come up and seeeng a song!" People began to clap. I waved and smiled. I could hear Lhesa laughing behind me. Someone brought over a book of songs and dropped on the table. People at a nearby table shouted, "Sing some Bon Jovi, Dude!" I smiled and looked through the book while the next performer took to the stage.

There wasn't a single Bon Jovi song in the book. I searched for any songs I might know. I saw Steppenwolf's "Born To Be Wild" and flashed back to Jon Bon Jovi getting onstage at Club Soda with Mike Behm and Frenzy to perform that song. I knew I could get through it. I gave my selection to the announcer.

After the contestant onstage finished singing the announcer called out, "Señor Bon Jovi, pleese come to the stage!"

The crowd chanted "Bon Jovi! Bon Jovi!"

I jumped on stage red-faced and smiling. I don't know if any of those people thought I actually was Jon or not, but I was more nervous than I had been for any performance in my career. "Gracias." I said into the microphone.

Then the song started blaring through the speakers. Four staff members joined me onstage sporting long wigs and pantomiming with wooden guitars and we all rocked out. I sang and the crowd was jubilant in their response. When the song ended they applauded and screamed. I was greeted by handshakes and high-fives all the way back to my table. At the end of the competition they made an announcement.

"Señor Bon Jovi is the grand weener of the eeevening!" The crowd clapped and whistled as I went up to accept the award – a 40-ounce bottle of Tequila.

"One more song Señor Bon Jovi," he shouted.

I wanted to give back to these wonderful people and sing something in Spanish, but my Spanish was terrible and I couldn't think of a single Spanish song I actually knew, anyways.

I selected Carlos Santana's "Smooth" and they rolled the music. When the song started, the audience cheered even louder. My selection was appreciated and understood. They jumped to their feet and sang along with me. It was one of the most humbling outpourings of unbridled happiness I had ever been witness to, and it struck me deeply. I thanked everyone in my awkward Spanish and shook hands with everyone in the courtyard.

Lhesa came by and took the huge bottle from me saying she would take it upstairs to our room. I nodded, hugged elderly women, and shook hands with little kids. She returned a few minutes later, still holding the giant bottle. Her face was as red as her hair.

It just so happened that several people in the resort were coming down from their rooms after hearing the commotion at the karaoke event. Lhesa had been standing in the lobby clutching the giant bottle of tequila when some people exited the elevators, saw her, and began shouting "Parteee Cheecka!"

They howled with laughter at the little redheaded woman with her "muy grande Tequila." Once everyone filed by, there was the hotel doctor who had treated her earlier that day, staring at Lhesa and the giant bottle. Lhesa was mortified.

"I was going to try to explain," she said. "But he just walked away, looking back over his shoulder at me."

I laughed like I had never before. Imagining my demure, non-drinker wife mistaken as a party girl was beyond hilarious. I hugged her and tried my best to ease her embarrassment. Ever since then, "party girl" has been one of my favorite pet names for her.

In the fall of 2002, things were rolling along as scheduled. Lhesa discovered she was pregnant again and our life just kept getting sweeter. My practicums were going well, Lhesa's job was working out great, and I started playing hockey again. I hadn't played since I was 12.

I started real slow – going to drop-ins at the local rink and getting my wheels and my wind back. Then I joined the Kwantlen University team and started skating with guys who were 15-20 years younger than me. It was frustrating at first, but each day I found myself being able to keep up a little more. Since I was older than everyone else I had to learn to play smart – not too much wasted skating, read the ice, and keep my head up. One day, while playing in a college tournament, I got nailed by a giant defenseman. I hit the ice hard. I woke up on my back with the guys standing around me. My head was killing me and my vision was blurred. I managed to make my way to the dressing room with help from my teammates and went home feeling nauseous. The next day I went to the doctor and he scheduled me for a series of tests. I had suffered a massive concussion and he told me that my hockey days were over. The next few months were foggy. I could only sleep for 45 minutes at a stretch and always had terrible headaches. There were times I wanted to knock myself out with a hammer just so I wouldn't have to deal with the pain and be able to sleep for a few hours. When things got bad I would go downstairs and lay my head on the cool concrete floor with an ice pack on top of my head.

Concentrating at school became difficult and I suffered from frustrating mood swings and memory lapses. To add to my discomfort, my left hip started hurting and I was feeling pretty beat. My aches and pains abated when I taught; however, sitting in theory classes was challenging. It was already a tough program and sometimes a difficult environment.

The woman who ran the teacher candidate program was tough and I knew from the beginning of the program that she wasn't fond of me. I didn't bother me too much as she wasn't particularly nice to some other candidates either. She was an imposing figure and many student teachers regarded her as "The Wall" that stood between us and our teaching certification. She was a large woman and wore thick layers of frosted blue eye shadow and bright red blush on her round face. She wore a sort of smile at all times, but it didn't really fool anyone. She operated the program from inception and had been a teacher some decades ago. She spent her days in her office dispensing judgment over prospective teachers and ruled the faculty with an iron fist. I was terrified of her and I cringed when she looked at me with that strange half-smile. The first time she spoke to me, I knew I was in her bad books.

"One of your fellow candidates tells me you used to be a musician," she said between labored breaths. I had no idea how to respond. The way she said musician, could just as easily have been molester.

I nodded and said, "That was a long time ago." From that

moment on, I knew I would have to tread carefully with everything I did. She regarded me with suspicion whenever I passed her in the faculty hallways. I avoided eye contact as best I could. I'm sure she felt she had lots of reasons to dislike me. I was a musician, I wore a leather jacket, and rode a motorcycle. I did not fit her idea of what a teacher should look like.

I worked hard, and hoped that would be enough.

My life skills helped me find creative ways to deal with challenges in the classroom. My mentor teacher told me I was a natural. I think this angered The Wall. No matter how well I did, she continued to regard me with disdain.

One day she called me into her office and told me that I needed to address my philosophy.

I asked what it was I needed to change. Her answers were vague and filled with rhetoric from the program brochures. She told me I needed to get back to basics – the tried and true methods that she had employed a millenia ago when she taught. I promised I would get in line.

She dogged me over the next month. I had made a powerful enemy. She was the last person in that program that you wanted to piss off. She had total control over who was recommended to the Teachers' accreditation body. In the teaching program there was no failing the course; you were simply asked to withdraw.

One day during my practicum, The Wall told me she had decided the only way for me to continue in the program was on a 'special contract' under which she would monitor my progress and assign me an assortment of readings to address the errors in my attitude and philosophy. At the end of the program, she would decide whether I had shown sufficient growth in my philosophy and professionalism regarding appropriate and responsible teaching.

In a last ditch attempt to salvage my chances I contacted the faculty, citing what I believed to be bullying behavior and personal discrimination. It turned out students were not the only ones powerless against The Wall. I received a response from the faculty saying they would not intervene. I would have to work it out myself. They told me I could withdraw from the program at any time. I was dejected and helpless in the face of politics and policy. I pushed on in the program for a few more weeks, but the idea of that contract scared the hell out of me.

I knew there was no way she would allow me to graduate, regardless of how well I did in my practicums or theory. The remaining tuition costs to finish the program would be in the thousands regardless of pass or withdrawal. I was certain The Wall would ensure I didn't receive recommendation to the College of Teachers. My student loans were running out, and at the end of the program, I would be broke. I had a wife, a daughter, and a baby on the way. I decided to cut my losses and get a job. The Wall happily accepted my withdrawal.

Lhesa was devastated. We had both worked so hard and made many sacrifices to keep me in school. She insisted she go down to the school to make an appeal on my behalf. Lhesa soon found out why The Wall got her name. Their conversation became heated, awkward, and uncomfortable.

"You should be ashamed of yourself!" she finally told The Wall. The exchange caught me completely off-guard. I had never seen Lhesa be so forceful.

The Wall smiled. "No, you should be ashamed of yourself."

The conversation was over. I managed to pry Lhesa out of there before things got worse and did my best to calm her on the ride home.

"I still have my degree." I told her. "I'll get a good job and apply to the teacher program at UBC in the spring. Everything will work out." Teaching would just have to wait a little longer. All I had to do now was find a job.

The job market at that time was lean in Vancouver and finding anything was tough. I sent out a hundred resumes and received just as many rejections. It was an employer's marketplace. I took whatever odd jobs I could get: single days working construction, odd shifts at the RV dealership, and selling perfume knock-offs out of a duffel bag on the street. My situation was dire. Thank goodness Lhesa was still willing and able to work during her full pregnancy. I felt guilt and shame for not being able to provide for my family. Lhesa supported me in every way and I was amazed by her cheerful determination.

People with university degrees who were lucky enough to be hired were taking jobs as dishwashers, waiters, and temporary laborers. I wracked my brain to find a way to get a competitive edge. One night, when I was reading Hannah a story about a giant radio that had actual musicians in it, I realized there was one thing I could do—I could always go on the road with a band.

I chuckled at the irony of rock 'n' roll being a dependable fallback position. Even though the gig markets had collapsed in the major centers, there were always remote areas with good-paying, long-term engagements.

I called Papa Woody to find some guys, any guys, that would be willing to travel and wanted to make some money. The band would have no aspirations other than to head out to parts unknown and rake in some cash.

Papa said a local guy named Sean Reynolds would play drums and another guy he knew named Dave Schriek would take the guitar spot. I found bassist Eddy Bugnut through a friend and the lineup was complete. After a few emails, things moved quickly. We figured out what songs each guy knew and I drafted a set list. There would be no rehearsal. The first night on the road would be our rehearsal. I called a couple local agents and got a gig on the second phone call for a two-month stay in Whitehorse up in Canada's Yukon Territories. I told them the name of the band was Big Radio Static.

Lhesa didn't like the idea that I'd be gone for two months, and neither did I, but it was a guaranteed paycheck and the money was good. We had lots of support and help from Lhesa's parents, and the baby wasn't due for several months. Everything would be ok.

CHAPTER TWENTY-THREE

B ig Radio Static flew up to Whitehorse that Sunday and started the following night. The band got tight fast, and we packed in the crowds. I started to make new friends and had fun playing with Sean, Eddie, and Dave. I enjoyed rocking out without the crutch of drinking. That first week was all about the joy of playing music.

As the weeks rolled by and the novelty wore off, I started partying with the locals. To freshen things up musically, we rehearsed new material during the day. The guys in the band were younger than me, and like most Generation X people they loved Grunge. We added songs from Nirvana, Pearl Jam, Stone Temple Pilots, and Soundgarden. I actually found an appreciation for the music style I had once scorned. The new material went over like gangbusters with the locals and we were the hottest ticket in town. People came in droves and the place was a zoo on any given night of the week.

Northern locales are often a setting for partying to excess and Whitehorse was no exception. Booze and drugs were readily available and offered free to the band every night. I kept myself in check for a while and found a way to not get sucked into the party vortex. Sometimes, I would succumb to temptations. I would repent and get sober again, but for fewer days each time. As the weeks rolled by my fresh outlook was drowned with drink and the partying was an every night occurrence.

The nights got longer and the days were comatose interludes of recuperation. Lhesa could tell something was wrong when I called home. Her voice became more and more concerned each time we would talk and I told her not to worry. She was very pregnant at this point and I felt horrible about falling back into the old party ways. I would straighten out and vow to stay that way. Then the weekend would come. By the end of our two-month stay, I was more than ready to go home.

Lhesa could tell I hadn't taken care of myself. I blamed it on poor eating habits and not enough sleep. A call came in the following week for a return engagement in Whitehorse. It started at the end of the month and the money was even better than before. There were still a couple of months before the baby was due and I would be back in time. I promised myself I would stay clean this time.

My resolve lasted most of the first two weeks. Playing music and drinking had become inseparable. I could no longer get through the night without partying. I rationalized that playing cover songs in bars was unfulfilling so I drank to make it fun. Two decades of hammering it out in the clubs had taken its toll and playing Top 40 in the frozen North wasn't exciting me anymore. If I was really going to play music perhaps I needed a project; an original project, something that could rekindle my creativity. It was either that, or I had to let go of playing completely. The partying wasn't going to stop, and I had to leave the party.

I decided I needed to get off the road again, get accepted into a different teachers' college and teach. I could book the odd in-town shows for the band and that would be it. As for my creative anxieties, they would have to wait. Right now, all I had to do was get through this gig, go home, and sober up.

When I got home I applied to the UBC Teacher's Program and managed to pick up a few local gigs for Big Radio Static. A small in-town scene had emerged from what was once the duo circuit in Vancouver and there was about a dozen or so of these gigs. The venues were small pubs and taverns now hiring three-piece bands to play on their cramped duo and single stages. I began getting steady dates from a local agent named Edie Perala. Edie was from the Bronx and an absolute delight to talk to. She and her husband Ante had worked the carnival circuit for many years and she had some wonderful stories that she would tell you in her thick New York accent. We were doing well at Edie's gigs and she started booking more and more local work for us until we had back to back weekends booked well in advance. The money was decent and it gave me time to prepare for school again and be with Lhesa and Hannah.

One day, I received a call from Papa Woody. He was recording some of his own songs and asked if I wanted to play the bass tracks. I thought it would be fun and he agreed to let me bring Doug Grant in to play the drum tracks. It was great to get a chance to play with Doug again and to rekindle our friendship. Papa played some tapes and we talked at length about where pop music had morphed over the past few years and where it might be heading. He agreed that grunge had made a huge impact on the musical landscape and more or less died along with Kurt Cobain. Post-grunge had come along to take its place with bands like Creed, Spacehog, and Nickelback. Some classic bands from the '80s were releasing records with more modern rock sensibilities.

I shared my observations about how Bon Jovi had found rebirth in the modern rock marketplace. It was a great example of how new life could be breathed into classic rock.

"So many people thought that Bon Jovi was down and out," I told him. "And they found a way to come back. Bon Jovi was virtually silent during the Grunge Years but they never relented."

I played "It's My Life" for Papa and we dissected the elements that made it palatable for new ears while it kept the band's classic sound. The post grunge qualities were evident in the production values and the mix, while Richie's trademark talk box harkened back to the band's "Slippery When Wet" heyday. There was a noise factor, a slightly darker hue to the sound, present in most or all of the new rock bands on the radio. Regardless, rock sensibilities had changed and it was likely they weren't ever going to be the same again.

I cautioned him. "You can embrace it and find your place in the mix or suffer the same extinction as the Jurassic Rock cronies."

We waded for hours through the sticking to your guns arguments, the obligatory function over fashion debate, and the ever-popular don't chase the radio cautionary tales. I played him Nickelback, Theory of a Dead Man, Audioslave, Seether, Creed, and a host of others. Papa was a quick study and found a host of fine details to apply to whatever worked well for his voice and playing style.

The results were stellar. The existing songs were more hard rock, with fresh modern sonic qualities and structures. His personality shone through and gave it a unique identity. We penned six songs together and found a sound we both loved. Papa insisted I produce the demo, and I got Ray Roper to engineer the tracks in his studio. When the songs were mixed, we knew we had something special. We made hard copies and prepared to shop them to the labels. All we needed was a name to put on the CDs. I suggested the name Chrome, as it was strong and sounded contemporary. He loved the idea, but wanted it spelled Krome. I loved it. I worked up a quick logo on my computer and the CD was complete.

The whole thing had been so smooth. I had never been this completely creatively satisfied with any other work of which I had been part. The songs, the sound, the recordings, all had come out just the way I had heard it in my head. It was the most successful recording session I had ever experienced and the results were amazing. We contacted the Vancouver offices of the major labels and they agreed to hear our demos. I couldn't wait to hear the reactions. Everyone would love it.

On the down side, I had not been accepted for the UBC 2003 intake and would have to apply for entrance in 2004. Lhesa and I were both disappointed. I tried not to let it bother me and focused on the potential for Krome. I would still be a teacher someday. It was a minor wrinkle in our plans.

That Christmas, I flew out to Toronto to see Mom and my brothers. I couriered the Krome demo to some labels while I was there and an A&R guy from a major label responded the following day. He said the label might be interested in offering Krome a contract in the spring when they were doing their new artist signings. He acknowledged our contemporary sound, loved the heavier side to the songs, and he felt our timing was perfect. I called Papa right away. He was thrilled, and said he would start finding a second guitar player to complete the line-up so we could rehearse the material and do some shows.

When I returned home in early January of 2003, Papa had hired a young guitar player named Jesson Nelson. Jesson had never been on the road and had very little band experience, but Papa figured he had a good grasp on the guitar and the rest would come along. Jesson was a decent guitar player and a sweet guy, and he played well with the band. When we showcased Krome in April at the Roxy we were in great form. The label rep was in the audience, said he loved the band, and would send a good report back to Toronto. We all rejoiced. The band was on its way

Sophie Thea Michalan Moore, my second miracle, was born the following month on May 29, 2003. My little family was growing. I now had a wife and two children, and I began to consider my future in a way I never had before. It was time to stop pissing around. I had to support my family. Whatever I was doing I had to concentrate on making it profitable and then, perhaps, I could speculate on the music business again - when I could afford it.

Krome's future seemed bright, but I was still gun-shy about any chances for success in music. I would be a teacher by 2005 and start making money then, but I needed decent paying work right now. The in-town scene was bringing in steady money for me, but I knew it could pay more. More rooms were hiring trios and four piece bands, but there were few of these acts to play the venues. Many bands made several appearances at each venue so I knew there was room for new bands in that scene. Most of the groups playing in the growing circuit were low-tech; no stage lights, small sound equipment, and played song lists replete with archaic rock standards. I pictured the pubs as a potential new Top 40 scene that was largely untapped. I decided to concentrate on developing my efforts in the scene to get as much money as I could. In the meantime, I could look for other temporary work while I prepared to go back to school.

I decided it was time to make Big Radio Static a better moneymaker and exploit the growing new scene as best I could. I stacked the band's sets with more contemporary rock, Grunge, and post-Grunge hits. I started bringing in cool lighting systems, bigger sound systems, and a smoke machine. Word got around, slowly at first, our calendar started filling up, and our money started to go up.

My guitar player had grown tired of playing cover songs and was leaving the band. I was referred to a local player named Robert Graves, a veteran rocker with long blonde hair who reminded me of Alvin Lee from Ten Years After. He had the same big red hollow body Gibson and wild onstage persona that was perfect for our new show. Most of the grunge and modern rock songs on the set list were foreign to him, but he was quite professional and learned the songs note for note. Robert brought some cool classic rock songs that he could sing to round out the show, and soon we had a great sounding three-piece behind me as the band's singer and front man.

I shortened the name of the band to Big Radio. I made large full-color venue posters and created a band website with photos of the band, our friends, fans, and venue staff we would meet at each show. Our stage show and setup was more elaborate than most of these pubs had ever seen. We were a rock 'n' roll spectacular compared to most other pub trios, and word of our big production and cool set list spread overnight. The band soon became the most sought-after group in the pub scene and began to set the standard for all other in-town groups.

Soon other bands were bringing in light shows, smoke machines, and bigger audio gear to compete. Pubs were rocking all weekend long. Soon the in-town scene was alive and healthy again. I felt proud of how things had developed.

In the meantime, things became complicated for Krome. The label balked on signing a record deal and told us they might opt for a lease deal on the masters of the album once we had it recorded. Papa shopped to other labels and there was some interest, but most of the companies were telling him they would only be interested in a similar type of lease-deal. The music business was changing and big record deals were a rarity. Many bands were recording albums on their own dime and then leasing masters. Papa decided to see if he could put together a lease deal for the finished product, and then tour like crazy. I told him it was unlikely I would continue as the band's bassist as I was going to go back to school and I didn't want to tour any more. He said he would find a replacement soon.

I was excited about going back to school, but I also felt some anxiety. I still loved the idea of teaching kids, but my experience with The Wall and the faculty body had given me cause for doubt. What would my future really be like in the education system? Were my frustrating experiences something that would continue when I became a full-time teacher? How could I guarantee life as a teacher would be different? Maybe it would all work out.

But what if The Wall was right? What if she'd done me, and every kid I would teach, a huge favor? Maybe she had saved me from a short, miserable career. After days of going over the "what ifs," I decided teaching would have to wait. I couldn't reconcile my fear about school administrators and educational politics and I knew I had to find my peace with it all before trying it again. I was not going to spend another $20, 000 in student loan money to gamble on a career that I might regret.

But if I wasn't going to teach, what the hell would I do? A career in teaching was my bid to change my life and give me some financial security. I would have to find another career, or at least a good job. I began to wrack my brains thinking about how to use my education to get a good-paying job. The job market was not much easier for a university graduate, and in fact, the competition was fierce. People much younger than me were coming out of school and into the work force, many of whom were taking unpaid intern positions just to get in the door with a good company. I could never support my family as a struggling intern, making three hundred bucks on weekends in a pub band. I was going to need a real job and a decent wage. Hopefully, my education would help me find something decent.

Producing the rest of the Krome album kept me busy, and I focused on the possibility the group would find success in a lease deal. I poured everything I had into that album and worked long hours every day trying to make this the best record of my career. The effort was worth it. The album was a great collection of radio-friendly hard rock, and there was a definite continuity and identity to the overall recording. With school off my radar, I agreed to go tour with Papa and help drive interest toward the band and the album. He was sure he could get a deal.

Lhesa tried to stay upbeat about the chances for the band and said she thought I had done a wonderful job as producer. But, I knew she felt it was a big mistake to forget about teaching. She thought I was scared and simply sabotaging myself. I knew she was probably right. Still, I clung desperately to any chances for Krome.

Papa sent the CD out to record companies and radio stations across the country. A few stations began to play the title track, "Acknowledge," and he borrowed money to have a radio tracker enhance the spins. We climbed the charts on a few radio stations in Canada and went on tour to chase the rising single.

We toured as far as Quebec, making stops in every province

along the way. We did interviews, in-store appearances, industry conventions, and shows in every small club that paid us for food and gas. It was not glamorous, but we felt momentum build by the time we hit Montreal. "Acknowledge" had cracked the Top 50 on the Canadian rock charts and we filled venues wherever we went.

It was taking off and we knew we'd get a deal any day now. We played the North by Northeast Festival and Conference in Toronto and hoped we could attract a label. We had minor interest from a couple of companies, but no one wanted to commit. They told Papa to keep playing and gaining ground in the domestic markets; they would keep the band in their sights. The cross-Canada tour lasted two months and we returned home tired, hungry, and broke. Although there was a good buzz about Krome, we didn't have distribution for the album. The only sales had been the few hundred we had sold at the gigs.

By the end of 2004, Papa was desperate to showcase the band anywhere. He insisted we play as many dates as he could find, anywhere he could find them, in exchange for $20 per day for food. We sometimes had to sleep in the van we travelled in, right beside our equipment.

Krome gigs were interfering with my ability to book paying gigs with Big Radio. It was becoming a financial nightmare. Lhesa was forced to pick up the slack, working like a dog at the hospital and taking care of the kids. I was losing faith in Krome and the Big Radio money wasn't enough to support me, let alone help support my family. Tensions between Papa and I grew. He was now leaving me out of the decision-making process. He told a Vancouver newspaper the entire Krome project was exclusively his brainchild and vision. When I picked up the paper the next day a local entertainment headline read: "Krome is a one-man show." Shortly after that, he and I got into a heated argument. He fired me on the spot.

I felt so stupid. You would think after all of my years in the business I would have covered my ass. I had done a handshake deal on trust and friendship. I had produced the album for free on the promise that I would receive a percentage of sales. My relationship with Papa came to an end. I gave up trying to contact him and accepted the loss as another lesson in life and business.

I needed money fast. Playing in bars would never bring in enough income and I had no employers banging down my door. I had a couple of interviews, but nothing materialized. A friend who drove tractor-trailer took me on a ride-along and put me behind the wheel to see if I might be interested in becoming a professional trucker. I loved driving the rig and I thought driving a truck was a good opportunity for a guy in my situation that needed work as soon as possible. The money was decent and the industry was starving for new drivers. Even if I changed my mind again and went back to teaching, I could drive truck during summer holidays. The plan sounded great to Lhesa too and her good credit got me $1,800 to upgrade my driver's license. I was confident that I would do well in the driver's course, get a job right away, and pay her back with my first month's salary.

The course was fun, theory was easy to learn, and the driving lessons went well. The day I got my license to drive semi I got a job with a company in Port Coquitlam, BC called Consolidated Fastfrate Inc. The company was strong with several terminals throughout Canada. It was a union workplace with benefits and a decent hourly wage. The first year I made more money than I would have on a teacher's salary and I paid Lhesa back.

For the first two years at Fastfrate I continued doing Big Radio gigs on the weekends. I wanted to keep making the extra money, but I enjoyed the gigs less and less. The crowds were reasonably responsive and the shows gave me a chance to let off some steam, but the new breed of twenty-something managers running these small pubs were difficult to deal with. Most of these tiny venues operated as sports bars during the day and weeknights. Rock 'n' roll bands were an irritation that managers begrudgingly relented to on weekends. The bands were often treated like a necessary evil. By 2007, I was tired of these places and I was afraid I might start drinking again out of boredom and frustration.

I drove for Fastfrate, Lhesa worked at the hospital, and our lives were rolling along. But our girls were growing and we needed a place to call our own. Lhesa's credit was in good shape and we bought a house 45 minutes outside of Vancouver in the city of Chilliwack. The distance to Vancouver made it tougher to keep playing with Big Radio and our shows became rare occurrences. The drinking and driving laws stiffened in British Columbia and so I played the shows straight. Crowds thinned a result of the crackdown on drinking drivers and gigs slowly disappeared.

The sober reality of the dying pub circuit was all too clear to me and I felt my days of playing in a band were finally ending. Several months passed without a gig and I realized it didn't bother me. I dug deeper into straight life. I was out of music, once and for all.

It wasn't nearly as devastating as it would have been a couple years earlier. God knows, I had given music a good shot and stuck with it long after most people would have given up. I was proud of that and I found it comforting. I had made peace with never grabbing the brass ring and I found myself more content each day with family life and working 9 to 5. The routine of getting up each morning, having breakfast with my family, and going to work was soothing.

I'd never known this kind of consistency and continuity before. Having Lhesa, Hannah and Sophie in my daily life gave me a renewed spirit. I appreciated the beauty of my world and the people in it. I was more forgiving and my optimism about the future flourished. Days spent alone in the cab of my truck gave me time to think both ahead and behind. In these moments of introspection, I remembered the past as a way to reconcile the mistakes as learning experiences and use them to keep moving toward a better future.

I didn't want to hate who I had been. But it was painful to remember some of the things I had said and done over the years and to think about the pain I had caused others. At first, it was difficult to re-visit the past and I was careful to not delve too deeply. I tried to look ahead more than back and concentrate on my present and future. I wanted to close the dark doors behind me.

The hiatus from performing gave me time and distance to think. My life had been a series of starting over.

The impetus for rebuilding each time was usually a complete destruction of what came before. Not this time, this time I was building on what I had.

I tried to face the truth about myself head on. I knew I'd allowed myself to fail at teaching. It wasn't The Wall, or the university, or the politics of Public Education, that made me quit. I did it to myself and I'd done the same with music. I blamed anyone and everyone for my lack of success.

One common element was present during all of those

disappointing turns and breakdowns: me. Sure, there was a bit of back luck and bad timing, but through it all I had made choices. My frustrated sense of entitlement, the chip on my shoulder; I was the wounded martyr. Enough.

It was time to step out of those roles and face reality. I was just a person living in the world.

Forgive yourself and then move forward. That's what people do.

Chapter Twenty-Four

By the summer of 2008, I had put enough distance and fresh perspective between my present and my past that most of my demons had been exorcized. Occasionally, bad memories would pop up at bedtime or sitting at a stoplight, and I would shudder less each day as I realized they would serve as cautionary flags. I remembered good things about my past and even allowed old friends to convince me I had, at times, been way too hard on myself. My job was going well, Lhesa and the kids were happy, and I felt good. I loved my new life.

The only complain I had was with my left hip. The pain from my hockey concussion never returned, but my hip had become progressively more painful and I walked with a limp. It had come upon me gradually, and I'd accepted it as something I might have to live with. But I could no longer press the heavy clutch in the truck without discomfort, and I couldn't play sports with my kids the way I wanted to.

I went to my doctor and he referred me to an orthopedic specialist. The abuse I'd taken playing hockey had broken down the cartilage in the joint and what little cartilage remained had calcified leaving only bone on bone. The specialist told me that, until recently, it was unlikely that I would have been a candidate for hip surgery because I was so young. I thanked him for that. He said that my hip joint was intact and would not need replacing, but there was a new procedure for cases like mine called resurfacing. He explained he would cut the thigh open wide, file down the mating surfaces of the hip and replace each contact surface with metal. It sounded gruesome, but I was excited about the chance to live without the pain.

The day soon came and I went under the knife for six hours.

When I awoke my doctor told me the operation was a success. I would have to stay in the hospital for a couple of weeks, but after a few months I'd feel better than I had in years. I wanted to get excited, but the morphine gave me headaches and messed with my head. I was a miserable patient. The catheter was a nightmare and the pain of physiotherapy was excruciating. There were also strange dreams and waking hallucinations brought on by the medication.

One night I was lying in bed listening to a movie in the room next door that I recognized as First Knight. The next thing I remembered was lying on a grass field looking up at a gray, cloudy sky. I could hear the sounds of cheering and hoof beats around me. My hip was hurting badly.

I was in a large jousting arena, wearing the same knight's outfit I had worn at my wedding. I had been thrown from my horse, which was pawing the ground beside me. I recognized the animal as the one I watched die on the Coquihalla summit. Breath steamed from his muzzle and I looked around me. People were both cheering and jeering as I tried to get to my feet. A spike of intense pain shot up from my hip and I looked down to inspect my injury. My left hip was swollen and the skin was torn wide open. The wound was covered in blood and I could see parts of the joint protruding through the jagged flesh. I was horrified and screamed for help. No one heard me. I screamed again. There was only the cheers and catcalls from the spectators lining the jousting track. I fell back and everything went black. I awoke on a table with two women in peasant garb pouring water onto my hip and dabbing the wound with blood-soaked rags. The pain was unbearable and I pushed their hands away, screaming at them to leave me alone. They ran from the room. I could see my armor and chain mail hanging from a hook on the wall. My sword was leaning against a small table next to where I lay and I reached out to grab the handle. The metal was cold and I strained to pull the heavy weapon from its sheath. I screamed against the pain in my hip and became enraged at my helplessness. I turned onto my right side and began hacking at the wounded hip with the sword. I couldn't feel it, yet it was cutting through the center of the joint. I got deeper with each swing until the severed leg fell to the dirt floor with a sickening thud. The pain disappeared. A wave of relief came over me and I looked down at my hip. My leg was gone. The wound was closed. There was no blood, fresh white rags covered where my leg had joined at the hip. I felt tears streaming down my cheeks. I lay my head down on the cold table and closed my eyes. It was done.

I woke up the next day, the dream still fresh in my thoughts. I ran the details back through my head and marveled at how graphic it was. I laughed at the thought of hacking my own leg off, and shook my head. Wow, morphine was something else.

I have vague memories of people coming to visit me; I have since asked them what I was like. The general consensus was that I was "miserable and mostly incoherent." It was an experience I never want to repeat. The next three months were a series of self-injected blood thinners, bandage changes, weeks with crutches, weeks with a cane, and finally back to work. Soon my hip was stronger than it had been in years and I was completely pain free.

My doctor said my recuperation had been remarkable and that my recovery was ideal. I felt blessed. I hadn't realized how much pain I'd lived with for all those years. I thought about the amputation dream and formulated a hypothesis about its meanings.

In its most literal sense, I had freed myself from the pain of my damaged hip and was relieved. I remembered the sight of seeing my body, no longer whole and feeling remorse about the missing appendage. I wondered if the relief was an analogy to the way my life had become so much better after saying goodbye to music. It too was an amputation of sorts. I had cut music from my life to divorce myself from the pain.

Lhesa told me many times she thought my decision to leave music completely had been harsh and extreme. Why did it have to be all or nothing? I explained how I was disappointed in playing in pubs and how my drinking went hand in hand. She argued that other guys were probably doing it for the enjoyment and extra cash. They were able to separate the party from the show, and so could I. She was right, but I knew it would only be a matter of time before the joy wore off again.

Still, there had to be a way I could enjoy music. Lhesa asked me to think about what I wanted from music and picture myself there. The conversation got me thinking. My head was in a much better place now that I was living life without pain, both physically and emotionally. It was fun, for the first time in a long time, to think back to the joys that years of performing had given me. I steered clear of ruminating on the disappointments and pitfalls and concentrated on what was good. I thought about the pure joy of singing, going on KISS expeditions with Les Starkey, and bringing the rock 'n' roll caravan to all those towns. I imagined a life where I could go out on short jaunts around the world, sing to happy audiences of thousands, stay in wonderful accommodations, eat good food, and make decent money to do it.

But how could I do that? I didn't have any hit songs. I wasn't a star. But, I could sing and perform. There must be a way to create the ideal situation I imagined. I tried to conjure up scenarios where I could make my fantasy career a reality. It was harmless fun and a great way to occupy myself in the cab of my truck for 10 or 12 hours a day.

One day Lhesa's brother, Jim, announced he was getting married. He and his fiancée, Shannon, had arranged to have the ceremony in Las Vegas at one of those little chapels, and Lhesa and I were asked to attend as maid of honor and best man. We stayed at the Monte Carlo hotel, on the main strip. It was a fabulous way to spend a week, visiting the attractions, trying my hand at gambling, and walking up and down Las Vegas Boulevard.

We all went down to the cabaret to watch a show. The group performing was a tribute to Prince, called Purple Rain. It was a good show and the cast paid a lot of attention to detail. The lead singer was not a dead ringer for Prince, but his costumes were authentic, his moves were well executed, and he was an accomplished guitar player. I watched the band and the response from the crowd. People were dancing, singing the words, and their expressions were those of pure joy. Prince had quite a few hits, and these guys were as close as you could get to seeing the actual artist in concert. And it only cost 10 bucks to get in the door. You couldn't see the real Prince for even 10 times that price. As much as I appreciated Prince as a composer, entertainer, and musician, this tribute band was close enough for me. I'd enjoyed the Prince experience, and I figured that was also what most of these people would take away from this evening.

I looked around at the magnificent cabaret: this was the kind of gig I had pictured in my fantasy dream-gig-scenario. People enjoyed the band and it was all in a fun atmosphere. It was reminiscent of my karaoke night in Mexico. Everyone was on vacation. There was dancing, singing, and everyone was there to have a good time. That was the kind of audience I wanted. I allowed my eyes to blur and let the atmosphere envelope me. And then it hit me.

This was it! This was what I was looking for! It was perfect. I looked around at the band, the room, and the audience one more time and realized I had found the answer: I didn't need a hit song; I didn't need to find joy performing in depressing bars. I was a singer and a performer. And that was the true essence of what my joy had been all along. It was what I wanted to do since the opening night of Old King Cole. I didn't care about a hit record then and I realized I no longer cared about it now. What I wanted from music was to feel the joy of performing again. I wanted to share something with an audience that would make the evening just like the one I had seen in Las Vegas and that night in Mexico. I reeled with excitement as I envisioned the path in front of me like the yellow brick road. I wanted the music, the adventure, and the beautiful ecstasy of shared joy. And now, I knew how to make that desire come true. Euphoria overtook me. I couldn't wait to get started.

CHAPTER TWENTY-FIVE

I n the days that followed, my long hours in the truck were spent hatching my plans. I thought about which artist to create my tribute to and how I would build the band's career. It was fun and I realized how much I had missed the process of building an act.

As a young artist I had decided on my goals and set out to achieve them. Although my ideas for success had been different then, I knew the tools I had acquired for building a band would serve me well. I would handle the business myself. This was not a record deal I was chasing. There would be no manager. I was building a band, once again, and I would use all of my experience to make it successful. I began to plot out a lucid plan for success.

I knew from the moment I started to build the tribute project I would have to crystallize my goals and draw a path directly towards them. I established a number of checkpoints in the form of short-term goals, and established what the markers would be and how to recognize them. The procedures I learned while making business plans in university gave me new tools for business and I decided to apply those methodical approaches. My plan included:

- Market research - who was doing what where and with what level of success
- Which artist would yield the largest potential market share
- Legal issues?
- Timeline for the project
- Mission/Philosophy
- Musicians
- Test Market

- Capital/Start-up costs
- Web Presence
- Showcase for agents and buyers
- Use feedback, online fan numbers, and gig attendance to ascertain growth
- Create solid benchmarks for success

Once I felt the band was ready we'd head out and spend six months establishing the domestic market. After that we'd have to do research for immigration and visa requirement for US ventures. We could use the income from domestic dates to finance showcase opportunities for the international market. I set a goal to play Las Vegas and at least two major US markets within the first 24 months. That would raise the band's price in the marketplace, and leverage opportunities for venturing overseas. Within five years I planned to have a solid, lucrative calendar consisting of Canadian dates during the warm summer months, and migrate to warmer, international locations during the cold, Canadian winters.

The process of building a new band's career path had never been so clear. I could see the five year plan unfold in front of me. With my new found clarity, I knew where I was going and how to get there. I knew what signposts to watch for, and I could envision all of the yardsticks I would use to measure the project's success.

I began to refer to my business plan as the simple plan, even though it was a tall order. Put a band together, market it properly, make some clever calculated risks, and use the markers and the finish line ahead to guide my way.

Although it would require a lot of hard work, some measures of luck, and a good band, the plan was sound. I found out as much as

I could about tribute bands and the tribute marketplace. I scoured the Internet for articles. I even went to the library to find a how-to book on forming a tribute band. There weren't any. Online sources offered articles about celebrity impersonators and tribute bands, but nothing existed that could be considered a how-to book.

I knew tribute bands were not new, but it seemed rock tributes, like the Prince show in Las Vegas, were fairly new. Rock 'n' roll fans were older now. The '70s teenagers who rocked out to Led Zeppelin and Aerosmith were now in their 50s. They were the ones in the casinos and Las Vegas show lounges.

The only rock tribute artist I knew during my club days was Guy Jones. Guy had an Alice Cooper Tribute show that was spectacular. He had figured out a way to simulate hanging himself using a harness and had at least one huge snake wrapped around him at any given time. Guy had the makeup and clothing that lent an authenticity to the whole show. There were a few others I considered who might be able to help, but in the end I decided to do it on my own. I found links to thousands of tribute bands, but there was little information about the growing tribute phenomenon or the history behind the movement.

Rock and Country superstars dominated the list of the celebrities that were the target for many tributes, while scores of others paid tribute to a variety of other musical genres. Tribute artists and bands attempted to evoke the spirit of the original artist by creating look-alike, sound-alike presentations and found a viable market niche in the business of live entertainment. The first tribute artists and bands rose in response to a desire to experience the faux representation of acts that were either dead, or had stopped touring.

One of the first things that struck me about the viability of tributes in the marketplace was the cost of a tribute performer relative to what the actual artist would cost. My Purple Rain ticket had been a fraction of the price I would have paid to see Prince, and I knew the economic model wouldn't be lost on entertainment buyers. Tribute bands could offer the same songs and a similar experience to the original artist; in turn, the ticket price was lower, and smaller venues could host the event without having to have large attendance numbers to offset costs.

The end result was the buyer had a higher margin of profit, the music fan enjoyed an affordable evening with an ersatz version of their favorite artist, and everybody went home happy. Well, almost everybody.

Tribute bands and the artists who have come to enjoy success in impersonation careers have been regarded in infamy in the hearts and minds of many of the emulated entertainers, their fans, and many musicians. Many perceive celebrity doppelgängers as a pox on the face of original creativity. I read a caustic diatribe from a well-known Vancouver journalist how tribute bands and singers were nothing but failures as composers, and he slammed tribute bands and the ever-expanding tribute marketplace as a vulgar, lecherous cash-grab.

The article berated tribute musicians for sacrificing their musical integrity and artistic merits while condemning tribute artists as both inferior and less valid than singers and songwriters of original compositions. The writer wasn't citing any plagiarism by the performers, but rather they were adopting the songs and likeness of a popular artist for what he deemed was an opportunistic exploitation for personal gain. He argued that a tribute is an insidious flattery at best and suggests a lack, or wanting, of personal creativity on the part of the tribute performer. I'm paraphrasing, but his version was equally brutal.

When I first played clubs in 1979, I had never seen a tribute band and I wasn't really conscious of them. I'd only seen some celebrity impersonators on TV, but mostly they were cheesy satires of sequined-jumpsuit wearing Elvis Presley lookalikes singing to blue-haired old ladies in Las Vegas cocktail lounges. Impersonator acts were considered cliché in the social conscience and had been relegated to D-list and carnival sideshow status. Musical impersonators had met with much criticism from music aficionados and the entertainment industry alike and their opinions were strong on the subject. Tribute bands were copycats without integrity. They were leeches riding on the coattails of others and unable to create their own art.

I'd heard so many passionate conversations on what real art was. I remembered my own stuffy elitism during certain periods of my musical growth. I would listen as people waxed on ad nauseam about art vs. commerce, original songs vs. covers. It was all so inane.

True art was the product of original work, period, some would decide. Everything else was just mimicry, as far as they were concerned. Even then, I knew it was an old argument. There is a long-standing stigma put on artists who perform the songs of others. I didn't play covers because my songs were shite; some of my songs had done well and were played on the radio. All I knew was that I liked singing and playing. I enjoyed the exploration of music regardless of whose songs I played.

I knew I would have to face the possible onslaught of detractors and suffer the derision of copycat haters everywhere. But I was determined to make the very best tribute I could and then damn the torpedoes. I wasn't going to hurt the artist I was saluting. If nothing else, it raised awareness about an artist's music.

It didn't take long before I left the nagging artistic quandaries behind. The decision to build the band was no longer in question. I had other concerns. It was a marketplace I barely knew and I would have to learn fast. There was the work of researching the particular artist, finding players perfect for the job, then replicating the look, sound, and concert presentation values that would satisfy even those fans that had seen the real artist in concert. First of all, I still had no idea which artist I would cover.

Back to the computer I went. A keyword search for tribute bands produced a staggering list of results. I waded through days of reading with my initial focus on learning which artists had been covered the most. At the top of the list were: Elvis Presley followed by The Beatles, Abba, and Neil Diamond. It was logical as these were all multi-million selling artists with a wide appeal. There was no way I was going to enter that over-crowded fray. (I didn't really look or sound like any of those guys anyways.) I knew what I chose would have to be heavy enough to satisfy my rock urges, while also being middle of the road and versatile enough to appeal to a large age range in a variety of venues and settings.

I thought about all of the bands who fell into those categories and whose material I would enjoy performing. The list was shorter than I hoped. I considered artists like Tom Petty, Bob Seger, John Cougar, and Billy Idol. I could do a pretty good imitation of those artists, as I had performed a lot of their material in my day. I could make a decent attempt at looking like anyone of them. I thought about Eddie and The Cruisers, but there wasn't enough hit material to fill a show. Then it hit me. Bon Jovi!

I'd been compared to Jon Bon Jovi ever since "Runaway." I had fielded hundreds of comments about the similar sound of our voices. I thought back to the kids who had made those comments in school and I recalled my Mexican honeymoon as Señor Bon Jovi. I felt I had found my answer, or perhaps it had found me. Either way, I decided to form a Bon Jovi tribute band. I knew at once I couldn't have made a better choice.

Chapter Twenty-Six

Building a tribute band was some of the most difficult work I had ever undertaken. After all the years I had spent performing in bands, putting bands together, keeping them alive, learning and rehearsing songs, and becoming a better performer I was about to be put to the test building a completely new kind of band. I was launching a tribute to Bon Jovi. I would have to learn about Bon Jovi, get a band to look and sound like Bon Jovi, and I would have to learn to sing like Jon, move like Jon, look like Jon, and if possible, even think like Jon. I was nervous, but resolute. I was going to build the best Bon Jovi Tribute in the world and we would be successful. All I had to do was figure out how to be the best. It was time to start some research.

Thanks to the Internet, I could find most of the information I would probably need. The rest could be found in books, magazines, interviews and live shows.

I started looking at other Bon Jovi tributes to see what my competition was doing. There were quite a few Bon Jovi tributes already in existence and I was disappointed to see my tribute choice was anything but original. Upon further investigation, I found several were no longer in existence and many performed in languages other than English. Almost two-thirds of the bands were from Europe. One or two of them sounded somewhat authentic and had one or two guys that looked like their Bon Jovi counterparts. The same was true for a handful of North America Bon Jovi tributes. In most cases, the singer was more or less reminiscent of Jon and sometimes they would have a good Tico look-alike, or maybe their Richie looked similar to the real Sambora. But there were no Bon Jovi tribute bands where the whole band looked similar to Bon Jovi, and certainly none that coupled this with an authentic sound.

I narrowed my field of study down to five or six Bon Jovi tributes that appeared to have put forth some effort. I looked at their websites to assess the effectiveness of their marketing. As a guy who had been part of the modern computer revolution from the start, I knew how powerful the Internet had become as a sales tool. Some of the other tributes' online ideas were decent and got me thinking about how I could improve upon them. The videos of other Bon Jovi tribute bands were grainy live footage. Some of their artwork was alright, but most were hand-drawn, or anemic vector graphics. The only higher-end graphics were obvious rip-offs of actual Bon Jovi artwork.

I researched litigation or copyright infringements. The only one I found was an Internet story about how Jon Bon Jovi had issued a cease and desist order against an all-female Bon Jovi tribute band called Blonde Jovi. The article said the Bon Jovi organization argued the name Blonde Jovi was too similar-sounding to Bon Jovi and it might cause confusion for consumers regarding the Bon Jovi brand. Blonde Jovi subsequently changed their name and I couldn't find a link to their new identity.

Other than that, there was no further information regarding any real action taken against a tribute band. No legal precedents had been set to prevent tribute bands from performing the material of popular artists while simultaneously presenting the material dressed in the same likeness as the original artist. I took this as a good sign. The market was free and clear of any potential litigations and requirements for legal compliance. Legally, tribute bands were the same as any other cover band, playing someone else's songs for money.

I believed a tribute act was much more than a band playing cover tunes; it was a musical homage to an artist with a legions of loyal fans. I felt creating a tribute to such an adored artist constituted a huge responsibility and it was one I took seriously. What I had to figure out was how to effectively communicate to Bon Jovi's fans that I wasn't doing this as a parasitic cash grab.

Over the years I'd heard stories about how rabid Bon Jovi fans are. Those who loved them – really loved them. Fans were protective and territorial. How would my tribute sit with them? Authenticity was a crucial element. I hoped if it was obvious to Bon Jovi fans that a great deal of educated effort went into creating my show then I had to believe that they would respond positively. In order to do that, I had to become an expert on Bon Jovi. I also needed Bon Jovi fans to know my tribute was an homage and that I respected there was only one true Bon Jovi.

I was mulling all of these things and I came up with a slogan I thought would help. Under the name of my band, I would put the tag line: "Proudly second best – only Bon Jovi does it better." I liked the phrase as it served to illustrate our deference for Bon Jovi, and assert we were unmatched in our field. It was perfect.

Even without being a Bon Jovi expert I knew my reverence toward the band was genuine. I figured the only challenge with using that tag line would be that I would have to make sure the band I created was the best; at least in as much that I believed it was true. For this to happen I would need to put together a killer band, but before I went looking for players, I needed to learn all I could about Bon Jovi. In order to teach four other guys about Bon Jovi I would have to learn a great deal more about the band before I could teach anyone else.

The first step was to study as much Bon Jovi concert footage that I could get my hands on. I watched over 50 concerts, interviews, music videos, and miscellaneous segments from their earliest shows to their most recent: I had full-concert videos, bootleg camcorder videos, studio shot MTV-style music videos, as well as VHS and DVD professionally-shot videos. I had a lot of material to review.

YouTube was a great source and gave me a sampling of the years of interviews that Jon and the band had done since the '80s. I watched the oldest videos first to make some sort of chronological sense to how the band had progressed in terms of clothing style and presentation.

The first full video I watched was a concert from Tokyo in 1984. This was footage from part of a tour for the first and second Bon Jovi albums when the band's only big hit was "Runaway." This was the Bon Jovi I remembered as a young musician. The show was a parade of spandex, makeup, teased hair, and kitschy poses. This would not be the direction for my tribute band.

I still didn't have a concrete decision on which phase of Bon Jovi's career I would focus on for my band's presentation. I was not a young man anymore, and neither was Jon. There was no way I was going to try and look like a pretty-boy twenty-something. Besides, one look at a middle-aged man prancing about in feathered hair and spandex would send even the most rabid old-school Bon Jovi fans running for the exits.

After the Tokyo 1984 videos, I watched the Slippery When Wet era. The band had matured both musically and in their look. Songs were cleverly crafted with giant hooks and more sophisticated lyrics. Their image was more refined yet still had the glam sensibilities of the period. The Santa Fe affectations were now present, most notably in "Wanted Dead or Alive." The rapport between Jon and Richie was evident and a big part of the group's live allure.

I moved into the New Jersey videos and there was little difference from the Slippery When Wet videos. Fans and critics have suggested these two albums are somewhat interchangeable. They had been released close together and not a lot of growth was evident.

The video Tokyo 1988, showed Bon Jovi at their best to this point. The big concert tricks were finely honed and the material was played flawlessly. What they did, they did well. Each guy had their role and the band was a cohesive unit. There was still enough bombast in the group and presentation to make them outrageous enough for '80s hard rock sensibilities, yet the maturity of the group showed in their performance.

Keep The Faith was the biggest departure the band had made from their past. It wasn't just the haircuts; the music was darker, more introspective, and more polished. The band had grown up and Jon had come into his own as a bona fide international icon. The Blaze Of Glory album and videos featured musical guest stars on the recordings and from the Young Guns film. You could tell Jon had said goodbye to his pretty boy days and had matured as a songwriter and entertainer. The rock 'n' roll cowboy image was manly. It was a great place to start thinking about the image for my tribute.

These Days featured the guys with slightly longer hair length and I felt this snapshot in time would work well as part of a composite idea I had been formulating. I wanted to create more of a blended overall presentation that would satisfy both classic Bon Jovi fans as well as those more in tune with Bon Jovi's contemporary look and sound.

Musically, I knew in order to present a show that would satisfy both types of Bon Jovi fans, it would have to contain material from the beginning to present day. As I continued to watch the videos I made notes of the specific elements that made up the overall feel of the band at those points in history.

The 1995 DVD Live From London blended the Bon Jovi's past songs and their new, more substantial direction. The 2000 DVD The Crush Tour showed even more evolution, and I felt it contained the tightest live performances I had heard the band play.

I watched a VH1 video called One Last Wild Night and it was the best song line-up I had seen. Although the songs were quite up-tempo compared to the original recordings, the flow from song to song was amazing. I jotted down the order. It was the perfect set list that addressed a great cross section of the band's catalogue.

Now I had the perfect sample of videos to give to the new players to establish what I was looking for in costuming, approach, and song flow. Interviews gave a sense of the various personalities in Bon Jovi, and I made a DVD of a number of them to help my guys research their Bon Jovi counterparts.

It was starting to feel like I would be able to effectively communicate this project musically and visually, as well as get a good sense of the spirit and camaraderie that was in Bon Jovi.

After months of research I realized Bon Jovi was far more than just a band to many of their fans, – they were an institution and a way of life. This was much more than building a band. It was building an ode to a philosophy, a spirit, and a beloved icon.

Chapter Twenty-Seven

The idea of putting together a Bon Jovi tribute band was definitely scary. Here was a band that had captured the hearts of hundreds of millions of people, sold over a hundred million records, and forged an iconic place into the social consciousness of popular culture. During those months of research I gained much respect for their work ethic. I admired their resilient camaraderie, and I marveled at their vision, foresight, and adaptability to change.

Bon Jovi was a world-travelled outfit that effectively navigated decades of success and struggle. They managed to stay solid and musically relevant. They kept all (or most) of their original fans and constantly added new ones. Through it all they'd stayed faithfully connected to their roots and to the blue-collar ethos that appealed to the masses. They were down to earth rock stars; a bunch of guys you could probably easily talk to without feeling insignificant.

Many of the groups that sprang from the glam era were poster boys for excess, decadence, and nihilistic over-indulgence. Bon Jovi passed through that period and come out the other side un-jaded by the spoils and accolades of the crazy '80s. They remained sensible people who appreciated their fans, their roots, their country, and the plight of the larger world.

I knew I would have to indoctrinate my guys into these sensibilities. It was important they all understood I wanted authenticity in look, sound, and spirit. It was also important to communicate to our audiences that we were Bon Jovi *fans*.

Bon Jovi has a way of making you want to be a part of them and what they do. They are a great live band with likeable songs and their harmony and humility is endearing. The guys in Bon

Jovi love and appreciate their fans as much as their fans love and appreciate them. That is the essence of Bon Jovi – mutual respect and admiration. Emulating that spirit would be the cornerstone of constructing the band and the show.

I started to assemble a list of the criteria my line-up needed. First, I wanted the band to travel out of Canada so I needed players with clean passports. This narrowed my list immediately. Then I needed guys who could look, play and act like their Bon Jovi counterparts. They had to be able to travel, be mature, responsible and they had to be able to sing. My list was now very small, but at least I had some ideas for the kind of guys I was looking for.

Shopping for players in clubs and luring members from other bands is an oft-used avenue for finding players. Jon Bon Jovi gathered his band by meeting other musicians in bands around the New Jersey scene. He enlisted bassist Alec John Such from New Jersey locals Phantom's Opera. Through Alec, Jon met Tico Torres who also played with Phantom's Opera. He was able to convince the two of them to join his band.

Richie Sambora had played with a New Jersey club band called The Extremes and then later with Alec John Such in The Message. One night he came down to a club where Jon was performing and was enthralled by Jon's performance. After the set was over, Richie approached Jon and declared, "I am going to be your new guitar player." Jon hired him on the spot and the rest is history.

By 1983, Jon had assembled the now-famous Bon Jovi line-up that has, with only a single member change, remained together for over 30 years. (Alec left as bass player in 1994 and was never replaced by a permanent member.) As a rock fan, I think this is remarkable. As a bandleader, I am amazed. Putting a band together is challenging, being in a band is difficult, but keeping one together is almost impossible. As I researched Bon Jovi's career, I empathized with Jon's challenges and respected the way he endured the pitfalls and stumbling blocks. He kept that band strong and they took on the world together. I knew this was no easy feat. So many things could break up a band. So many times, it was the band itself.

In his legendary collection of Star Wars films, George Lucas described the Old Republic as "The Republic of Legend…" He envisaged this galactic union as impervious to any forces against it – yet could be destroyed from internal struggles. "Like the greatest of trees, able to withstand any external attack, the Republic rotted from within…"

I have recounted a paraphrased version of this to many musicians over the years. Rock 'n' roll bands become a republic. They are tribal groups of once disparate individuals united to pursue a common goal. As strong as the union becomes, inner turmoil often causes its demise. If you're lucky, a band can become like a family.

I wanted my new band to be strong. I needed mature guys that were not mentally over the hill and in good physical shape. I wanted them to have ambition and a desire to succeed. My list was getting more comprehensive each day and I finally decided it was time to find players. So off I went, searching for Bon Jovi doubles.

Doug Grant had been with me since the late eighties and I knew that I wanted him on drums. He had a clean passport, was an awesome player, and his look was pretty close to Tico Torres. Doug had the reputation of being consistently reliable over the past two decades. It was hard not to love the guy. He was a well-respected drummer, and one of the nicest people you will ever meet. I needed him in my band.

I gave him my whole song and dance about learning about tributes, Bon Jovi, my philosophy, and the philosophy I wanted for the band and Doug understood it all right away. He said he loved the idea and thought it was brilliant. He was in.

Now I needed a guitar player. Randy Robertson was one of the coolest guys I'd ever met. It didn't hurt that women liked him too. He had long, dark hair, and facial features that were similar to a modern-day version of Richie Sambora. I knew he could play guitar well and I was confident he would also be able to sing Richie's challenging vocal harmonies too. He was my first choice.

I asked Doug if he thought Randy would be interested, and Doug said "It all depends how you sell it to him, I guess."

I didn't want to have to go through all of the philosophy and machinations behind my thinking, as I'd done for Doug. Randy wasn't the kind of guy for long, drawn out explanations about things. He was an intellectual and pragmatic in the way he viewed life and music. He was also a songwriter and still interested in playing original music. I decided I needed to show Randy my plan for a band that was going to do well in the marketplace, then he could make his own decision.

I made a Bon Jovi tribute poster on my computer to give the impression it was a working band. The graphics were not the best in the world, but the overall feel of the poster was professional and belied a sense the band was established and credible. I arranged a meeting with Randy under the guise that I wanted to talk about picking up some casual work here and there doing a few pub gigs together.

Randy was interested and I called Doug, told him about my

ruse, and asked him to let me do all the talking at the meeting.

When we were all together, I told Randy I had made the decision to come out of retirement. An amazing opportunity had come my way as the vocalist for a new Bon Jovi tribute band. I showed him the poster and raved about how the band was going to do very well in the tribute marketplace. Randy congratulated me and said he felt tributes were the way to go these days. He thought my timing was excellent, and believed the tribute market was only going to get stronger. He asked me about the guys in the band and I told him how the drummer was a dead-ringer for Tico, the other guys were decent, but I felt the Richie guy was the weak link. I saw Doug squirm as he tried not to laugh. I kicked him softly under the table.

"Man, I so wish you were the Richie guy." I said with a nice touch of regret.

"No doubt!" Randy replied without any hesitation. "Maybe you should tell them that."

That was all I needed to hear.

Doug burst out laughing. "Ted, you're such a jerk!"

After he stopped laughing, Doug and I took turns giving Randy the short version of the spiel. It only took a couple sentences before Randy said, "Sign me up!" The three of us laughed at my hokey, but effective, ploy.

Now we needed a bass player. Mike Champigny was referral from Robert Graves of Big Radio days. He was a great bass player and a good singer. I found Mike on Facebook and his photos reminded me of Hugh McDonald, (Bon Jovi's unofficial replacement for Alec John Such) when Hugh performed on the Live From London DVD.

With the same beret and sunglasses that Hugh wore in that video, Mike would pass as a good facsimile. Doug knew Mike and said he was a good guy. He offered to make initial contact and soon arranged a meeting. Mike had a peaceful nature and a sweet disposition, and I liked the guy right away. Mike was everything Robert had claimed. His bass playing and vocals were great and I was inspired by the potential for this line-up.

The four of us got together for a drink and began to talk about rehearsal plans and discuss who we thought who would play keys. The guy I thought would be perfect in the role of David Bryan was already busy with a popular Canadian recording act. He'd told me straight up that he wouldn't be able to commit to any other projects right now. Doug and Randy reminded me about a keyboardist that had once come up and jammed with us at a gig. He was a decent guy, but came with some warnings. Rumor had it he wasn't that reliable and had backed out of a few gigs at the last moment, but we decided to audition him anyway. I had often heard rumors about guys and later found out they weren't true. The least we could do was check the guy out.

He had the basic requirements, clean passport, and he even had blonde, curly hair like David Bryan. He was great player. His sounds were excellent, and for the most part, he seemed decent. He came from an affluent background and there was an air of elitism to his personality, but overall he appeared to be reasonable person. He was a bit morose at times and he sometimes reminded me of Eeyore, the depressed donkey from Winnie The Pooh. I figured as the project moved forward he would become inspired and hopefully warm up to the rest of us. It would just be a matter of time.

Chapter Twenty-Eight

I'd been rehearsing alone for weeks in my basement. Jon's vibrato was similar to mine and I tuned into it right away. His tone, annunciation, and affectations would take some time to master, but I understood the place that most of this came from for him. The process of singing like Jon was enjoyable and I soon realized the potential rewards that this project held for me. Jon was a great singer and this tribute would give me plenty of opportunities to showcase my own voice.

The other two big tasks of getting into the role of Jon Bon Jovi were establishing wardrobe and copying his onstage moves. I noticed the way Jon moved onstage was similar to how I moved. The way he grabbed the microphone was close enough, although the way he stood in front of it was different.

His walk, his gait, and his general mannerisms with his hand gestures and various rock posturing were also a little different from what I did, yet there was a familiarity in what he was doing. I didn't move exactly the way that he did, but I understood it. The way Jon bounced up and down while singing at the microphone was something I had seen before. I scoured my brain trying to think where this had presented itself to me until I came up with the answer. It was Springsteen! All of those years I spent doing the Middle America thing with The Boss and Eddie and the Cruisers I had inherited some familiarity with New Jersey rock sensibilities. The bounce, which I have heard referred to as the Jersey Bop, was evident in Eddie Wilson, The Boss, and now in Jon Bon Jovi and Richie Sambora. I adopted it as part of my new approach when singing at the microphone.

My voice was getting closer to Jon's each day, and I practiced my Jon moves in front of the mirror until I had them down pat. My daughters, Hannah and Sophie, would sometimes join me and sing along while I practiced. The project had given our whole family a cool thing to share and we became die-hard Bon Jovi fans together. Soon the girls knew the words to all of the songs as well as I did and I used them as sounding boards for my progress in adopting Jon's vocal style and his moves.

I found a video called Learn To Play Bon Jovi and I practiced all of the guitar songs I would perform in the show. In more recent Bon Jovi concert videos, Jon had switched to a Takamine from the Ovation he had played in his earlier years. I learned the AP carved on his guitar was a salute to Al Parinello, the man who had rekindled his interest to play guitar again when he was a kid.

I went down to my local music store and tried out a few Takamine instruments and some Ovations too. I played several guitars from both makers and I found that I favored the Ovation look and feel. I purchased a black one and practiced with it over the next few weeks until I had Jon's guitar parts mastered.

I went down to the laundry room one day, where Lhesa was folding clothes, and got down on one knee and performed an intimate version of "(You Want To) Make a Memory" for her. It felt amazing to be able to share my joy with her. For several weeks now, Bon Jovi songs had been booming from the basement as a constant soundtrack to our lives and our house had become the House of Bon Jovi. Our neighbors had commented about it and their remonstrations regarding our constantly rocking house told me it hadn't escaped their notice.

Now I had to think about costumes. Wardrobe ideas were easier now that I had narrowed my focus down to those three specific concert videos. I found some fringed leather jackets that would suggest an ode to Jon's '80s days. I attacked my wardrobe choices from a song-by-song perspective and tried to find things that would serve each period. As a general rule, I would wear black leather pants - I still owned three pairs of those - and I also had a great pair of black leather chaps I could use as a throwback alternative. I got a couple of jean jackets and faded them with bleach in my bathtub until they looked just like ones Jon wore.

I knew a hairdresser from my bar days in the '80s named Alanah who was a huge Bon Jovi fan. She and I sat hours talking about Bon Jovi and I let her in on my tribute project. Alanah thought I would be perfect in the role as Jon. She was a great example of a Bon Jovi die-hard fan and it felt like a genuine affirmation for what I was doing. I told her I was in the process of gathering costuming and she showed me her impressive storehouse of Bon Jovi collectibles and clothing.

Alanah had purchased a black leather Bon Jovi 25th Anniversary jacket from the Bon Jovi organization and it didn't fit her, so she sold it to me. It was a beautiful, black lambskin with "Bon Jovi 25th Anniversary" embroidered on the back and the same cut as many of the leather jackets Jon often wore. It was a huge score and one I knew would be a staple of my wardrobe. Alanah also had a white-fringed leather jacket and she lent it to keep for as long as I liked. It was a perfect fit and I thought it would be ideal for a more vintage look when I performed older songs, such as Runaway, during the show.

She also had a bowling shirt from the Bon Jovi merchandise collection and said I could have it if I wanted it. It wasn't exactly something I could wear onstage, but it said Bon Jovi on the back and I envisioned how it might look if I had the sleeves removed. Jon often wore sleeveless shirts and I decided to take it to a tailor, along with some photos of Jon in one of his sleeveless shirts so she could duplicate it. There was also a Bon Jovi football jersey, a Slippery When Wet belt buckle, and a Bon Jovi coffee mug. I was blown away. I told Alanah how I appreciated her generosity and how I was grateful she believed I would do a good job at portraying Jon.

Before I left, she told me that she would cut my hair just like Jon's and she guaranteed that it would bring my overall look as close to Jon's as possible. We arranged to meet again soon and I went home that night feeling much better about where things were heading.

I had the book Jon Bon Jovi: The Biography by Laura Jackson. There was a picture of Jon on the front cover. I held the book next to my face in the mirror. I tried to find physical similarities between the two of us. We were somewhat closer in appearance nowadays than in previous years. Seeing Jon in terms of the man he had become was huge in putting my fears to rest about our resemblance and I made the decision to accept the positives. I dressed up in my Jon clothes and put my guitar around my neck. I grabbed my new Jon sunglasses that looked like the ones he had worn in the "One Last Wild Night" video and stood in front of the mirror. I swept my hair from right to left and smiled wide. Even I had to admit that if I saw me from a distance, I could be mistaken for Jon Bon Jovi.

I had the look, I was nailing the voice closer every day, I could play the parts on guitar with little effort, and I felt empowered more than I had been at any step of the project. It had already been months of work to get this far and it had all been worth it. As I looked in the mirror I began to think about how at my age this would probably be the last time I would spend this much effort in building a new project. It was, in all likelihood, my last kick at the can trying to create something successful on any level in music and I was going to give it everything I had.

I would create a whole band that had enough Bon Jovi sensibility and allusion that those who loved Bon Jovi would recognize and appreciate the effort, while those who were more casual fans would see a show that was dynamite. I was so excited. I was going after this with everything that I had left in tank. It was probably my last shot and I wanted to go out in a blaze of glory.

It was at that moment I knew I had found the name of my band.

Chapter Twenty-Nine

Now we just had to rehearse the songs. The first rehearsal was "You Give Love a Bad Name," and as soon as everyone was set up and ready we began to play. From the first bar of song, I was struck by the power of the band. I had been to enough first-time rehearsals to know not to get too discouraged by humble beginnings, but this was extraordinary from the top. I could see the other guys looking around as we played. They were surprised too!

We ripped through the song from beginning to end in one pass and it was obvious everyone had done their homework. When the song was over everyone commented on how cool it had been. We played it again to be sure it hadn't been a fluke. The song was even better the second time around. When it was done, Doug called out "Next!" and everyone laughed. We spent the next hour or so jamming bits and pieces of some other Bon Jovi songs that the guys knew collectively.

Afterwards we sat down and talked about the project. Eeyore was concerned about having to work too much as he had a job that paid him well and he didn't want to jeopardize it. I promised everyone that we would make the thing work for everybody and we all left that night feeling great. It was an amazing first rehearsal. This was real now and it was actually going to happen. I couldn't wait to get started rehearsing the rest of the songs.

Over the next nine months we rehearsed once each week, sometimes twice. Two or three times each month we met at someone's house and watched the three videos and discussed our characters and the various elements of the show we wanted to incorporate in ours.

Each guy spent time on their own perfecting their own parts and assembling costumes. Everyone got haircuts to match the look of the Bon Jovi guys in the three concert DVDs. I went to Alanah to have her craft me a Jon hairstyle. She understood completely my idea of compromise between the different looks Jon had in the mid-1990s up to present day and when she was done I was amazed. I walked into rehearsal the next day and the guys were blown away. Everyone looked good with their new hair, and we were even more inspired and excited.

***

Doug, Randy, Mike and I had grown close over the months, but Eeyore, despite fleeting moments of camaraderie here and there, gave the general impression that he was holding us and the project at arm's length. The guys approached me individually about it on a few occasions, but I dismissed their worries by telling them once we got out and played a few shows things would work out. A part of me wasn't so sure. The spirit of Bon Jovi had seeped into the hearts of the rest of us and we made it a point to invite Eeyore to every social event that we went to. Sometimes he came along and enjoyed himself, other times he was distant. He explained his relationship was taking a toll on him. We decided to leave things be and hope for the best.

The time came to get out and play a show. I booked a gig through a local agent to play a small club in Kamloops, BC called On The Rocks and on August 21, 2009, Blaze Of Glory made its debut.

We were so excited on the way to Kamloops. Morale was high

and we knew this was something big. After sound check we all had dinner and talked about how forming this tribute band had had such a great effect on all our lives. Eeyore thought it was all gobbledygook. He would roll his eyes and then go play with his equipment while the rest of us talked. Doug, Mike, and Randy had adapted to a group system that we were already seeing dividends from.

One of the things we had discussed was our behavior while we went anywhere as a band. Each member was an ambassador of the band and that we would be often perceived as a whole by any one member's behavior. It was critical to be pleasant and professional to everyone that we met. The waitresses and bar staff had remarked how nice everyone was, so we must have been doing something right—at least most of us had. Eeyore was a bit rude and often dismissed staff as though they were menials, but we attributed that to his affluent upbringing. We did our best to deflect it with mild jokes and redirection, and for the most part, we pulled it off.

After supper, a couple of the guys came to my room with concerns about Eeyore's behavior. I told them what we needed to do now was concentrate on the show. It was time to get ready.

I had my shower, did my hair, and put on my stage make up. I reached for the first shirt I would wear that night and looked at myself in the mirror. I couldn't believe it. A year of planning and now I was about to go on stage as Jon Bon Jovi. I put on my shirt, pulled on my leather pants and looked in the mirror again. I smiled. Nine months of watching videos and singing and dancing in my basement and rehearsing with my new band. It all came down to this one night. I grabbed my sunglasses and headed out the door.

Energy radiated from the guys was as we marched together and arrived at the club. The place was jumping inside and music blasted through the door as Doug went in to tell the manager we were ready to go on. I was nervous, but we all knew our parts. I kept my voice strong and even and said, "Have a good show, boys." We all bumped knuckles and exchanged words of encouragement.

Then we heard the DJ. "And now... from Vancouver... Blaze Of Glory!" The crowd erupted with cheers and applause as I called out, "Just do what we practiced!"

As soon as we entered the room every person in the over-packed house rose to their feet, screaming and whistling. The energy was palpable. I took a deep breath and smiled. People patted our backs, high-fives reached out from the crowd, cameras flashed, and girls yelled out "We love you!"

Once we were all in place, I looked over the crowd, waiting for the noise to die down. It was evident that wouldn't happen, so with my heart pounding, I motioned to Doug to count in the first song. We launched into "Raise Your Hands" and the music took over. I got swept up in the energy and was amazed as the crowd sang the words back to me. I looked back at the bar, no one was pouring drinks, and no one was ordering drinks. Everyone faced the stage. They all just cheered and sang for the entire first song.

When the first number ended I had to stop for a second to let the crowd applaud, but mostly so I could catch my breath and my composure. That four-minute song had gone by in what felt like 45 seconds. The rest of the evening was wonderful; but if I said I remembered every minute of it, I'd be lying. We played our hearts out and just let it all happen. These were die-hard Bon Jovi fans and they sang along to every song we played. When we tried to leave the stage, the crowd wouldn't let us and called us back for two long encore sets. They were still cheering as we left the club.

After we cleaned up, we went to Doug's room to celebrate. We were all in shock. The crowd had been so appreciative of the show. It was obvious to all of us they'd understood the intentions behind Blaze Of Glory. It was an affirmation we had communicated precisely what we had talked so much about during those months of rehearsal. We were onto something big.

The next morning, with the sound of the crowd still ringing in our ears, we went home victorious and inspired. We talked about what went well and what needed improving. It was the beginning of a process of rehash and tweak that we repeated for every show thereafter.

A couple of smaller local shows were booked to tighten up a few things. Then I reviewed the business plan. We had to increase our online presence, get promotional materials and get a promo video together. I had some experience in website design and making posters, but I was a rookie compared to Randy.

He ran a business creating websites and artwork on a commercial level and made us an amazing poster and website. We had little start-up capital, but I got a neighbor, an avid photographer, to shoot us in exchange for the photo credit. I arranged a free show at a local casino where some friends we knew would film us with their video cameras. The photos were great, the video was good too, and soon our website was at least as good, if not better than our strongest competitors.

Profiles were created on Twitter, Facebook, My Space, Reverb Nation, Sonic Bids, Gig Salad, Gigmasters, YouTube, and a number of tribute band websites. I called all the agents around town to drum up more gigs. The buzz about the band had reached most of their ears, and we got gigs well into 2010.

The gigs got larger and the spirit of the band grew larger. We were a band of brothers, almost. Eeyore's personal life was a constant struggle and his moods were unpredictable. The harder we tried to reach out to him, the more he pulled away. It was as if our Bon Jovi-fueled positivity was an annoyance to him and he was often distant whenever we explored deeper into our philosophies. On drives to gigs we would be so excited to share new revelations we had thought of or learned from Bon Jovi interviews, and he would sit in the back of the van with his headphones on, watching movies on his laptop, or working with his software programs.

He had created a complex system for his equipment setup and refused to play on any gear other than his own. We had grown past the point of having to haul a bulky backline with us and we had a nice rider that provided for all of our needs. Yet, on every trip we would pack Eeyore's enormous rig in the van. The guys had no problems expressing their concerns and resentments to me about his attitude and refusal to adapt to our way of doing things. His rig had become so complicated that it often took half of sound check before he was ready to play, and the rest of us had to wait around before we could finish and go for supper. At suppertime, he would be still brooding about his technical woes. As time went on his elaborate equipment became so problematic that it often malfunctioned, and he attempted to solve his problems by throwing more money at them.

Despite all our efforts to simplify, he kept spending more money and complained about how much the band was costing him.

He was quite vocal about how much of a liability the band was for him, and we believed he would quit if we didn't do something.

I approached Eeyore a couple of times and expressed my concern about how I didn't want any resentment between him and the rest of the band. He was defensive and argumentative and claimed I was exaggerating. His moods had begun to affect everyone in the band to such an extent we had to distance ourselves from him so as not to dampen the amazing experience the rest of us were having.

We were enjoying the time of our lives and we all had a sense that things were really taking off for the band. We didn't want Eeyore's problems to become our problems, and the whole thing became a dark secret that we were covering up. I urged the guys to continue reaching out to him and in the meantime I would be proactive and see what our options might be for a replacement.

The band grew leaps and bounds over the summer of 2010. The world was focused on Vancouver for the Olympics. We now played corporate shows and the band developed an upscale reputation in the marketplace. I searched for bigger and better gigs by combing the Internet and sending letters to hundreds of casinos across North America and overseas. I found a posting online advertising a callout for showcase acts to perform in Las Vegas for a convention. It was to be held that fall, and coincided perfectly with the period I had planned to play in the city.

Showcasing a band in Las Vegas was like high stakes poker with the odds definitely in favor of the house. The preparation proved to be expensive, and I began saving money from the gigs. I convinced Lhesa to loan me some money, as she had done before.

It was another huge leap of faith and it was not an easy decision for either of us. I did my best to explain the potential return on investment for the band, and ultimately for our family, but speculating on the music business was a tough sell. Lhesa finally relented and I promised to do everything I could to minimize the amount of money we would invest. Rooms at the convention hotel were expensive so I reserved cheaper ones down the street. The band would travel light so we didn't need a van, and we'd book the cheapest flights possible. The biggest expense for the trip would be the showcase fees. If we could find a sponsor that was an exhibitor, the costs would be substantially reduced. I combed the exhibitor's list on the convention roster to find potential names to solicit. I sent a letter of introduction to eight of them, citing some of the more prestigious events we had played over the past six months.

Edwin Rojas from Rojas Talent Group, an entertainment booking agency in Florida, returned my email within the hour. I was impressed with his prompt reply and how much he knew from the Blaze Of Glory website. I wasn't used to such immediate and thorough responses. He continued to impress me with his quick replies and jovial manner in our follow-up conversations. I was honest with him about how I was looking to reduce my costs and he appreciated my candor.

We made up a written agreement where he would sponsor Blaze Of Glory at the convention in Vegas in exchange for a percentage of any jobs we were offered from the showcase performance. We hadn't even been officially accepted yet, but he assured me we would. He had been to the conference a few years in a row and felt we were superior to any other rock act he had seen there.

Within a few days we were confirmed acceptance into the showcase. The band was ecstatic when I told them. It even seemed to lift Eeyore's mood somewhat and I hoped that a weekend in Las Vegas might be just the thing to show him he was in the right band and maybe he would start to embrace us more. I did research into visas and immigration for travelling to the US and soon found out why a lot of bands don't do it. It was a logistical nightmare and required the coordination of several agencies, filing of many forms, and a lot of smaller costs that added up to a much larger total.

I considered the expenses for this trip as an investment capital on my part and I looked at it as something that every new business owner has to do to some degree to speculate on the futures of his or her company.

I was so grateful for Lhesa's support and her belief in me. I felt a huge sense of responsibility and determination to make sure things went as well as possible. I pleaded with everyone in the band to be on their best behavior and they promised to deliver the best show of their lives. Everyone understood this represented the biggest opportunity the band had been given in our short existence and hopes ran high. The year had seen a steady climb in Blaze Of Glory's domestic market share and we were taking out first leap into the international marketplace. So far, my plan was working. The band was established, had a great local reputation, and we were going to Las Vegas - right on schedule.

CHAPTER THIRTY

The trip to Las Vegas was the coming-out party for Blaze Of Glory. Everyone was far more excited than we'd been for our Kamloops debut. When we landed in Vegas, we felt like rock stars. Anyone who has been to Las Vegas knows how exciting it is at night. We checked into our hotel and went for a walk down the strip. The sights and sounds of the boulevard fueled our anticipation for the show and we spent the evening reveling in the experience.

The next morning we went to the Las Vegas Convention Centre, signed in with the event coordinators, and received our Showcase Performer badges. We felt so cool. There was a large concert stage in the open concourse of the Centre and we found our sound check and show times posted next to the stage. Our show would be a 15-minute slot at 6:30 that night. We spent the day cruising the exhibits, visiting every table and dropping off the business cards and info sheets. I met Edwin Rojas and he was as warm and genuine as he had been in our correspondence. We talked about the band's showcase hopes, and he said he would help me follow-up after what he knew would be a stellar reception from the industry folks.

He was confident we would do well and I thanked him for everything he had done to make the trip happen. We went back to the hotel, grabbed our instruments, and returned for sound check. Everything went smooth and the crew was impressed.

"You Canadians are all so damned polite," the soundman told us and we laughed and joked about how the stereotypes of gentle Canadian etiquette had preceded us. After sound check, I talked with the guys about how this ubiquitous perception about Canadians was something that would continue to work in our favor if we just did what came naturally. Everyone had been polite at the airport, going through customs, and the processing of our visa had gone well. We'd been received at all points of our trip with returned courtesy and now we had all seen the rewards of our good behavior in another country. Our journey had been a textbook perfect execution and I was proud that everyone had brought their best.

All that was left was to do a killer show. I picked three songs, two rockers and a ballad to go between them. Six-thirty rolled around and it was our turn. We waited backstage for our introduction. We were impressed at how much the announcer knew about our band as he spoke to the crowd.

It had become a tradition and a customary prompt for my guys before each show that I would say "Have a good show, boys," and when I said it that evening, it had a more prophetic meaning. We had executed the steps of our journey, not just the ones to get here this weekend, but for the entire year and we had made it to Las Vegas. All that was left was "Have a good show, boys."

The announcer called out to the crowd "And now from Vancouver, Canada – The finest Bon Jovi tribute anywhere – Blaze Of Glory! The opening drums of the New Jersey album that preceded "Lay Your Hands On Me" boomed and the band climbed the steps to the stage. This had become our regular entrance bit and it was a nice impact to have the band go onstage ahead of me so the crowd could cheer for them. Then when I came up it was a second opportunity for more cheers. It worked tonight just as perfectly as it always had, and instead of our regular first song being "Raise Your Hands" we opened with "You Give Love A Bad Name."

It was my intention to give the crowd a massive hit right off the top and I knew the song had special significance to the band, being the first we had ever performed together. The crowd's response was excellent and people began to move closer to the stage. Everyone in the band had a huge smile on their faces. I looked back into the audience and saw a pretty, young blonde woman sitting alone at the front of stage right. She was looking up at the band smiling and I couldn't help but wonder why a girl like that would be sitting alone.

I had slated "Bed Of Roses" in the second spot, as I was so proud of the way the band delivered ballads. It also held special opportunities for me as a singer to exercise the intimacy of a ballad vocal performance and also to perform a classic Jon Bon Jovi concert move. During the song, Jon would go out into the audience and select a woman from the crowd to dance with during the guitar solo and I had adopted this for the Blaze Of Glory show.

When we reached that part of the song, I went out into the audience and asked the blonde woman to dance. She danced with me throughout the solo and the crowd cheered loudly as was the case whenever I would do this during the show. I bowed to her, helped her return to seat then climbed the steps to finish out the song onstage. We closed with "Living On a prayer" and knocked it out of the park. The crowd erupted and we knew we had done what we came to do. We had rocked the house.

Afterwards we went into the audience and shook hands with people and posed for pictures. The woman I had danced with introduced herself as Heather. She was a sales representative in the casino industry and a huge Bon Jovi fan. She was as nice as she was pretty and we spoke at length about the convention, Bon Jovi, and how our trip had been so far and exchanged information. She said she would be in touch and would spread the word about Blaze Of Glory.

Edwin was pleased with the band's performance and told us

all that we were going to do very well. We thanked him again for helping us and we left the hotel feeling like kings.

That night we let ourselves cut loose a bit and partied Vegas-style until the early hours of the morning. Everyone was a bit hung over on the flight home, but our morale was sky-high and we talked excitedly about following up and looked forward to the returns our well-received performance would bring.

Over the next two weeks I pounded social media with the triumph of our Las Vegas performance, and coordinated efforts with Edwin on following up with the industry people. The show had established Blaze Of Glory as a true marquis act and a band that could perform on the international stage. Our cachet increased exponentially overnight and led to a domino effect that garnered us offers for many more US dates. Edwin booked us to play The Yuma County Fair in Arizona and I began planning the trip. Heather Donovan, the woman I had met and danced with during Bed Of Roses corresponded with me on a regular basis and said she had sent news of our band to several of her contacts and received some interest. Over the next couple of months our friendship grew and I enjoyed countless discussions about our mutual love and respect for Bon Jovi.

Heather was the kind of Bon Jovi fan I had suspected many were; she was an even more significant example of how Bon Jovi's endearing spirit had touched people's lives. She had seen Bon Jovi perform almost a hundred times and her knowledge about the band rivaled and probably exceeded mine. She had met Jon and had pictures of them together. Her gentle and compassionate nature seemed so consistent with my own since I had been indoctrinated into the Bon Jovi family of admirers, and I was so touched that someone with this familiarity and love for Bon Jovi felt that Blaze Of Glory was not only acceptable, but outstanding in its delivery.

She remarked on our authenticity, my Jon-likeness and vocal resemblance, and how the band's collective nature as people was so congenial. She told me Bon Jovi would be proud to have a band and group of people like ours as ambassadors. It was the greatest compliment I had received since the project began.

As I planned the trip to Arizona I discovered that the visa for a paying gig required much more logistics and money than a visa for our unpaid showcase. Not only was the P2 visa, for receiving income as entertainers, reviewed by a more rigid bureaucracy, but there was now the added compliance of IRS red tape. The Arizona gig was booked for April 2011; I had to learn the ropes of touring in the US quickly if I was going to meet my deadline to submit the visa application in time. I didn't have money to pay a lawyer and I didn't know anyone in the business who had experience in US tours. I researched day and night, learning what I needed. I waded through scores of documents, agreements, forms and conventions of AFM requirements, IRS compliance, and US/Canada Tax treaties until I began to form a clear picture of our responsibilities to satisfy all of the appropriate agencies involved.

It was a frustrating and rewarding month. I finally got all of the documents filed, paid the monies and received the P2 visa just in time. The flights were booked, the vehicles rented, and the meals and accommodation were coordinated. Everything went like clockwork.

It was scorching hot in Yuma and we were a bunch of frost-bitten Canadian boys, just escaped from the cool spring weather of April in Canada. It proved to be a difficult climatic change for us all and it was a sometimes a challenge to stay cool sometimes, but we kept our spirits in check.

Eeyore did not fare as well. His equipment was giving him trouble again and he was snapping at everyone in the band and the technical crew during sound check. The rest of us tried to extend our support, but were met with outbursts of rage. He needed to calm down so I asked him to accompany me back to the trailer to talk.

When we got there I tried to appeal to him with how important this was to us and asked him to relax. We would all help him in any way we could. He just stared into space. Finally, he cut me off and told me no one in the band had the problems he had to face. He ranted. I listened. His gear frustration combined with the heat had brought him to the boiling point.

"I quit!" he yelled and slammed the door of the trailer on the way out. I knew I wouldn't get anywhere with him in his present condition, so I left him alone. He finally got his equipment working and we finished our sound check.

Over the course of the week we played three shows a day in the hot Arizona sun for the fair crowds and managed to salvage a nice time for the four of us and put on some great shows.

We let the Eeyore problem fade into the back of our minds and we ended up having a great time partying with the crew at the hotel and exploring the town. When we got home I talked with Doug, Mike, and Randy. Everyone agreed that we could keep Eeyore for the next few gigs, but we needed a replacement soon. His unpredictable moods and short fuse were a liability, even if he was professional onstage. A week later he called and apologized, but we still needed a replacement.

I was surfing the net and found an article online about a convention in Reno, Nevada, for the fair industry in the Western United States. The set up was similar to the one we had played in Las Vegas and I was excited about the potential to get the band into the fair and festival circuit in the US.

I still hadn't paid Lhesa back all the the Las Vegas money and I knew we had no more to invest, so I called up the guys in the band, told them about the convention, and asked for funding ideas. Randy said he would ask his mom and I prepared a financial prospectus for what the expenses would be. His mom was business-minded and was impressed with the Blaze Of Glory. She agreed and understood the potential for what the fair convention could do for us. Just as we had done in Las Vegas, we travelled to Reno, did a killer show, and met a lot of new contacts.

Once home, I received a call from a Sacramento-based booking agency called That's Entertainment International. They loved the band's showcase set and offered us a number of gigs at fairs, festivals, and casinos in California and Nevada. Edwin had no problem with me accepting dates from them and said he "didn't begrudge anyone for trying to make a living." I knew he was disappointed that he wasn't the agent booking the dates. Our agreement was only for shows arising from the Vegas convention gig. We agreed that our west coast dates would ultimately help him sell the band on his side of the country as we were both convinced the band's impressive calendar would help us to move forward.

Heather Donovan had sent a letter to a huge casino in upstate New York called the Turning Stone and it served to help Edwin close a great deal for us to play there in the Fall of 2011. Edwin said he would get some other shows in the area and we could make a small tour out of it. The Turning Stone was part of a large chain of Native-owned casinos in the US, and I was excited that a good report from them might secure other Native-owned casinos as well.

I posted our upcoming California and New York shows on our website and began to use them as leverage to reach out to other venues in my letters of introduction when soliciting dates on my own. I got a call from a booking agency based in Vancouver called Canadian Classic Rock (CCR) who had exclusive Canadian representation for many international recording artists, and I arranged a local show where they could come out to see the band. I knew Bruce Bromley at CCR from when he worked for Sam Feldman during the '80s and I knew Bruce's partner, Bernie Aubin, the drummer from The Headpins. Bernie came out to see the band and loved the act. CCR offered to book the band in Canada and I accepted right away as Canada was the only place in North America I didn't have representation.

In discussion with the guys in Blaze Of Glory, we often listed the pros and cons of playing local. We agreed it was great to play Vancouver for our family, friends, and fans to see us as long as we were not in danger of overplaying our hand. I maintained we didn't want to oversaturate the local marketplace so it was sustainable for us in the coming years. Many of the gigs we were offered in Vancouver were bars and pubs. We resisted the temptation to make easy money as it would serve as a detriment to the band's cachet in the marketplace. We resolved to play less, be patient, work some part-time straight jobs to fill-in the financial holes, and stick to fewer and larger local venues.

The plan worked well and soon we found ourselves in the fortunate position of playing some of the most prestigious local venues. We played the Pacific National Exhibition (PNE), The Cloverdale Rodeo, and Canada Day in Surrey – three of the biggest annual events.

Then we were invited to perform in Asbury Park, New Jersey. When Edwin called and told me, I was flabbergasted. I knew there was a Bon Jovi tribute in New Jersey, and another one right next door in New York. I questioned it briefly and then jumped at the offer. What Bon Jovi tribute band would turn down the opportunity to play in the very place where Bon Jovi had their roots?

Edwin hooked up another New Jersey gig at Mexicali Live in Teaneck. Then he told me about an impressive offer to be the first rock band ever to play at the Katherine Hepburn Cultural Arts Centre in the legendary actresses' hometown of Old Saybrook, Connecticut. I almost dropped the phone. I've been a Kate Hepburn fan all of my life and the gig sounded wonderful to me. The whole tour sounded so cool, I couldn't wait to tell the guys. They were floored. The timing was such that we would have the New Year's Eve, off so we decided we could go down to Times Square that night and watch the ball drop. It was going to be amazing.

The dates looked brilliant on our calendar, and added to a growing list of impressive schedule of fairs, festivals, and casinos throughout California and Nevada.

CCR kept us busy throughout the summer playing fairs and festivals throughout BC and Alberta, and we balanced these with the shows in the Western U.S.

My simple plan was coming to fruition. We were on schedule, if not ahead of it. The shows were flawless and we added new songs from more recent Bon Jovi albums. The crowds reacted with joy and appreciation. We thrilled audiences from age 2 to 92, and the band was becoming closer than any other I'd ever been a part of.

Eeyore's moods were still volatile, but we shielded him from the public when he was off stage. Occasionally, he would disrupt a sound check, and we would try to avoid any witnesses. He quit the band three times that summer and always came back with an apology. We ignored his resignations and kept a lookout for anyone who might fill-in if we were abandoned without notice. Eeyore's name was on the work visas and the flight itineraries and we were committed to keeping him around, for now. We went through periods of caring about his pain and then not caring, each of us drawing strength from the other three. In spite of it all, the four of us were having the time of our lives.

During one of our gigs that fall, I connected with Darcy Nybo, an old friend from the '80s. She'd been good friends with Fast Eddie and had made friends with the band girlfriends from The Cool Front and Ted Moore and the Border days. Darcy was one of those normal people; with a house and a job, who loved rock 'n' roll. I invited her out to dinner with the band and we spent the evening before the show reminiscing and laughing about our crazy rock 'n' roll days.

After a few stories, Doug looked at me and said, "Ted, you should write a book."

"Yeah Ted, write a book," Darcy chimed in. We all laughed a bit more. When the laughter died down Darcy looked me and said, "I'm serious Ted. I own a small book publishing company now. You write it, I'll publish it."

I laughed again and promised I'd think about. I had so much on my plate; there really wasn't any time. And besides, who would read it anyways?

Chapter Thirty-One

Christmas of 2011 was wonderful, and we were all excited about our trip to New York, New Jersey, and Connecticut. I told the guys to invite their wives and girlfriends to join us for the tour. I knew it would be a great way for the Blaze Of Glory family to get closer; besides, I figured the New Year's Eve experience in Times Square was something couples should be together for. Doug's wife wasn't able to get the time off from work, but the rest of the girls would fly down and meet us at our hotel in Paramus, New Jersey, which would serve as our home base while we played the four shows on the tour.

Our first show was at The Turning Stone in Verona, a small town in Upstate New York. The casino was a beautiful complex and we were treated like royalty by the staff and management.

Heather Donovan texted and said she was coming to the show and bringing some friends. It was nice to know we would have familiar faces in the crowd. The wives would miss this show as they weren't landing until the following day, so we took the opportunity to party with just the band as it was likely we'd be distracted with tourist stuff over the next few days. Although we had planned some outings with the whole crowd, we all wanted to show our significant others some special attention.

We talked about how nervous we were about having Eeyore and his girlfriend together at the shows. They were volatile, and had broken up and gotten back together more times over the past two years than any of us could count. We vowed to stay on high alert for anything that would publicly compromise the band. Sound check went well and that night was the best show the band had ever played. After the show the entertainment manager said the owner and his wife had made a rare appearance that evening and loved our performance. They wanted us back next year.

"To New York!" I toasted, and we clinked our drinks together. "If we can make it here, we can make it anywhere!"

The humor of the cliché wasn't lost on anyone, and we laughed and talked for a while about the following day's itinerary. A monumental show awaited us in Asbury Park the next day so we said our goodnights and went to our rooms. I nodded down the hall at Doug as he opened his hotel room

"Next stop, New Jersey," he said and closed the door behind him. I got into bed and lay awake for over an hour. My dreams were coming true. I finally drifted off and slept like a king.

The next day involved a full afternoon of travel and we ended up unable to meet the girls at the hotel. We told them to get a cab and head down to the club and we would meet them, but they were tired from the trip and said they would see us after the show.

***

It was just before sundown when we rolled into Asbury Park. The five of us had been crammed into a van with six guitars and nine suitcases for over seven hours. The setting sun cast a marble orange and red hue stretching across the New Jersey coastline as we followed Asbury Avenue west toward the ocean. This was the first time any of us had been to the Jersey shore, and we all pressed against the windows to take in the surroundings. I had only seen Asbury Park in pictures and movies. I was expecting the beach and carnival town immortalized on Bruce Springsteen's debut album "Greetings from Asbury Park, NJ." But the fabled seaside community that had once been an iconic vacation spot for millions showed many signs of urban decay. One of the guys piped up on how he had read the carousel at the pier had been sold to an amusement Park in Myrtle Beach and many of the boardwalk pavilions were all boarded up. You could see signs that reconstruction and renovation to some of the buildings were underway, but neglected and demolished areas stood as testimony to the economic downturn and the loss of a once healthy tourism industry.

Still, Asbury Park had an amazing musical heritage and was home to venues that had helped launch the careers of bands like Southside Johnny and the Asbury Jukes, Bruce Springsteen, and of course, Bon Jovi.

We rounded the corner at Ocean Avenue, and drove until we spotted our long-awaited destination – the legendary Stone Pony. It had taken three years and seven hours to get here. We cheered and clapped as we pulled to a stop alongside of the club.

"Check it out!" I called the guys' attention to the myriad of gig posters plastered along the sidewall of the building. Dozens of promo shots and glossy show bills advertised legions of artists that had played inside the famous venue.

"Let me out…" someone pleaded from the back. Although it was December 29, and the temperature had dropped steadily that day, the fast food containers, hangover breath, and sweaty feet had produced an epic raunchiness in the van such that we all wanted to vacate the vehicle as quickly as possible. We ignored the cold and piled out of the van as fast as we could in our jeans and t-shirts to get a closer look at the playbills. We huddled together, oohing and aahing over the acts that appeared to be bands and artists from the New Jersey music scene, both past and present. Each of us took turns calling out the famous and obscure names from the pictures while the reality of where we were sank in.

We were a Bon Jovi tribute band and we had arrived in Bon Jovi's neighborhood. We had made our way to the very place Bon Jovi had their roots and tonight we would enjoy a milestone that was the culmination of careful planning, determination, and hard work. Playing this gig would be the perfect ode to all we had invested in Blaze Of Glory. We would play in rock music's jewel of New Jersey. We all agreed that we had done something remarkable. We had been invited to bring our own faithful rendition of the Bon Jovi show across the continent to the birthplace of the world famous band.

Standing there on the streets of Asbury Park I recognized how far we had come. Blaze Of Glory tours had taken us through dozens of shows from clubs in Western Canada to fairs in California, with glorious stops in Las Vegas and Reno, while the milestones and critical acclaim gathered behind us. We were relative newcomers to the tribute band marketplace, but we had already carved a wider trail than any project I had ever been a part of. There had been few victories for me over the years – few moments when I felt I had accomplished something special. My pursuits in music had given me some small measures of success: I had heard my songs on the radio, I had played some great gigs, and I had been offered a couple of nice deals. But nothing quite compared to what I had experienced in the last three years with Blaze Of Glory.

We pressed our noses against the glass like a bunch of country kids ogling toys through a store window at Christmastime. I shivered and looked around at the setting sun fading behind the buildings along the shoreline. I imagined Bruce Springsteen,

Southside Johnny, and Jon Bon Jovi strolling these very sidewalks. I was revved up. It was going to be so special to sing the show tonight. We were going to celebrate a beautiful success story.

Blaze Of Glory had hit the ground running and kicked ass right out of the gate. Even people who weren't hard core Bon Jovi fans had been generous with their compliments, and we prided ourselves on converting folks who admitted that they hadn't been Bon Jovi fans before.

It was just over three years, but for me, this journey had taken a lifetime. This success was part of a larger dream that had played out since my earliest memories. Building this band changed me. Emulating Bon Jovi changed me. I loved the new me and I was so grateful to Blaze Of Glory and Bon Jovi for this opportunity.

I was happy that Lhesa was here to share this with me. She had been my godsend and I looked forward to spending New Year's Eve with her. Doug called my name and I shook free from my daydream.

"There's been a mistake, Ted." Doug laughed and I recognized that laugh. In all the years I had known Doug and whenever plans changed or fell through in the music business, he would laugh that same way as if to say – if you don't laugh you might cry.

"We've been double-booked." He laughed again. "There's some kind of college fraternity thing going on in the Stone Pony tonight so we've been moved to the Wonderbar down the street."

For a moment I was downhearted, but then I realized that playing down the street was better than having no gig at all for the night. Besides, we were still in Asbury Park, Bon Jovi Land, playing on the Jersey Shore just like Eddie and The Cruisers, and that was good enough for me.

We drove down the street to the Wonderbar and were greeted

at the door by the beverage manager, Catherine. As the band set up their gear, she told us Bon Jovi stories and directed me to a cabinet with some pictures of Jon, Richie Sambora, Bruce Springsteen, and other famous musicians from the New Jersey scene.

"They all come here pretty regularly," she said. "Bruce Springsteen was just onstage here with his band last week and Jon's been onstage to sing with bands here a few times as well."

She told me how her husband had been the guitar player for a band with Tico Torres as their drummer. Apparently Jon had come into the club one night and asked Tico to join his band. Catherine said her husband told Tico not to do it. He said the kid's band wouldn't amount to anything, but Tico joined up anyways.

"And the rest is history," she laughed. She was an awesome woman with a wealth of Bon Jovi trivia. All of the Bon Jovi guys were vacationing with their families and the staff said they wouldn't be coming down to the club that night, but if we came back another time, we shouldn't be surprised if one of them showed up and jammed with us.

The doorman told us he had been there for ten years and he had never seen a Bon Jovi tribute band play the club. "I never even knew there was any," he laughed. "If Jon and Richie were here, you'd have them onstage with you the whole night."

After sound check, we took to the stage, the stage where Bruce Springsteen had stood only days before. The same stage where Bon Jovi jammed when they were in town. Here we were, a tribute band from Canada, playing Bon Jovi songs in the Bon Jovi holy land.

We started our set and immediately noticed a difference in the crowd. These were more than Bon Jovi fans; these were his neighbors. They sat and clapped when we finished a song and would clap again when we'd launch into the next one. As I played, I felt even more of a connection to the songs.

The rest of the show was great and it was cool to talk to people afterward who knew the Bon Jovi guys. They said Bon Jovi would have been impressed with us. They all had stories about the guys in the band and how they were still seen locally all the time.

"They never forgot their Jersey roots," an older guy told me while I was sitting at the bar. I talked with him for a while on how we thought their down to earth nature was such a big part of their charm and enduring fan loyalty. The management loved the band and said we were welcome to come back anytime. I thanked him and said it was awesome to have played there.

We headed to the hotel in Paramus where Lhesa and the girls were waiting in our rooms. Lhesa was disappointed that she had missed the show, but I told her all about the two shows and promised she would love the following night's show at The Katharine Hepburn Theatre.

"The Kate," as the staff and locals called the theatre, was a beautiful, two-story heritage theatre adorned with antique fixtures, plush draperies, stunning acoustics, and the amazing Katharine Hepburn museum located on the ground floor. The audience that came to the show was a collection of season ticket holders, individuals and families, who were all part of the theatre society in Connecticut. They were a wonderful and appreciative crowd. We were the first real rock band that had performed at the theatre and I think they were as excited as we were. It was a different audience than we had ever played for before in that they were all dressed in formal attire and sitting quietly in theatre seats. Our presentation was now a polished and chic performance and we were especially gracious that evening. It was a joy to have the band play a venue such as this, and I felt it was a strong testimony to the versatility I had so hoped the act to have.

The show was very well received, and although in a much different way than we were used to, it rocked the house. The audience was wonderful at the meet and greet afterwards and management invited us to return anytime. That night gave us affirmation that Bon Jovi music, and Blaze Of Glory's presentation, would work anywhere, for any crowd. We could play any gig and we felt empowered.

The next three days in New York were spectacular. I was thrilled to share this experience with Lhesa, and we crammed as much tourist stuff into our time as we could. We would take the Hoboken train to Penn Station and then ride the subway or walk to destinations in the city. We went to the Rockefeller Centre, took the Staten Island Ferry, walked down Broadway several times, and had an awesome tourist's eye view of New York.

The highlight of the trip was New Year's Eve in Times Square. We stood with a hundred thousand others on those streets and watched the ball drop. I could barely believe it. I kissed my wife at the stroke of midnight and hugged the guys. We had made it to New York. Some buyers throughout the state had seen our shows in New Jersey and Connecticut and called Edwin to ask when we would return. Edwin started work on lining up a follow-up tour and we were ecstatic that we would return to this amazing place. It was a sweet victory, and we went into the last show in Teaneck with morale at an all-time high.

The show was mostly good that night. There was a guy on the crew that gave us the cold shoulder and it wasn't until later we found out that he was close friends with another Bon Jovi tribute band. He was impressed with our band and perhaps that's what bothered him. I understood the guy's feelings. The idea of resentment from competitors was not new. We were the new kids in town and we were moving in on their turf. Since we had broken into the international marketplace we'd become targets for various attacks from other bands. Aggressive competition wasn't a new idea and I'd seen many examples during my music career, but some of the most intense and nasty demonstrations of competitive behavior came after I formed Blaze Of Glory.

Don't get me wrong, I love the idea of competition in any business field and I believe competition is healthy for both businesses and consumers. Ideally, competition keeps a business honest. It makes you maintain a product of good quality and it makes you strive to always be better – which invariably spurs innovation. Competition also has a negative side, and there have been many examples of unscrupulous behavior throughout history by competitors in their pursuit for stronger market shares. Some guys get real nasty about it.

Other Bon Jovi tributes had sent threatening letters, called venues where I was booked and offered to play for less money, and even disguised themselves as potential buyers, both online and over the phone.

When these attacks came to my attention, I talked with my guys and said we should always take the high road and not respond in any way other than to stay aware and keep building what we had. Some attacks were blatant and vicious, but I knew it would not serve us well to step into the ring. Besides, there was plenty of work to go around and eventually the novelty of beating on the new guys would wear off.

None of us really knew what the ceiling was for a tribute band. There weren't any limits or end in sight. We were just doing the best we could and it kept getting better and better. Still, we had to do something about Eeyore. It was like our beautiful rolling wheel had a broken spoke. During the last night of the New York tour, he and his girlfriend had a huge fight in the lobby of our hotel, causing a scene in front of staff and guests. We lost all hope of salvaging anything with him and we resolved to replace him when we got home. He flew home with Doug and Mike while Randy and I flew to Anaheim to attend a fair conference as delegates with That's Entertainment. We met with new buyers and solidified our presence in the California fair market. We had one more show to play in San Diego, and after that I would let Eeyore go. He had to find his own way. Nothing we said or did helped. He needed to help himself.

CHAPTER THIRTY-TWO

Back home, I thought about other markets for Blaze Of Glory. I'd received a deluge of phone calls and emails from bands, agents, and other industry people asking how I had brought Blaze Of Glory to such heights. I remembered my conversation with Darcy, and thought maybe she and Doug were right. Maybe I should write a book. It could be about one singer's journey from relative obscurity in Canada to a successful career as an international tribute artist. The book would address many questions people had asked me about the tribute phenomenon and how I'd built Blaze of Glory. I connected with her, signed a nice contract, and began to write.

Blaze of Glory now had established pockets on both US coasts. I turned my attention to spreading our net overseas. I had sent letters to all the cruise ship lines letting them know we were available as a feature on world cruises. As the feature, the gigs required only 10 days on board, instead of the three months or more as a regular act, which would have proven prohibitive for my players that were working straight jobs. I sent repeated emails to Royal Caribbean, Princess, and Carnival. Edwin proved to be my ace in the hole and negotiated a series of cruises for us with Royal Caribbean. The first date was booked for March of 2013. I could leverage this victory with my existing roster of dates. It meant more shows, better money and wider markets.

Now to replace Eeyore. A guy named Mark Olexson called to say he was available, but for a limited time period as he was starting an original band. I arranged a rehearsal and it went well. The band was impressed with his performance and we all enjoyed his demeanor.

I went home that night feeling like a huge weight had been lifted. We had one last show to play with Eeyore. The trip went quickly and he was in a good mood. The four of us managed to have a good time knowing things were going to get a lot better after this weekend. When we returned to Canada I told him I had to let him go. He said he was going to quit again anyway. Fair enough. He could make the mode of departure his choice.

Our next scheduled trip was the Caribbean cruise. It was the perfect place for Mark to start. We would be at sea for 10 days and it would give us all a chance to spend time getting to know each another in close quarters. It was a nice way to start a new guy in the band. It was an impressive first gig, the money was good, and the show was only 45 minutes. He'd only have to learn a short set for now. From my perspective, it was the best-case scenario.

All five of us met at the airport. We were all excited to play our very first cruise ship gig and to play it with our new fifth member. We flew to Montego Bay via Toronto and stayed overnight at the Ritz Carleton. Royal Caribbean had taken care of everything, and we felt like rock stars in our 5-star hotel in Jamaica.

That night we went down for supper in the dining lounge where a Calypso group was playing. The band was awesome, the food was great, and the surroundings were beautiful. After dinner we all went down to the shore and watched the sun set. I looked around at the guys and saw nothing but smiling faces. As the setting sun stretched out on the water I felt a calm come over me. I laid back in the chaise lounge, listening to the waves hit the shore. I closed my eyes. This was heaven.

The next morning a shuttle arrived and took us to the dock where the Freedom Of The Seas awaited us. The ship was the largest

I'd ever seen. It was 14 decks high and at least two city blocks long.
I had seen pictures on the Internet, but I was unprepared to stand
in front of something so massive. People were boarding and several
had stopped to ask if we were the Bon Jovi band that was playing
that night. Everyone was so excited to see our show. They asked to
take photos with us and our excitement grew as well. We knew that
first night would be amazing.

There were several checkpoints and details to go through before
we got onboard. I watched Mark and he was a perfect gentleman
at every point in the process. My confidence built and I looked
forward to our show with unfettered anticipation. Finally, we were
firing on all five cylinders. There could be no stopping us now.

It felt strange wandering the hallways of the ship as I made my
way to my stateroom. I had seen Titanic many times, and I couldn't
help but think what this massive ship would look like under water.
I couldn't shake the thought that there was a chance, no matter
how remote, that I might be swimming through these corridors,
darkened and filled with freezing water, trying to find a way to
escape. Damned Titanic.

I arrived at my stateroom on Deck 12 and opened the door
to a large deluxe suite with a king-sized bed and a large balcony
that looked out onto the blue ocean. I had a walk-in closet and a
full-sized bathroom with tub and shower. It was a far cry from the
cramped quarters I'd heard about. I immediately understood I was
being treated very well. I sat down on the bed to take it all in.

Then it was time for sound check. The theatre was an
astonishing sight. The balcony held over a thousand people and the
main section held at least two thousand or more. The crew was very
professional and said it was exciting for them to have an act that was

such a departure from what was typically presented at the venue. Most of the shows were of the Cirque de Soliel variety, and no rock acts had ever graced the stage. Blaze Of Glory had been sent in as a tester to see how a cruise ship theatre would react to a rock band as the feature act.

There was no mistaking how calculated Royal Caribbean had been in their choice for this experiment. I had reached out to all the cruise lines two years earlier and initially my emails were, for the most part, unreturned. Some stoic polite replies had hit my inbox a few times over the following months with invitations to stay in touch. Royal Caribbean had watched Blaze Of Glory over the past two years to see if we were the kind of act they wanted onboard ship.

They had ultimately decided on a Bon Jovi tribute for many of the same reasons I had decided to build one. It was a good crossover demographic, a large catalogue of hits, and the relevance of a band still touring and making albums. I knew the cruise ship giant had lots of Bon Jovi tributes to choose from. When I originally started the band there were almost 50 Bon Jovi tribute bands worldwide, and now there were over 60 – two of which were using the name Blaze Of Glory. The fact that Royal Caribbean had chosen our band out of all those options was a huge compliment. There were at least 10 or 12 geographically closer than us and flight costs would have been far less for them to fly one of the groups from New York, New Jersey, or Eastern Canada. Still, they flew us in from the furthest, most diagonal point across the continent.

We had always been theatrical in our presentation; we were adept at working large crowds and all-ages audiences. Several videos of the band were available in a myriad of online locations featuring me in the crowd singing to elderly ladies and young kids and I was sure this was a big selling point for our band. Our calendar was well-controlled and free from venues that might prove unfavorable. I'd made sure the band had never played pubs, bar rooms, or steak pits. We were strictly at festivals, fairs, casinos, and theatres, and on a large international scale. We had been in Las Vegas and Reno and played from New York to California and beyond. It certainly helped that Edwin was confident we were the perfect act for this job. He had been aboard the cruise ships himself for many years and knew what we did would be a great fit. Still, this would be a test gig and there was a lot riding on how our first one would go. We were more than up to the task.

At our first sound check I noticed there was a hydraulic lift in the stage floor. I asked the production manager if I could appear from beneath the stage at the start of the show. We rehearsed it a couple of times to get the timing right with the band's intro. I was certain it would be a great entrance. That night I went with the security guard down below the stage, through the cramped, darkened corridor to take my place on the waiting platform.

I could hear the large crowd chattering as they waited for the show to begin. The lights went down the crowd roared and I heard the intro music start. I couldn't see anything, but I could picture each band member walking onstage as the cheers grew in reaction to their appearances. The band started into "Raise Your Hands" and lights filled my dark hiding place. The platform started to move upwards and I raised my fist in a triumphant Jon–like manner as I rose from below the stage. The crowd screamed their appreciation. I stayed perfectly still until the riser stopped at stage level. Every seat in the giant theatre was filled and thousands of people were smiling, clapping and cheering. I grabbed the microphone and sang the first line. I could hear my voice from every corner of the theatre and the band was in perfect form. Each of the guys' faces wore an expression of pure joy. My nervousness was gone and we rocked through the set like clockwork and nailed every section. Forty-five minutes went by in a wink.

After the show, the Cruise Director met us at the side of the stage and called to the audience for a last cheer. People screamed their appreciation. We were elated and relieved as we'd done exactly what everyone had hoped – Blaze Of Glory had brought down the house. We went up to the lobby after the show, signed hundreds of autographs and posed for pictures as the throngs emerged from the theatre. Everyone offed stellar accolades for our performance and many promised they would return for the second show. Two hours later we performed the set again and the response was even more enthusiastic. That night after the meet and greet we gathered in my stateroom and celebrated our victory.

"Nice show, boys," I said calmly and everyone laughed at my understated delivery of what had been a spectacular experience. We dressed in more formal attire and went down to the promenade to mingle with the passengers. Almost every face was familiar and they had all seen at least one of our performances that evening. We signed more autographs, shook hands and posed for photos with hundreds of people while they patted us on the back and raved about the group. It was humbling and heartwarming. We were all proud of what we'd done and grateful for the experience. It was everything we worked towards and the feeling of accomplishment was not lost.

Late that night, when most of the passengers had retired for the evening, the five of us ventured to the very front of the ship. It was pitch black and it took our eyes a minute to adjust to the light from the moon and stars. A hundred feet below, we could hear the waves crash against the side of the massive hull.

Then Doug called out and pointed to the sky. A magnificent shooting star, unlike any I had ever seen before, streaked across the night sky. It was an affirmation of our journey thus far, and a perfect salute to our stellar achievement.

The second show was not for another week, so we spent the next five days mingling and enjoying the ports of call. By day five, I was surprised to find that I was feeling homesick. I had always felt like I was built for touring and I couldn't remember a time when I would rather be at home than out with my band. Here I was, on a cruise ship in the Caribbean, longing for home. But now I had someone to miss. Lhesa and the girls were at home waiting for me. I wished they'd been here to see this.

The last shows went even better than the first two and we ended our voyage on a perfect note. The Cruise Director and Production Chief told us we would have a great future on cruise ships and we flew home feeling like champions.

Edwin was able to parlay our first trip into another one right away. Our cachet had taken another huge step forward and greater offers started to come in. We signed on with Major League Baseball to play shows at the games. They confirmed our first show in Miami when the Marlins hosted the Washington Nationals. It was good money and excellent exposure for us. We did a TV interview the day we flew into Miami and watched it on the giant screen during the game. The Marlins had given us a VIP box at the top of the massive ball park and we felt like kings of the world when we saw our faces 10 stories tall during the seventh inning stretch.

Doug was a huge baseball fan and he was having the time of his life. I was overwhelmed as I watched the expressions of joy during the game and our performance afterward. I was so proud that I was able to share this with him. He had been my trusted companion for so many years and it felt amazing to see him enjoying something so dear to him. We kept every one of those 28,000 people on their feet singing and cheering and went home feeling like the world was our oyster.

Mark Olexson had left the band about a month earlier, just as he warned us he would. We were lucky to get a very well-respected Vancouver keyboard player and studio owner named Kevin Williams to join us. Kevin was a really cool guy and worked his way into the group dynamic in no time. We felt like a pretty tight group and everyone was happy to be enjoying this new experience of everyone being happy.

Our calendar had also taken on a different dynamic. I began accepting less shows for the upcoming year to leave room for cruises and more baseball performances. We had another cruise from Antigua to Barbados and more would be coming in for the following year. The world was opening up for me in ways I'd only dreamed. I was seeing places I'd only heard of in movies and as a kid gazing at maps. I was making my dreams come true.

The tribute marketplace had changed a great deal in those five short years since I built Blaze Of Glory. There were tributes to just about any band you could name, and there were multiple versions all over the world. I was certain the over-crowded tribute market would eventually collapse from the bloat of so many bands and I began to think how I might move Blaze Of Glory into a different realm before we found ourselves drowning in the muddied waters of over-supply.

I looked at the competition and saw acts that augmented their shows in different ways. Adding video images was an expensive proposition and seemed to be the domain of larger dollar groups such as Rain, (a Beatles tribute act) and specialty acts like Legends of Rock. It had been something we had discussed with Blaze Of Glory, but the logistics of travelling with screens was a nightmare and renting them at each city was too expensive. We agreed that it was an idea we might revisit later.

Some acts added Top 40 sets in addition to their tribute set; others still had started doing tributes to more than one act during their performance. That wasn't where we wanted to go. In the long run, the band's identity wouldn't be watered down.

I personally liked the idea of multi-band tribute shows. It offered a wider range of entertainment for the audience, and if well-selected, the lineup could complement each other to make the evening a more exciting event.

We had done shows with a couple of other bands on the same bill in 2011. It had worked great. Blaze Of Glory had opened the show, followed by an Aerosmith tribute called Aerosmith Rocks, and then Who Made Who finished the night with a tribute to AC/DC. The evening was so well received that I followed up with the other two bandleaders and discussed the possibility of more shows together.

Danny Deane, the Steven Tyler character from Aerosmith Rocks, and Scott Folkerson, who played Angus Young in Who Made Who, were veteran performers and we fell into easy conversation with one another as we discussed the business of tributes and the potential for our three acts to band together. I talked with them more and more as the months went by. Danny and Scott were kindred spirits. They understood the deeper philosophies of the business and marketplace. We became strong allies over the next year and began to probe deeper into the advantages of putting the three-band show together.

Our mutual Canadian agent, Bruce Bromley, was instrumental in selling the package to a number of buyers and we started playing regional shows for a test market. Danny had been toying with the idea of calling the package Monsters Of Mock – as a salute and obvious wordplay to the Monsters Of Rock festivals. We all loved the name and agreed that Monsters Of Mock would be the moniker we would travel under. Danny, an accomplished web designer, created a great website, Scott financed brand new videos of Who Made Who, and I flooded the media with radio and newspaper interviews.

The lineup made so much sense. Blaze Of Glory opened – being the most family-friendly, all-ages act. Aerosmith followed Bon Jovi nicely, bringing a slightly heavier, sexier theme to the evening. Then AC/DC capped it off perfectly for a crowd that was sufficiently lubricated and ready for some head-banging.

Each band had five guys and our instrumentation was such that we could all share the same gear. Our riders and accommodation requirements were also virtually identical and it made us a more streamlined package for the buyer. I assembled a comprehensive itinerary for the three bands and we hit the ground running.

Monsters Of Mock gathered a great reputation and the shows were a blast to perform. When you put 15 rock 'n' rollers together on a tour all sorts of things could happen. Lucky for us, everyone got along famously and each member of the tour was an excellent ambassador under the Monsters Of Mock banner. We consolidated and coordinated our meet-and-greets and merchandise sales. Everyone was kept in the loop regarding all business aspects of the package. Each bandleader was paid separately, but it was understood and agreed that no one act would receive preferential compensation above the others. We also agreed if any other bands were brought into the package to replace one of us that was engaged elsewhere, that no other AC/DC, Aerosmith or Bon Jovi tribute would be used. We were united in our loyalties to the package and its integrity, we kept in close touch with our philosophies and desires regarding the business.

Now with Royal Caribbean, Major League Baseball, and Monsters Of Mock, Blaze Of Glory's future is as iron-clad it can get in an over-crowded and aggressive marketplace. No matter where you see the band you will know we are doing what we love to do and each one of us is having the time of his life. Who could ask for more?

I know I will probably never get rich playing in a tribute band, but through the process of building Blaze Of Glory my life has become enriched in ways I had never imagined. My relationships with my wife, my band, my family and friends are wonderful and fulfilling and I have earned the respect of my colleagues. My general outlook is better than it has been for as long as I can remember and I know the Bon Jovi spirit played a key role in the changes that spurred my metamorphosis as both a person and a performer. My dreams have come true and success has never looked so good. I can honestly say, for the first time in my life, I have finally made it.

CHAPTER THIRTY-THREE

You may find it strange that an artist or a band could affect someone's life in such a profound way. I think that is one of the miracles of music. In my case, the messages of hope, determination, and resilience in Bon Jovi's lyrics and philosophy, along with Jon's altruism and indomitable spirit, awakened something inside me and became a huge catalyst for change in my life. I must have been ready for it. Middle age had crept up on me and my perspective was in desperate need of reconstruction. The demons and substance abuse of my past are long gone and I am able to remember the good things I have experienced along the way. All that I have learned has given me strength and focus to realize and create a wonderful, successful life and career. Through building Blaze of Glory I experienced a new clarity about what was important in my life and what I wanted to accomplish with music. I wanted to share love, happiness, camaraderie, and a sense of purpose with everyone I could. Anything else seems unimportant to me now.

All those years I had been so bent on trying to change the world. I was going to slay the dragon to save the princess and the kingdom, while all along what made me most fulfilled was to bring joy to those closest to me in my life and those I performed for.

On one hand it could be said that I was born shit poor, struggled my whole life in self-perceived failure, and almost ended that life because I couldn't face the world one second longer, but then found the truth of my desire and learned to love myself and my life.

On the other hand, it could also be said I was born and raised a happy kid who fell in love with music, found a way to embrace life through adversity, and fell in love with an amazing woman who knew I was worth saving. Then, with the spirit of an altruistic rock star and his band's messages of hope and inspiration as my guide, I became exactly what I wanted to be – successful and happy.

No matter which story is truer, the end result is the same. I refined my ideas of success and realized they were well within my grasp. I just had to get out of my own way.

Today I live life looking forward to every minute of every day with my heart and my mind wide open. I love with all of the strength in my heart and I am resolute and resilient in the face of struggles that will always exist. My new world is a beautiful place filled with wonderful days and the promise of even better tomorrows.

I give Bon Jovi much credit for helping me find happiness and success. I think for anyone who moves from darkness into light there is something or someone that, in some way, shines a beacon. For me, it was a band from New Jersey who helped nudge me in a new direction and I am grateful.

Now you know how I came to be in a Bon Jovi tribute band and why it is I continue to do so. If a guy like me can make such an amazing change, then so can you. Find whatever it is that sets you on the right path and then follow your dreams.

Thank you Jon, Richie, Tico, David, Alec, and Hugh. You helped steer me toward a direction I had trouble finding on my own. I repeat this mantra to myself as I sit backstage waiting to go on.

I hear my cue. It's time to go. Another beautiful, sunny California afternoon and the atmosphere of the midway floods my senses. I hear the sound of the crowd as the band starts up. It's time to go sing. It just doesn't get any better than this.

TED MOORE

Acknowledgements

To all of the musicians
I have ever worked with,
for your talents
and your loyalty.

To my family,
friends, and fans,
for more love
than my heart could hold.

To my Mom,
for your
courage, wisdom, and faith.

To Lhesa, Hannah, and Sophie,
for saving me.

To my enemies,
for keeping me
vigilant and honest.

To God,
for sparing me...
for now.